Mellanie Queen

The Other God
The Judas and the Hidden God

Copyright © 2022 Luiz Santos
All rights reserved.
No part of this book may be reproduced in any form or by any means without written permission from the copyright holder.
Cover image © LS Studio
Review by Marco Villar
Graphic design by Clara Mendonça
Layout by Ricardo Almeida
All rights reserved to:
Luiz A. Santos
Category: Gnosis

Summary

Prologue 5
Chapter 1 The Gospel of Judas 6
Chapter 2 The Context of Gnosticism 12
Chapter 3 Judas as the Chosen Disciple 18
Chapter 4 Jesus' Revelations 23
Chapter 5 The Concept of Demiurge 29
Chapter 6 The Supreme God and Divine Fullness 35
Chapter 7 Divine Hierarchy and Intermediate Beings 41
Chapter 8 The Dual Nature of the Universe 47
Chapter 9 Creation and the Material World 52
Chapter 10 Judas and the Sacrifice of the Body 58
Chapter 11 The Gnostic Path of Salvation 64
Chapter 12 Jesus' Revelations about the Spirit 70
Chapter 13 The Pursuit of Self-Knowledge 75
Chapter 14 The Role of the Soul and Consciousness 80
Chapter 15 Spiritual Enlightenment 85
Chapter 16 The Concept of Spiritual Archetypes 90
Chapter 17 The Duality of Good and Evil 93
Chapter 18 The Role of Ignorance in Suffering 98
Chapter 19 Judas's Journey 103
Chapter 20 The Secret of the Divine Kingdom 108
Chapter 21 Gnostic Mysteries 113
Chapter 22 Gnostic Meditation Practices 118
Chapter 23 Spiritual Visualizations 123
Chapter 24 Connection with the Inner Divine 128

Chapter 25 Awakening Consciousness 133
Chapter 26 Exploring the Aeons 138
Chapter 27 The Journey of the Soul After Death 143
Chapter 28 Rituals of Spiritual Liberation 148
Chapter 29 Practices of Reflection and Contemplation 153
Chapter 30 The Mystery of the Cross 158
Chapter 31 Development of Spiritual Love 163
Chapter 32 Transformation of the Ego 168
Chapter 33 The Quest for Absolute Truth 173
Chapter 34 Releasing Material Attachments 178
Chapter 35 The Role of Intuition 183
Chapter 36 Purification of the Soul 188
Chapter 37 The Meaning of Suffering and Trials 193
Chapter 38 Communion with the Supreme God 198
Chapter 39 Rejection of the Demiurge 203
Chapter 40 Integration of Spiritual Knowledge 208
Chapter 41 The Return to the Pleroma 213
Chapter 42 Achieving Inner Peace 218
Chapter 43 The Spiritual Ascension of Judas 223
Chapter 44 The Legacy of Gnosticism 228
Chapter 45 Daily Gnostic Practices 234
Epilogue 243

Prologue

As you open this book, you find yourself standing on a rare and profound threshold, where the past, the present, and the eternal intertwine in mystery and truth. There is something here that transcends the visible—a journey to the depths of hidden realities that call for your attention, a singular opportunity to unveil concealed layers of your own soul. With each page, it's not merely a narrative that unfolds but a transformative possibility, a revelation that leads you to question what you truly know about the sacred and the profane.

This book grants you the role of a privileged observer, bringing to light a secret buried in the sands of time, where Judas Iscariot emerges not as a traitor, but as a bearer of wisdom and revelations that transcend ordinary understanding. Here, however, you are not merely a reader: this knowledge exists as if it were delivered to you personally, as a calling long waiting to be answered. It is an invitation to witness Judas under a radical prism, as someone who navigated light and shadow, discovering a truth that few dared to see.

In these pages, you are not about to encounter a simple story of redemption or condemnation. Instead, this is a map to a challenging and complex spiritual journey, where the very idea of good and evil dissolves, giving way to a reality where the divine and the human blend and transform. Each word invites you to question the certainties you've been taught, to break with the conventional, and to open your mind to the deeper possibilities of existence. What is salvation if not the very act of understanding what we truly are, beyond appearances and judgments?

On this path, you will encounter the concept of the "Hidden God," a silent and grand presence operating beyond the limits of matter and refusing any earthly definition. Here, Judas emerges as a companion on this path, a bearer of hidden knowledge that surpasses common understanding. This journey is not one of blind faith; it is a journey toward self-knowledge and spiritual freedom, a quest for "gnosis"—the transformative wisdom that liberates the soul from illusions.

As you read these pages, prepare yourself for a shift in how you see the world and yourself. Let the mystery of this story reveal the shadows and lights of your own existence, showing that what we judge as betrayal may, in fact, be the noblest of callings. Allow yourself to dive into the revelation that Judas, perhaps, was not a traitor, but a divine emissary chosen for a role that transcends the notions of good and evil. Who knows if, in the end, you might find in Judas a mirror of your own quest?

This book, now in your hands, is a portal inviting you to cross a veiled boundary. Within it, historical time dissolves, and you are taken to the core of wisdom as old as humanity and as deep as the cosmos itself. What you will find here is not only the story of a man but the resonance of a universal truth, an echo reaching through the ages, waiting for one who dares to awaken.

Let yourself be captivated. This is the beginning of a journey where each page is a step and each word, a key to the unknown. If you are ready to question, to transcend, and to awaken, then proceed. This book is yours, and it awaits you with the mystery of one who knows the secrets of the ages.

Chapter 1
The Gospel of Judas

In the deserts of Egypt, in the remote and ancient sands near Al Minya, a buried secret emerged, one that would resound through the world of religious scholarship and ignite the imaginations of those seeking to understand a hidden and complex spiritual past. The Gospel of Judas, a lost text veiled in mystery, was rediscovered in a fragile manuscript, offering a rare glimpse into a world of theological debate and spiritual rebellion. Unearthed in the late 20th century, this text revealed a narrative previously unknown, or perhaps intentionally obscured, within the traditional Christian canon.

The Gospel of Judas quickly stirred controversy, offering an unorthodox perspective on Judas Iscariot—the disciple historically remembered as the betrayer of Jesus. Yet in this gospel, Judas is not cast merely as the villain but as the trusted confidant, entrusted with a profound secret. This unique portrayal was unlike anything the Christian orthodoxy had accepted or permitted, forcing a reconsideration of Judas's role and what his relationship with Jesus might signify within a broader, more complex spiritual landscape. For centuries, the Orthodox Church had maintained a steadfast narrative, where Judas was the betrayer, the symbol of treachery, and his story was irrevocably linked to darkness. But here, hidden beneath layers of ancient text, was a version of Judas as a figure on the path to enlightenment—a figure who dared to step beyond conventional understanding in a quest for ultimate truth.

The journey of the Gospel of Judas into modern hands was far from straightforward. Originally composed in the second century CE, it likely circulated within a small community of Gnostic Christians, individuals who sought a deeply personal and mystical understanding of the divine. Written in Coptic, a language adapted from Egyptian with Greek influences, the manuscript was fragile, its pages worn and fragmented. At some point in history, it was hidden away, possibly by those who recognized its danger or by those who hoped that future seekers might one day unearth it and be transformed by its teachings. By the 1980s, the manuscript had surfaced on the black market, passing through the hands of collectors and traders who only saw its value in monetary terms, unaware of the immense spiritual implications it held. The text languished in a bank vault in the United States for years, deteriorating as it awaited rescue. It was not until 2006, after painstaking restoration and translation, that the world could read this ancient manuscript and contemplate the secrets it contained.

Scholars from around the world gathered to study this Gospel, delving into the meanings behind its cryptic language and trying to piece together the full picture of its significance. The words were challenging, poetic, and imbued with a sense of reverence for the mysteries they conveyed. The Gospel of Judas speaks in a voice familiar to Gnostic traditions—a voice that emphasizes hidden knowledge (gnosis) as the key to spiritual salvation. Rather than advocating for faith alone, as many orthodox teachings do, the Gnostic path suggested an inner journey, one where wisdom and understanding lead to transcendence and liberation from the material world's confines. This gospel did not ask its readers to blindly believe; it invited them to look within themselves, to question reality, and to transcend it.

The Church, however, did not receive this text as revelation or sacred truth but as a threat. Gnostic ideas, particularly those found in the Gospel of Judas, directly challenged the established orthodoxy that the Church worked so carefully to build. In the early centuries of Christianity, there was no singular, unified belief system; rather, there were diverse and often competing schools of thought. While some Christians found comfort in rituals and the teachings of a singular divine authority, others sought a more direct and personal connection with the divine, which did not always align with the dogmas that were gradually forming. The Gospel of Judas, with its revolutionary ideas, was soon declared heretical.

The rejection of the Gospel of Judas by early church leaders had profound implications, influencing the trajectory of Christian doctrine for centuries to come. By the late second century, influential figures such as Irenaeus, a bishop in what is now France, wrote vehemently against the Gnostics, condemning their texts as dangerous distortions of true Christian faith. In his work *Against Heresies*, Irenaeus explicitly mentioned the Gospel of Judas, casting it as a work of deception. He argued that Gnosticism led believers astray, away from salvation and toward a fractured understanding of God. For the burgeoning Church, Gnostic texts threatened not only theological integrity but also the unity and authority of their institution.

In this time of theological struggle, Judas himself became a symbolic figure of all that the Church wished to renounce. To the orthodox, Judas was more than a man; he was a representation of betrayal against Jesus and against the emerging Church. The Church framed him as a lesson—a cautionary figure whose name would forever evoke treachery. But the Gospel of Judas offered an alternate interpretation, suggesting that his actions were not acts of betrayal but rather a necessary step in a divine plan. The idea that Judas could be chosen, perhaps even favored, for his role in the Passion of Christ was anathema to those who preached a faith based on loyalty, obedience, and clear moral lines. If Judas's betrayal was divinely sanctioned, it blurred the distinction between good and evil, a line the Church worked tirelessly to delineate.

But what if Judas, as the Gospel suggests, was indeed chosen for a role only he could fulfill? The text portrays Judas not as an enemy of Jesus but as his confidant and co-conspirator. Here, he stands apart from the other disciples, who are depicted as misunderstanding Jesus's teachings, focused on the material rather than the spiritual. Judas, however, is singled out for his deeper understanding, his willingness to transcend conventional beliefs, and to embrace a difficult path. In this portrayal, Judas becomes a symbol of the seeker, someone who is willing to question, to sacrifice, and to bear the weight of judgment in the pursuit of truth.

In the context of Gnostic belief, Judas's actions can be seen as a liberation—both for Jesus and for humanity. According to the Gospel of Judas, it was Judas who helped release Jesus from the material world, allowing him to return to the divine fullness, the Pleroma, beyond earthly constraints. This concept is quintessentially Gnostic. The Gnostic worldview often regards the physical realm as a place of entrapment, overseen by a lesser deity known as the Demiurge, who keeps souls bound to matter and ignorance. Liberation from this realm, therefore, requires an awakening—a willingness to see beyond the material and recognize the divine spark within.

This understanding of Judas as a liberator rather than a betrayer aligns with Gnostic values that prioritize inner knowledge and spiritual freedom over ritualistic adherence and blind faith. To the Gnostics, salvation was not granted by faith alone, nor was it a reward for obedience to a strict moral code. Rather, salvation was an act of recognition, an awakening to one's divine nature and the interconnectedness of all existence. Judas's actions, then, might be viewed as part of a greater cosmic mystery, a sacrifice that transcends human judgment and opens the path to enlightenment for those who dare to follow.

The Gospel of Judas challenges its readers to question not only Judas's motives but the entire foundation of the relationship between humanity and the divine. It asks us to consider whether salvation is truly something that can be granted by an external authority, or whether it is, at its core, an individual journey of self-discovery and transformation. Through this lens, Judas's story is no longer one of simple betrayal. It becomes a tale of courage and transcendence, a portrayal of a soul that dared to confront the unknown in pursuit of ultimate truth.

In the shadows of history, the Gospel of Judas remained hidden, its teachings buried under centuries of condemnation and misunderstanding. But its resurrection in modern times serves as a reminder that there are always hidden paths, forgotten voices, and ancient wisdom waiting to be rediscovered. This gospel offers not only a different view of Judas but also an invitation to explore the mysteries of Gnosticism—mysteries that challenge the boundaries between light and darkness, good and evil, and the physical and the divine. The Gospel of Judas beckons us into a world where the answers are not prescribed by an external authority but lie waiting in the depths of one's own soul, in the journey toward self-knowledge and spiritual liberation.

As we turn our gaze to the Gospel of Judas and the world of Gnosticism, we begin to see that this ancient text offers more than an alternative narrative. It is a guide, a map of the soul's journey through a world of illusion and truth, light and shadow. Through Judas's story, it hints at a path for those willing to seek, to question, and to awaken. The true journey is not one of betrayal, but one of discovery—the discovery of one's place within the vast, interconnected mystery of existence.

Chapter 2
The Context of Gnosticism

In the intricate web of ancient beliefs, where gods were plentiful and mysteries abundant, a different kind of understanding began to surface—one that would later be named Gnosticism. Rooted in a sense of divine mystery and an insatiable quest for truth, Gnosticism emerged as a spiritual movement intent on peeling back the visible layers of existence to reveal a hidden, transcendent realm beyond. This was a belief system that viewed the cosmos not through the eyes of obedience and ritual but with a radical focus on self-knowledge and spiritual awakening.

Gnosticism arose in the early centuries of the Common Era, a time of cultural and spiritual ferment in the Mediterranean world. The Roman Empire was at its peak, a sprawling power that brought together diverse religions, philosophies, and languages. Within this melting pot, ideas flowed freely across borders, cultures, and disciplines. Greek philosophy, Eastern mysticism, and Jewish apocalypticism all mingled, their ideas weaving into each other, creating a tapestry of thought that would profoundly shape the lives of those seeking deeper understanding.

Amid this backdrop, early Christians began to shape a new religious movement centered on the life and teachings of Jesus of Nazareth. However, even within this burgeoning faith, there was no single "correct" interpretation. Instead, there were multiple voices, each interpreting Jesus's teachings in different ways. The Gnostics were one of these groups, a collective of thinkers and seekers who read Jesus's message not as a call for simple faith but as an invitation to a transformative, inner journey. To them, the

Christ was more than a savior; he was a guide, a revealer of secrets, and a beacon leading them back to a divine origin hidden beyond the material world.

The term *gnosis* itself is central to understanding the essence of Gnostic belief. In Greek, *gnosis* means "knowledge," but it is not knowledge in the usual sense. It is not the acquisition of facts or the intellectual grasp of doctrines; rather, it is an experiential, transformative understanding that awakens the soul to its true nature. Gnostics believed that within each individual lay a divine spark, a fragment of the Supreme God, obscured by the illusions of the physical world. This world, they believed, was not the true creation of the highest God but rather the work of a lesser deity, the Demiurge, who ensnared souls in matter and ignorance. To find salvation, one had to awaken, to pierce through the illusions of the Demiurge and realize the spiritual essence trapped within.

This concept of salvation differed radically from that of early Christian orthodoxy. For the orthodox Christian, salvation was primarily an act of faith in Jesus Christ as the Son of God, whose death and resurrection redeemed humanity from sin. The Gnostic, however, sought salvation through gnosis—a direct, personal revelation of the divine. They believed that this knowledge could only be achieved through introspection and spiritual exploration, a journey into the depths of one's soul where the true God, hidden from the material realm, might be encountered.

The Gnostics held that not all individuals possessed the same potential for gnosis. Some, they believed, were predisposed to see beyond the physical world, to perceive the divine truths hidden beneath the illusions of daily life. These individuals were known as the "pneumatics" or "spiritual ones." Then there were the "psychics," souls capable of moral and religious life but not of true gnosis. Lastly, the "hylics" were bound to the material world, unable to perceive or aspire to anything beyond physical reality. This spiritual hierarchy was not a matter of judgment but of capacity and readiness. For the Gnostic, spiritual enlightenment was not a state to be imposed on others but an awakening that came only when the soul was ripe for revelation.

The Gnostic path, then, was a journey that few could undertake fully, a path of rigorous self-examination, mystery, and at times, secrecy. Many Gnostic texts describe initiation rituals, sacred oaths, and teachings given only to those deemed ready. These mysteries were not shared lightly, for the Gnostics believed that the truth they sought was sacred, and to share it without discernment was to risk desecrating its purity.

But Gnosticism was more than a solitary quest; it was also a worldview that saw existence itself as a duality, a cosmic struggle between light and darkness, spirit and matter, knowledge and ignorance. To the Gnostic mind, the material world, though alluring and seemingly real, was a shadow, a prison crafted by the Demiurge to keep souls bound to physical desires and illusions. True reality lay beyond this, in a divine fullness known as the *Pleroma*, where the Supreme God dwelled in eternal harmony. The Pleroma was the source of all being, an overflowing wellspring of pure consciousness and love, untouched by the limitations of the physical realm.

In this cosmic structure, the Demiurge served as a false creator, a figure who fashioned the physical universe but lacked the wisdom and benevolence of the Supreme God. This Demiurge, sometimes identified with the God of the Old Testament, was a tyrannical and ignorant being, mistakenly worshipped by those who could not perceive the higher reality of the Pleroma. To Gnostics, the Demiurge's creation was a flawed and transient imitation, an elaborate illusion designed to trap souls in an endless cycle of birth, suffering, and death. Salvation, therefore, was not found in aligning with the Demiurge's creation but in escaping it—ascending beyond the world of forms and returning to the true, eternal light of the Pleroma.

This worldview set the Gnostics at odds with the emerging Christian orthodoxy. Early church leaders, seeking to define a unified doctrine, found Gnosticism's emphasis on individual revelation and its disdain for the material world unsettling.

Orthodoxy, rooted in communal faith and ritual, relied on a set of doctrines accessible to all believers, emphasizing the collective over the individual. Salvation, according to orthodox Christianity, was granted through faith in the church's teachings, through sacraments and the authority of tradition. Gnosticism, however, emphasized the individual's inner journey, a solitary quest for gnosis that could not be granted or mediated by any institution.

The contrast between Gnostic and orthodox beliefs extended to the nature of Christ himself. Orthodox Christians saw Jesus as the incarnate Son of God, both human and divine, who walked the earth, suffered, and rose again to redeem humanity. For many Gnostics, however, Jesus was a spiritual figure who came to awaken souls to their own divinity, revealing to them the false nature of the material world and the path to liberation. Some Gnostic texts even suggest that Jesus did not suffer or die in the physical sense but only appeared to do so, as the physical body was ultimately an illusion, unworthy of divine reality. This concept, known as *docetism* (from the Greek *dokein*, "to seem"), was heretical to orthodox believers, who viewed the physical death and resurrection of Jesus as central to their faith.

In Gnostic mythology, the figure of Christ often appears not only as a teacher but as a revealer of cosmic truths, a being who descends from the Pleroma to guide lost souls back to their divine source. This Christ is a luminous being, often portrayed as emanating light and wisdom, an emissary from the realm of true divinity. His role was not to atone for humanity's sins but to dispel the ignorance that kept souls bound to the material world. His message was a call to awakening, urging those with ears to hear and eyes to see to seek beyond the Demiurge's deception and reclaim their place in the divine fullness.

The orthodox response to these ideas was swift and uncompromising. Church leaders like Irenaeus, Tertullian, and Justin Martyr worked tirelessly to combat Gnosticism, labeling it as heresy and warning believers against its seductive allure. Irenaeus, in particular, devoted extensive writings to dismantling Gnostic doctrines, arguing that they were blasphemous distortions of the true Christian faith. To him, and to many others in positions of authority, Gnosticism was not only theologically incorrect but spiritually dangerous, a path that led followers away from the Church and toward a fragmented, individualistic faith.

Yet despite the Church's efforts to suppress it, Gnosticism persisted, its teachings hidden within secret communities, its texts buried in the sands or passed from hand to hand among the faithful. Gnostic sects like the Sethians and Valentinians developed their own interpretations of scripture, their own rituals, and their own interpretations of salvation. For these groups, the journey toward gnosis was not an abandonment of Christ's message but a deepening of it. They believed that Jesus's teachings, when stripped of orthodoxy's dogmas, revealed a profound truth: that the kingdom of God lay not in an external heaven but within the soul, accessible only to those willing to seek it.

The Gnostics did not reject Christianity; rather, they sought to expand it, to plunge its mysteries into the depths of the soul. They believed that knowledge, not blind faith, was the key to liberation, and that this knowledge could not be handed down by priests or councils but had to be discovered within. For them, the soul was a divine traveler, a spark of light moving through the shadowed world, longing to return to its source.

This path was not easy, nor was it without its dangers. The Gnostic journey was fraught with paradox and uncertainty, a struggle to discern reality from illusion, to awaken to truths that lay beyond the mind's grasp. The Gnostic seeker had to confront the Demiurge's deception, the illusion of the material world, and the darkness within their own soul. Salvation, in this context, was not merely a promise of a better afterlife but a radical transformation of consciousness, a breaking free from the chains of ignorance and awakening to the divine light within.

As the centuries passed, the Gnostic movement faced increasing persecution. The Church, solidifying its power and doctrine, sought to erase the "heresies" that threatened its unity. Gnostic texts were burned, their followers exiled, and their ideas condemned. Yet the spirit of Gnosticism endured, finding new forms in later mystical traditions and resurfacing whenever seekers found themselves yearning for a direct experience of the divine, unmediated by ritual, doctrine, or institution.

The Gospel of Judas stands as a testament to this resilient spirit. In it, Judas represents not a simple betrayer but a figure of profound spiritual courage, one who steps beyond the orthodox understanding in pursuit of the divine mystery. This text, and the Gnostic worldview it embodies, calls readers to a path less traveled—a path where salvation is not granted but realized, not bestowed by an external authority but discovered within. Gnosticism beckons those who seek not only to believe but to know, to awaken to the truth that lies beyond the veils of this world, in the eternal light of the Pleroma.

Chapter 3
Judas as the Chosen Disciple

In the canon of Christian tradition, Judas Iscariot has long been fixed as the arch-betrayer, the one who, for thirty pieces of silver, delivered Jesus into the hands of his enemies. He is the symbol of deceit and betrayal, an infamous figure condemned to shadows and scorn. Yet in the pages of the Gospel of Judas, a different story emerges—a narrative that challenges this depiction and reimagines Judas not as a villain but as the chosen disciple, the one entrusted with a profound, if difficult, role in the cosmic scheme. Here, Judas is not the one who turns his back on Jesus but rather the one who steps forward with knowledge and intention, bearing secrets that are too complex, too spiritually perilous, for the other disciples to understand.

The Gospel of Judas casts Judas in a role that is uniquely paradoxical. He is both the betrayer and the enlightened one, the one whom Jesus singles out as capable of receiving certain revelations. This dual identity is difficult for many to reconcile, yet it is precisely this tension that makes Judas's story resonate so powerfully in the Gnostic tradition. For the Gnostics, whose teachings challenge traditional dichotomies of good and evil, light and dark, the idea of Judas as both traitor and chosen disciple aligns with their belief in a layered, complex universe where truth is rarely as it seems.

In the Gnostic worldview, the material world is a realm of illusion created by the Demiurge, a flawed, ignorant being who fashions existence in his own image. Those who are bound to the Demiurge's world are trapped in a cycle of birth, suffering, and death, blind to the reality of the spiritual universe that lies beyond. For the Gnostic seeker, salvation means seeing beyond these illusions, recognizing the divine spark within, and embarking on a journey of awakening. In this context, Judas's role becomes not that of a betrayer but that of a liberator, someone who helps to break the chains binding Jesus to the material world so that he may return to the true divine realm, the Pleroma.

The Gnostic understanding of Judas's actions reframes the concept of betrayal itself. In the Gospel of Judas, Jesus reveals to Judas truths that he withholds from the other disciples. He speaks to Judas in private, disclosing secrets about the nature of God, the universe, and the role of humanity in the divine scheme. These are not teachings that can be easily grasped; they are complex, transcendent truths that require an openness and courage to confront mysteries beyond conventional understanding. Judas, in this narrative, possesses that openness. He is willing to embrace a difficult truth, to bear the burden of a path that will lead to his own condemnation in the eyes of others.

Jesus's choice of Judas as his confidant is, therefore, deliberate and purposeful. He recognizes in Judas a unique quality—a spiritual potential that goes beyond mere loyalty or obedience. Judas is willing to step into the role that others would fear or misunderstand. This willingness to pursue knowledge, even at great personal cost, is a central theme in Gnostic thought. For the Gnostic, the journey toward gnosis, or spiritual knowledge, is not a safe or comfortable path. It is a journey that may lead one into confrontation with the very foundations of reality, challenging the truths that others accept without question.

The Gospel of Judas goes further, suggesting that Judas's role in Jesus's fate was not only foreseen but essential. Unlike the other disciples, who are depicted as preoccupied with earthly concerns and unable to perceive the higher truths Jesus reveals, Judas is attuned to the mystical dimensions of Jesus's teachings. He understands that Jesus's mission involves more than preaching or performing miracles—it is about liberation from the material plane. This liberation, however, requires a final act of separation from the flesh, a release from the bonds of the physical body. In Gnostic terms, the body is a prison for the soul, an earthly vessel that traps the divine spark in a world of corruption and decay. For Jesus to return to the Pleroma, his true divine origin, he must be freed from this prison, and Judas's actions make that possible.

To fully understand Judas's role, we must delve into the symbolic significance of his actions. In the Gnostic perspective, Judas's "betrayal" becomes a kind of sacrificial act, one that mirrors the archetype of the wise individual who dares to transcend ordinary morality in pursuit of a greater truth. This act of handing over Jesus to the authorities is not a betrayal of Jesus's mission but rather a fulfillment of it. Judas's willingness to fulfill this role, knowing that it will mark him as a traitor in the eyes of others, speaks to his unique spiritual maturity—a readiness to shoulder the scorn of humanity to advance the divine plan.

In the Gospel of Judas, there is a conversation between Jesus and Judas that highlights the depth of their connection. In this dialogue, Jesus acknowledges Judas's distinct understanding, referring to him as "the thirteenth spirit" who will be set apart. This reference to the number thirteen carries profound symbolic weight. In the ancient world, thirteen was often seen as a number of transformation, of moving beyond the constraints of ordinary reality into the mystical or transcendent. By calling Judas the thirteenth, Jesus signals that Judas's path is different from that of the other disciples. He stands on the boundary between worlds, a liminal figure who holds the key to bridging the material and spiritual realms.

This privileged position, however, comes with a heavy price. Judas's journey is not one of earthly rewards or recognition but of sacrifice and isolation. Unlike the other disciples, who seek glory, power, or security in their relationship with Jesus, Judas is willing to step into the shadows, to be misunderstood and reviled, in order to fulfill a role that only he can play. His story becomes a Gnostic parable of the soul's quest for liberation—a journey that is fraught with misunderstanding, resistance, and sometimes the ultimate sacrifice of one's own reputation or identity.

For Gnostic thinkers, Judas's role also challenges the conventional ideas of sin and redemption. In the orthodox tradition, Judas is seen as irredeemable, a soul lost to damnation because of his act of betrayal. But within the Gnostic framework, Judas's actions are part of a divine mystery, a necessary step in the soul's journey from ignorance to enlightenment. Gnosticism holds that true sin is not a matter of individual actions but of remaining in ignorance, of failing to seek the higher truths that lie beyond the veil of the material world. Judas, by embracing his role in the divine plan, transcends this ignorance and becomes an instrument of Jesus's liberation.

The significance of Judas's role in this Gnostic narrative extends beyond the historical or theological. He becomes a symbolic figure representing the seeker of wisdom, the individual willing to confront uncomfortable truths, to accept paradox and ambiguity in the pursuit of enlightenment. His story resonates with anyone who has struggled to break free from convention, to pursue a path that others might not understand or accept. Judas, in this sense, is the archetypal outsider, a figure who sees beyond the surface of things and dares to act on that vision, even at great personal cost.

This portrayal of Judas as a chosen, even honored, disciple was anathema to the orthodox Christian authorities. It threatened the clear moral narrative they sought to establish, one in which loyalty and faith were rewarded and betrayal condemned. The notion that Judas's betrayal could be part of a divine plan, that it could carry a hidden wisdom, was incompatible with the teachings of a Church that emphasized obedience, order, and the rejection of heretical ideas. For the orthodox authorities, the idea that Judas might have acted with divine sanction undermined the foundational narratives of sin, repentance, and redemption upon which they built their doctrines.

In the centuries following the formation of the Christian canon, the Church worked diligently to suppress texts like the Gospel of Judas, condemning Gnostic ideas as dangerous and subversive. The orthodox view of Judas became fixed in the minds of believers, casting him forever as the traitor, the condemned soul. But the Gospel of Judas survived, hidden and eventually rediscovered, offering an alternative vision—a vision that speaks to the mysteries and complexities of the spiritual journey.

To consider Judas as the chosen disciple is to challenge our assumptions about loyalty, sin, and the nature of spiritual truth. The Gospel of Judas invites readers to look beyond surface appearances, to see Judas not as a villain but as a figure of profound courage and insight. His willingness to embrace a role that leads to his own condemnation reflects a spiritual depth that resonates with the Gnostic ideal of gnosis. For Gnostics, the path to salvation is rarely straightforward; it is a journey through darkness, a confrontation with the unknown, and a willingness to sacrifice ordinary comforts in pursuit of ultimate truth.

Judas's journey, then, becomes a reflection of the soul's journey toward the Pleroma, the divine fullness that lies beyond the Demiurge's creation. In fulfilling his role, Judas not only frees Jesus from the bonds of the material world but also illustrates the Gnostic ideal of transcending the illusions that bind us. His story serves as a reminder that the path to enlightenment is often fraught with misunderstanding, that those who seek the truth may find themselves isolated or condemned by those who cannot understand.

The Gospel of Judas offers a glimpse into a world where betrayal and sacrifice are not opposites but intertwined facets of a larger spiritual mystery. In this world, Judas becomes a model for the Gnostic seeker, an individual willing to bear the weight of his role, to face judgment and rejection, in the pursuit of a hidden, higher knowledge. His journey reminds us that the path to the divine is often shrouded in paradox and that those who are called to it may find themselves walking alone, misunderstood yet chosen, bearing the secrets of the soul's liberation.

Chapter 4
Jesus' Revelations

In the dimly lit pages of the Gospel of Judas, a world of whispered secrets and hidden wisdom is unveiled. It is here, in this delicate text of Gnostic origin, that Jesus speaks words too bold, too enigmatic to fit within the confines of orthodox teachings. Here, he shares revelations not with the disciples as a whole, but with Judas alone—a figure prepared to understand, a soul ready to grasp the profound mysteries lying beyond the illusions of the material world. These revelations, which shatter the familiar image of Jesus as the gentle teacher and guide, instead paint him as a revealer of hidden truths and cosmic mysteries, a teacher of realms invisible to the ordinary eye. In this gospel, Jesus unveils concepts that challenge the traditional view of God and creation, offering Judas a vision of divine reality and the enigmatic forces that shape existence.

As Jesus speaks to Judas, he unveils the existence of a true God—an essence so transcendent and unfathomable that it exists beyond the grasp of human understanding. This Supreme God is not the deity worshipped by the masses nor the familiar figure painted in traditional texts. Rather, it is a boundless source, a luminous presence that exists beyond form and definition. It is a God beyond gods, a being so pure and perfect that it lies beyond all material creation. This Supreme God is the origin of everything that is real and eternal, and yet it is distant, veiled from the created world, residing in a realm known as the Pleroma. Within the Pleroma, there is no suffering, no duality, and no separation. It is a realm of divine fullness, a realm of eternal harmony and unity—a realm that transcends even the concept of creation.

In contrast to the Supreme God, Jesus describes another figure—the Demiurge. This being is the creator of the material world, but it is not a creator in the sense of an all-knowing, benevolent deity. The Demiurge is portrayed as a lower, flawed entity, a cosmic architect who fashions the material world out of ignorance and arrogance. In Gnostic thought, this Demiurge is a false god, one who believes himself to be the only divine presence, yet lacks the wisdom and purity of the Supreme God. Blind to the true light of the Pleroma, the Demiurge creates a world of form and matter, a world governed by cycles of birth and death, of pleasure and suffering, of light and darkness. It is a world that traps souls within the limits of physical existence, a place where the divine spark is hidden beneath layers of illusion.

This duality between the Supreme God and the Demiurge represents the central conflict in Gnostic cosmology. The Supreme God embodies the realm of spirit, unity, and truth, while the Demiurge represents division, ignorance, and the imprisonment of the soul in the material world. Jesus's teachings in the Gospel of Judas suggest that salvation lies not in allegiance to the Demiurge or the structures of the world he created, but in awakening to the true God—a reality that lies beyond all material confines. The journey to this Supreme God is not one of conventional worship or ritual but a path of inner knowledge and spiritual awakening, a path where one learns to see through the illusions of the Demiurge's world and recognize the divine spark within.

In his conversations with Judas, Jesus speaks of the divine realm as a place of radiant light, inhabited by entities known as Aeons. These Aeons are aspects of the Supreme God, expressions of divine fullness that emanate from the Pleroma. They are not beings in the human sense but embodiments of divine qualities, manifestations of love, wisdom, truth, and beauty. These Aeons exist in perfect unity with the Supreme God, and through them, the divine essence flows into the universe, reaching out to those who have the eyes to see and the heart to understand. They are the bridge between the human soul and the Supreme God, guiding seekers beyond the confines of the material world toward spiritual liberation.

In revealing these truths to Judas, Jesus emphasizes that most people—including his other disciples—cannot see the reality of the Supreme God. The other disciples, he explains, remain mired in their beliefs, locked into the worship of the Demiurge and unable to perceive the deeper mysteries of existence. They follow the visible, the tangible, clinging to rituals and doctrines that bind them to the material world. Jesus explains to Judas that the other disciples, though devoted, are trapped in a spiritual blindness that prevents them from grasping the true purpose of his mission. They see him as a messianic figure who will bring political liberation, an earthly savior who will establish a new kingdom in the world of flesh and blood. But Jesus's message is far more transcendent. His mission is not to overthrow earthly rulers or establish a kingdom of this world, but to awaken souls to their divine origin, to reveal the path back to the Pleroma.

For Judas, this revelation is both a blessing and a burden. He alone among the disciples is given the knowledge of the true God and the Demiurge, and he alone understands the nature of Jesus's mission. Jesus tells Judas that he will ultimately be set apart from the other disciples—that he will play a role that will be reviled by the world yet sanctified in the realms beyond. This separation marks Judas as the chosen one, the disciple who bears the secret knowledge necessary to fulfill the divine plan. In essence, Judas becomes an agent of the Supreme God's purpose, a figure whose actions, though misunderstood in the physical world, resonate with the deeper truths of the spiritual realm.

Jesus's revelations to Judas also involve a vision of cosmic order, a hierarchy that extends beyond the physical and into the spiritual. This hierarchy begins with the Supreme God and flows downward through the Aeons, each emanation reflecting a different aspect of divine fullness. At the lowest level of this hierarchy is the Demiurge, a being disconnected from the

Supreme God's wisdom, who creates a world of illusion and suffering. Humanity, situated within the Demiurge's realm, is bound to this lower reality, its divine spark trapped in flesh and ignorance. Yet within each soul lies a dormant connection to the Pleroma, a hidden pathway to liberation and return to the divine source.

Through this vision, Jesus offers Judas a path to transcendence, a way to move beyond the constraints of the Demiurge's creation and return to the Pleroma. This path is not one of moral obedience or religious observance but of gnosis—direct, experiential knowledge of the divine. The journey to the Supreme God requires a stripping away of illusions, a willingness to look beyond the visible world and into the hidden depths of spiritual reality. It is a journey of inner transformation, where the soul awakens to its true nature as a fragment of the divine.

To aid Judas in this journey, Jesus describes the illusion of the material world and the nature of the human soul. He explains that the soul is trapped in the cycle of life and death, a process governed by the Demiurge and his minions. These minions, referred to as archons, are the rulers of the material realm, beings who enforce the laws of the physical world and keep souls bound to ignorance. In Gnostic tradition, the archons are portrayed as agents of the Demiurge, forces that work to maintain the illusion of the material world and prevent souls from seeing the truth. They control human destiny, influencing thoughts, desires, and actions, creating a world where people are focused on wealth, power, and pleasure rather than spiritual growth.

Jesus's teachings to Judas reveal that true liberation comes from breaking free from the influence of these archons, from seeing through the illusion of the material world and connecting with the divine spark within. This spark, the remnant of the Supreme God's essence, lies buried within each soul, waiting to be awakened. To awaken this spark, one must reject the false promises of the material world and seek the inner path to enlightenment. For the Gnostic, salvation is not about redemption from sin but liberation from ignorance—the ignorance imposed by the Demiurge and his archons.

The path Jesus describes is not an easy one. It requires a detachment from the physical, a willingness to confront the darkness within and around oneself. It is a path of solitude, of questioning, of turning inward to discover the divine truth obscured by the Demiurge's lies. This journey is one that few are willing or able to undertake, and this is why Jesus shares these revelations only with Judas. The other disciples, though sincere in their faith, are not yet ready to perceive the world beyond the material, to see that their worship of the Demiurge keeps them bound to the realm of illusion.

The conversation between Jesus and Judas culminates in a moment of profound realization. Judas, understanding the truth of Jesus's mission and the nature of the Supreme God, accepts his role in the divine plan. He recognizes that his actions, though misunderstood and condemned, will serve a higher purpose. In surrendering Jesus to the authorities, Judas will enable Jesus to shed his earthly form, freeing his soul to return to the Pleroma. Judas's act, then, is not a betrayal but a sacrifice, a conscious decision to assist in Jesus's transcendence beyond the material world.

For the Gnostic reader, this exchange between Jesus and Judas serves as an invitation to seek the hidden truths within their own lives. It challenges the conventional notions of sin, loyalty, and divinity, urging the seeker to question the nature of reality and to look beyond appearances. The Gospel of Judas presents a vision of Jesus not as a redeemer of sin but as a revealer of mysteries, a teacher who invites his followers to awaken to a higher reality. In this vision, Judas becomes a symbol of the seeker, a figure who is willing to confront uncomfortable truths and to bear the consequences of pursuing spiritual knowledge.

Through Jesus's revelations, the Gospel of Judas illuminates a path of awakening, a journey beyond the Demiurge's creation and into the realms of divine fullness. It invites readers to consider a reality that exists beyond the visible, a realm where the soul is freed from ignorance and returns to its source. In this journey, Judas stands as a figure of profound courage, a soul willing to embrace the mysteries of the divine, even when those mysteries lead him into darkness and sacrifice.

In this gospel's vision, the true purpose of Jesus's teachings is not to create a following or establish an earthly kingdom, but to guide souls back to the Supreme God, beyond the illusions of the world. Jesus's revelations to Judas are a testament to this mission, a reminder that the journey to truth often defies convention and requires a willingness to walk a solitary path. Judas, as the chosen disciple, exemplifies the Gnostic ideal of the seeker—one who is not satisfied with simple answers, who looks beyond the physical to find the ultimate truth, and who dares to act in alignment with the divine, no matter the cost.

Chapter 5
The Concept of Demiurge

In the Gnostic worldview, there exists a figure both creator and captor—a being who fashions the material world, not from wisdom or love, but from ignorance and arrogance. This being, known as the Demiurge, is a deity with a fractured understanding of divinity, a god who believes himself supreme but is, in truth, blind to the true source of creation. Unlike the Supreme God, who exists in a realm of pure spirit and light known as the Pleroma, the Demiurge is bound to the limits of matter and form. He is an architect of illusions, weaving the world as a prison for the souls caught within it. The Gnostic tradition portrays the Demiurge as a figure central to the suffering and entrapment of souls, a deity who represents the very opposite of the liberation and enlightenment that the Supreme God offers.

To understand the Demiurge is to understand the Gnostic view of the cosmos as a place of spiritual exile, a reality marred by imperfection, deception, and constraint. For the Gnostic, the material world is not a divine creation but a flawed construct—an elaborate façade that conceals the truth of the Pleroma, the realm of divine fullness and eternal light. Unlike the traditional religious view that celebrates creation as a reflection of God's love, the Gnostic perspective sees the material world as a realm of shadows and chains, a place where souls are bound to cycles of birth, suffering, and death. The Demiurge is the architect of this world, a being who believes his creation to be the ultimate reality, yet remains ignorant of the spiritual truth that lies beyond it.

The term *Demiurge* originates from the Greek word *dēmiourgos*, meaning "artisan" or "craftsman." In classical thought, the Demiurge was seen as a creative force, a being who shaped the material universe with skill and intent. However, in the Gnostic reinterpretation, the Demiurge becomes a figure of limitation, a god who lacks true understanding and thus creates a flawed world. The Gnostic Demiurge is not evil in the traditional sense of malice or malevolence; rather, his evil lies in ignorance. He is a being who believes himself all-powerful and all-knowing, yet his knowledge is partial, and his power is limited to the material realm. Blind to the existence of the Pleroma and the Supreme God, the Demiurge imagines himself the highest authority, creating a world that reflects his own confusion and vanity.

In the Gnostic mythos, the Demiurge is often associated with the God of the Old Testament, a deity who commands obedience, imposes laws, and punishes those who defy him. This association reflects the Gnostic view that the material world, with all its structures, rules, and hierarchies, is a reflection of the Demiurge's nature—a realm where order is imposed, freedom is restricted, and the divine spark within each soul is suppressed. For the Gnostics, the laws of the Demiurge are not expressions of divine will but instruments of control, mechanisms that bind souls to a reality of limitation and separation from their true, divine essence.

According to Gnostic cosmology, the Demiurge was not created by the Supreme God, nor does he represent a true emanation of divine essence. Instead, he is a being who arose out of an error, a cosmic accident in the realm of the Aeons. In some Gnostic texts, the Demiurge is described as the offspring of Sophia, the Aeon of Wisdom, who sought to know the Supreme God more fully but acted without the consent of the divine fullness. This act of independent creation resulted in the Demiurge, a being born of curiosity and separation, disconnected from the true source of divine knowledge. The Demiurge, in turn, fashioned the material world in his own image, a realm governed by ignorance, division, and illusion.

The story of Sophia's creation of the Demiurge is a powerful parable within Gnostic tradition. It speaks to the dangers of seeking knowledge without spiritual insight, of creating without understanding the true nature of reality. Sophia's action, though born of wisdom, led to the birth of a being who embodied ignorance—a being who could not comprehend the fullness of the Pleroma and instead fashioned a world of shadows. The Demiurge, in his ignorance, believes himself the only god, unable to see the divine reality that exists beyond his own creation.

As the creator of the material world, the Demiurge is also the ruler of the realm of matter. He is not alone in his task; he is surrounded by entities known as archons, rulers who assist him in governing the physical universe. These archons are his servants, beings who enforce his laws and work to maintain the illusion of the material world. In Gnostic belief, the archons are powerful entities who influence human thought, emotions, and actions, keeping souls bound to the desires, fears, and distractions of the physical realm. They are the agents of the Demiurge, shaping human consciousness to keep it focused on the material and away from the spiritual. Through the archons, the Demiurge maintains his grip on the world, ensuring that souls remain blind to the divine spark within them.

The Demiurge's world is one of duality, a realm where light and darkness, good and evil, life and death are constantly in conflict. This duality is a reflection of the Demiurge's limited understanding, his inability to perceive the unity of the Pleroma. In creating a world of division, the Demiurge traps souls in an endless cycle of opposites, a cycle that prevents them from realizing their true nature as fragments of the divine. For the Gnostic, this duality is an illusion, a construct designed to keep souls bound to the material realm. True reality lies beyond these divisions, in the undivided light of the Pleroma, where all is one, and the distinctions that govern the material world dissolve in the fullness of divine unity.

The relationship between the Demiurge and humanity is complex and fraught with tension. The Demiurge sees humans as his creations, beings he fashioned from the dust of the earth, infused with a life-force that he claims as his own. Yet within each human being lies a spark of the divine, a fragment of the Supreme God that the Demiurge cannot control or fully comprehend. This spark, the essence of the soul, is the true source of life and consciousness, a reminder of the Pleroma and the soul's ultimate origin. For the Gnostic, the presence of this divine spark is both a blessing and a burden. It is a reminder of the true home that lies beyond the material world, yet it is also a source of alienation and longing, a sense of being trapped in a world that does not reflect one's true nature.

The Demiurge, however, is determined to keep souls bound to his creation. He has crafted a world filled with distractions, pleasures, and pains, all designed to capture human attention and prevent souls from awakening to their divine nature. The archons, his servants, work tirelessly to maintain this illusion, influencing human desires, shaping cultures, and establishing systems of control that keep individuals focused on the material. Religion, politics, and social structures become tools of the Demiurge, institutions that enforce obedience and submission to his rule. In this context, the Gnostic path becomes an act of rebellion, a quest to see through the illusions of the Demiurge's world and awaken to the divine light within.

For those who seek gnosis, the knowledge of the Supreme God and the true nature of reality, the Demiurge is an adversary—a being whose ignorance and arrogance must be overcome. Gnosis, the spiritual knowledge that leads to liberation, is the key to breaking free from the Demiurge's control. By recognizing the illusions of the material world, by seeing through the desires and fears that bind the soul, the Gnostic awakens to the truth of the Pleroma. This awakening is not merely an intellectual realization but a profound transformation of consciousness, a shift from seeing the world as a prison to perceiving it as a temporary stage in the soul's journey back to its divine source.

The Gospel of Judas illuminates this struggle between the Demiurge and those who seek gnosis. In the text, Jesus reveals to

Judas the truth of the Demiurge's world, the prison that holds humanity in ignorance. He speaks of the need to transcend the material, to release the soul from the bonds of flesh and illusion. Judas, in his role as the chosen disciple, is given a unique insight into this reality, a glimpse of the Pleroma and the Supreme God who lies beyond. By entrusting Judas with this knowledge, Jesus sets him on a path of liberation, a path that leads away from the Demiurge and toward the divine fullness.

The concept of the Demiurge also raises profound questions about the nature of good and evil, light and darkness. In the Demiurge's world, these forces are in constant opposition, creating a reality where suffering, death, and conflict are inevitable. The Gnostic sees this duality as a reflection of the Demiurge's ignorance, a symptom of his separation from the true God. Yet within the Pleroma, there is no duality, no conflict, only unity and light. The Gnostic path involves transcending the Demiurge's world of opposites, moving beyond the limitations of good and evil to a higher understanding of divine unity. This journey is not a rejection of morality but an invitation to see beyond it, to recognize that true reality lies in the oneness of the Pleroma, where all distinctions dissolve in the presence of the divine.

For the Gnostic, the Demiurge is both a creator and an obstacle, a being who has the power to shape reality but lacks the wisdom to do so with love or insight. His world is a place of shadows and mirrors, a labyrinth of illusions that can only be escaped through the awakening of the soul. This awakening is the ultimate act of rebellion against the Demiurge, a journey back to the divine source that lies beyond his reach. In the Gospel of Judas, Judas himself becomes a symbol of this rebellion, a figure who sees through the Demiurge's illusions and takes on the task of helping Jesus fulfill his mission of liberation.

In this vision, the Demiurge is not an equal to the Supreme God but a distorted reflection, a being who embodies the limitations of the material realm. He is a reminder of the dangers of ignorance, of the consequences of creating without true understanding. Yet even within the Demiurge's world, the spark of the divine remains, a hidden light that calls to those who seek truth. The Gnostic path, then, is not a path of rejection but of transformation—a journey that takes the soul through the darkness of the material realm and into the light of the Pleroma.

The Gospel of Judas presents this journey in all its complexity, a tale of spiritual awakening and cosmic struggle. It invites readers to consider the nature of creation, to question the structures and systems that govern the material world, and to seek the divine spark within. In this narrative, the Demiurge stands as a reminder of the obstacles that lie on the path to enlightenment, a figure who challenges the soul to look beyond the visible and embrace the hidden truths of the universe.

Through the figure of the Demiurge, the Gospel of Judas reveals a world where salvation is not given but earned, where freedom is not granted but discovered. It is a world where the soul, caught between the Demiurge's realm and the Pleroma, must find its own way home, guided by the light of gnosis and the call of the true God. The Demiurge, though powerful, is ultimately a creature of shadows, a force that can only hold the soul captive as long as it remains in ignorance. For those who awaken, who see through the illusions of the material world, the path to the Pleroma opens—a path that leads not to the worship of the Demiurge but to communion with the Supreme God and the divine fullness that lies beyond.

Chapter 6
The Supreme God and Divine Fullness

Beyond the realm of forms and matter, above the illusions and boundaries of the material world, lies the Supreme God—a being of incomprehensible purity, untouched by the limitations of creation. This is not a god of rules or laws, not a deity who demands obedience or sacrifice. The Supreme God is the source of all that is real and eternal, the infinite foundation of existence, and the silent wellspring of divine light and wisdom. In the Gnostic tradition, this Supreme God stands in contrast to the Demiurge, the ignorant creator of the material world. The Supreme God embodies a truth so vast, a purity so absolute, that it transcends even the concept of creation. To know this God is not to engage in worship as one might with the Demiurge, but to awaken to an understanding that lies beyond words and ritual, a unity that calls the soul back to its divine origin.

The Supreme God is often described in Gnostic texts as dwelling in the *Pleroma*, a term that signifies "fullness" or "abundance." The Pleroma is not merely a place; it is a state of being, an eternal and unchanging realm where all aspects of the divine exist in perfect harmony. Unlike the material world, which is fragmented and governed by the dualities of light and dark, good and evil, the Pleroma is a realm of unity, a domain where these opposites dissolve into the singular presence of divine love and knowledge. Within the Pleroma, all divine qualities exist in their purest forms, emanating from the Supreme God like rays of light from the sun, each ray representing a different aspect of the divine, each contributing to the infinite completeness of the whole.

The nature of the Supreme God defies human comprehension, for it is a reality that exists beyond thought, beyond form, beyond even existence as we understand it. This God is often described as *ineffable*, a word that signifies something too great to be expressed in words. In the Gnostic vision, the Supreme God is not bound by personality or limitation; it is a boundless sea of consciousness, an infinite source that contains all wisdom, love, and light. To the Gnostic seeker, the Supreme God represents the ultimate truth, a reality that stands in stark contrast to the material world's illusions and limitations.

One of the most intriguing aspects of the Supreme God is its profound transcendence. This is not a god who intervenes in human affairs or shapes history according to a divine plan. The Supreme God is so far beyond the material world that it remains untouched by the suffering, conflict, and decay that define existence under the Demiurge. The Supreme God does not create the world of forms and matter; instead, it exists beyond them, radiating a divine essence that is reflected in the Pleroma but obscured in the material world. For the Gnostic, the Supreme God's nature is one of complete otherness—a being so pure and vast that even to imagine it is to confront the limits of human understanding.

In the Gnostic cosmology, the Supreme God does not act or create in the way that humans might conceive of action or creation. Instead, it emanates, its essence flowing outward in a series of divine manifestations known as Aeons. These Aeons are not entities in the way that one might imagine gods or angels; they are aspects of the divine fullness, expressions of the Supreme God's qualities and attributes. Each Aeon represents a particular aspect of the divine, such as wisdom, love, truth, or light. Together, they form the Pleroma, a realm that reflects the Supreme God's nature in perfect harmony. The Aeons do not act independently; they exist as parts of a unified whole, each embodying a piece of the divine essence, each contributing to the infinite beauty and harmony of the Pleroma.

Among these Aeons, one in particular plays a significant role in the Gnostic narrative—*Sophia*, the Aeon of Wisdom. Sophia's story is one of both beauty and tragedy, for in her desire to know the Supreme God more fully, she inadvertently steps outside the Pleroma, creating a separation that leads to the birth of the Demiurge. This act of creation outside the divine fullness introduces imperfection and division into existence, giving rise to the material world. Sophia's fall from the Pleroma is a reflection of the Gnostic view that ignorance and separation lie at the heart of suffering and illusion. Yet, even in her fall, Sophia retains a connection to the Supreme God, a reminder that all beings, even those caught in the material world, are ultimately connected to the divine source.

The Pleroma and the material world represent two fundamentally different realms, one governed by unity and wholeness, the other by division and limitation. While the Pleroma exists in a state of eternal fullness, the material world is defined by absence, by a sense of lack and incompleteness. In the Pleroma, there is no need, no hunger, no death; it is a realm of pure being, where every aspect of existence is complete in itself, part of a harmonious whole. The material world, by contrast, is a place of yearning, of striving for something beyond reach, a place where souls are bound by desire and fear, trapped in the illusion of separateness.

For the Gnostic, the journey of the soul is a journey from the material world back to the Pleroma, a return to the fullness that lies beyond the Demiurge's realm of limitation. This journey is not one of physical travel but of inner awakening, a process of shedding the illusions and attachments that bind the soul to the material. Salvation, in the Gnostic sense, is not a reward given by an external deity but an inner realization, a remembering of one's true nature as a spark of the Supreme God. This realization is known as *gnosis*, a direct, experiential knowledge of the divine that transcends belief or doctrine. Through gnosis, the soul awakens to its origin in the Pleroma, recognizing that its true nature is not defined by the material world but by the infinite light of the Supreme God.

The concept of the Pleroma challenges conventional understandings of divinity, for it suggests a God who is beyond involvement in the world of matter, a God whose essence remains untouched by the suffering and conflict that define human existence. In this vision, the Supreme God does not demand worship or sacrifice, does not command obedience or seek to control. Instead, the Supreme God simply is, an infinite presence that invites souls to awaken to their true nature, to remember their origin in the divine fullness. For the Gnostic, this is a radically different view of salvation. It is not about appeasing a deity or earning favor; it is about transcending the illusions of the material world and returning to a state of divine unity.

The relationship between the Supreme God and the Demiurge is one of contrast rather than conflict. The Demiurge, in his ignorance, believes himself the only god, yet he remains blind to the higher reality of the Pleroma. His creation, the material world, is a flawed reflection of the divine, a place where light and dark, good and evil, life and death are locked in perpetual conflict. The Supreme God, however, is beyond these opposites, existing in a state of absolute unity and peace. The Pleroma is a realm without duality, a place where all aspects of existence are harmoniously integrated, reflecting the wholeness of the Supreme God's nature.

In the Gospel of Judas, Jesus speaks to Judas of the Supreme God, revealing truths that the other disciples cannot understand. He explains that the true God lies beyond the world of form and matter, a reality that cannot be seen or touched but can only be known through inner awakening. Judas, chosen to receive this knowledge, is given a glimpse of the divine fullness, a vision of the Pleroma that lies beyond the Demiurge's reach. In entrusting Judas with this revelation, Jesus invites him to transcend the material world, to look beyond the illusions of the Demiurge and recognize the divine light within himself.

The journey to the Pleroma, however, is not an easy one. It requires a profound detachment from the material world, a willingness to release the attachments and desires that bind the soul to the physical. This journey is a path of self-knowledge, of peeling back the layers of illusion to reveal the divine spark that lies hidden within. For the Gnostic, the path to the Pleroma is a path of awakening, a process of becoming aware of one's true nature as a fragment of the Supreme God, a process of remembering one's origin in the divine fullness.

In this vision, the Supreme God is not distant but profoundly intimate, a presence that exists within each soul, a light that calls each being back to its source. The Pleroma is not a far-off heaven but a reality that exists beyond the illusions of the material world, a realm that can be known through the inner journey of the soul. The Gnostic path is one of return, a journey back to the fullness from which each soul originated, a journey that transcends the boundaries of the physical and moves toward the infinite.

The Supreme God, in the Gnostic understanding, is a mystery beyond comprehension, a source that cannot be defined or limited by human thought. This God does not judge or condemn; instead, it offers a path to liberation, a way out of the suffering and ignorance that define the material world. To know this God is to awaken to a reality that lies beyond all fear, beyond all division, a reality where the soul finds its true home in the eternal light of the Pleroma.

In revealing the Supreme God to Judas, Jesus unveils the possibility of this return, a return not to a place but to a state of being, a state of divine fullness. He invites Judas to see beyond the forms of this world, to recognize the illusions that keep souls bound, and to embrace the path of inner awakening. For Judas, this revelation is both a gift and a burden, for it requires him to see through the lies of the Demiurge, to understand that the world as it appears is not the ultimate reality, but a shadow of the divine truth that lies beyond.

The Supreme God and the Pleroma represent the ultimate goal of the Gnostic path, a destination that lies not in the afterlife or in a distant heaven but within the soul itself. It is a journey that requires courage, for it means leaving behind the familiar, the comfortable, and the known. It is a journey into the mystery of the divine, a journey that leads beyond the Demiurge's world and into the eternal light of the Supreme God. In the Gospel of Judas, this journey is illuminated, a path marked by the call of gnosis, a call that invites each soul to remember, to awaken, and to return to the fullness from which it came.

For the Gnostic seeker, the Supreme God is the final reality, a presence that exists beyond creation, beyond form, beyond even the concepts of good and evil. To know this God is to know oneself, to recognize the divine spark within and to realize that one's true nature is not of this world but of the Pleroma, the realm of eternal light and unity. In this understanding, salvation is not about escaping punishment or achieving reward; it is about awakening to a truth that transcends all boundaries, a truth that calls each soul to return to the fullness from which it was born, to merge once again with the infinite, silent presence of the Supreme God.

Chapter 7
Divine Hierarchy and Intermediate Beings

In the Gnostic cosmology, the universe is far more than the visible world of forms and matter. It is a layered, intricate realm, rich with divine forces and intermediate beings who act as conduits between the Supreme God and creation. These beings, known as Aeons, Archons, and other entities, exist on different planes of existence and serve unique roles within the cosmic order. The Gnostic universe is structured as a grand hierarchy, an ordered system where each being and force occupies a specific place in relation to the Supreme God and the material world below. This hierarchy is not a mere structure of power but a chain of emanations, a series of reflections that bridge the Supreme God's unknowable essence with the tangible realm of creation.

At the highest level of this hierarchy is the Supreme God, dwelling in the Pleroma—a realm of pure fullness, unity, and divine light. From this God emanate the Aeons, who are the first and purest expressions of divine essence. These beings are not gods in the way we might understand; rather, they are aspects of the Supreme God, reflections of divine qualities such as wisdom, love, truth, and beauty. The Aeons together form the Pleroma, an interconnected web of divinity that reflects the Supreme God's nature in all its completeness. In the Pleroma, there is no separation or division; each Aeon exists in harmony with the others, together comprising a totality of divine perfection.

One of the most significant Aeons in the Gnostic mythos is Sophia, the Aeon of Wisdom. Sophia's role is central in Gnostic cosmology, for it is through her that the story of creation and fall unfolds. Sophia, whose name means "wisdom," embodies the Supreme God's attribute of divine insight, yet her curiosity and desire to know the depths of the Supreme God lead her to step outside the bounds of the Pleroma. This act of separation results in the birth of the Demiurge—a lesser creator deity who is cut off from the Pleroma and unaware of the Supreme God. Sophia's journey represents a cosmic descent, an event that gives rise to the material world and introduces imperfection and separation into existence.

Sophia's separation from the Pleroma is a tale of both tragedy and redemption. In her longing to know the Supreme God more fully, she unintentionally creates a being who embodies her lack of knowledge—the Demiurge. This being, limited in wisdom and understanding, believes himself to be the ultimate creator, and in his ignorance, he shapes the material world. Sophia's fall represents a cosmic rupture, a moment where divine unity fragments into duality, giving rise to the realm of form and matter. Yet, even in her separation, Sophia remains connected to the Supreme God, her essence retaining a spark of divine light that offers a path to redemption and reunion with the Pleroma.

As the Demiurge fashions the material world, he is joined by other beings—entities known as Archons. These Archons are his helpers, rulers of the physical and astral realms who assist in maintaining the structures of the material world. They are agents of the Demiurge, embodying his ignorance and limited perspective. The Archons act as gatekeepers, enforcing the laws of the material universe and keeping souls bound to the world of matter and illusion. In Gnostic thought, the Archons are seen as hostile forces, entities who prevent souls from perceiving the truth of their divine origin. They represent the obstacles that souls must overcome on their journey back to the Pleroma.

Each Archon has a specific role within this hierarchy of control. They influence human thought, desires, and emotions, binding individuals to the physical plane through attachments, fears, and ignorance. In many Gnostic texts, these Archons are portrayed as beings who control the planets and the stars, using astrological forces to shape human destiny. Their power lies in their ability to manipulate the material world and maintain the illusion of separateness, an illusion that keeps souls blind to the divine spark within. For the Gnostic, the Archons are forces to be overcome, adversaries who must be transcended through knowledge and inner awakening.

The Demiurge, though powerful within the material realm, is still subordinate to the Aeons and the Supreme God. His dominion extends only over the physical universe, and he remains blind to the existence of the Pleroma and the divine beings within it. While he believes himself to be the ultimate creator, his power is limited, and his realm is but a shadow of the true reality that exists beyond. The Demiurge's ignorance is his greatest flaw, for it blinds him to the higher truths of the Pleroma and keeps him bound to a reality of division, duality, and limitation.

This cosmic hierarchy, from the Supreme God and the Aeons down to the Demiurge and Archons, reflects the Gnostic belief in a universe that is both interconnected and hierarchical. Each level of being emanates from the level above it, with the Supreme God at the pinnacle, followed by the Aeons, the Demiurge, and finally the material world. The structure of this hierarchy is not meant to impose authority or control; rather, it represents a process of emanation, a continuous flow of divine energy from the Supreme God down to the lowest levels of existence. Each step in this hierarchy is a reflection of the divine, albeit in increasingly diminished forms.

The Gnostic seeker's path is a journey up this hierarchy, a return to the Pleroma through the awakening of the divine spark within. This spark, which is a fragment of the Supreme God, lies hidden within the soul, obscured by the illusions of the material world and the influence of the Archons. The journey of the soul involves recognizing this spark, nurturing it, and allowing it to guide the individual through the layers of illusion back to the truth of the Pleroma. This journey is one of knowledge, self-discovery, and inner transformation, a path that leads beyond the material and into the realms of divine fullness.

To ascend this hierarchy, the soul must overcome the influence of the Archons and see through the deceptions of the Demiurge. This is not an easy task, for the Archons exert a powerful influence over human consciousness, binding individuals to the cycles of desire, attachment, and ignorance. The Gnostic path requires a radical shift in perception, a willingness to let go of the illusions of the material world and seek the deeper truths that lie within. Gnosis, or spiritual knowledge, is the key to this liberation. Through gnosis, the soul awakens to its divine nature and begins to see the material world as a temporary stage, a place of learning and growth rather than a final destination.

In the Gospel of Judas, Jesus reveals these truths to Judas, inviting him to see beyond the superficial understanding of the other disciples. He speaks of the divine hierarchy and the nature of the Supreme God, the Aeons, and the Demiurge, offering Judas a glimpse of the Pleroma that lies beyond the reach of the material world. This knowledge sets Judas apart, marking him as the chosen disciple who understands the true nature of Jesus's mission. Through this revelation, Judas becomes a symbol of the Gnostic seeker, an individual who dares to look beyond appearances and seeks the truth that lies within.

The divine hierarchy in Gnosticism also highlights the concept of intermediaries—beings who assist in guiding souls back to the Pleroma. These intermediaries, who may include enlightened teachers, prophets, or spiritual beings, serve as guides on the path to gnosis. They are not worshipped but respected as fellow travelers who have attained higher levels of understanding and can offer wisdom and insight. In the Gospel of Judas, Jesus himself acts as such a guide, a being of light who descends from the Pleroma to reveal the path of liberation. His role is not to demand worship but to illuminate the way, to show souls the truth of their divine origin and the path back to unity with the Supreme God.

This notion of intermediaries speaks to the Gnostic view of salvation as an inner journey rather than a series of rituals or acts of obedience. Salvation, in Gnosticism, is a matter of awakening, a process of peeling back the layers of illusion that obscure the soul's true nature. The divine hierarchy exists not to impose authority but to facilitate this awakening, to provide a structure that helps souls understand their place in the cosmos and the path that leads back to the Pleroma. The Aeons, as emanations of the Supreme God, serve as reminders of the divine fullness that lies beyond, while the Archons represent the forces that must be transcended to reach it.

The Gnostic understanding of divine hierarchy also challenges conventional religious structures. In orthodox belief systems, hierarchy often implies authority, with God at the top, followed by angels, priests, and finally believers. In contrast, the Gnostic hierarchy is one of emanation rather than control. The Supreme God does not command or judge; it simply is, radiating divine light that flows downward through the Aeons and into the material world. Each being within this hierarchy plays a role, not in enforcing obedience but in reflecting the divine essence in different ways. The journey of the soul is one of ascension, a process of moving upward through the layers of existence, reconnecting with the divine qualities that lie within.

In the cosmic order presented by Gnostic thought, each soul has the potential to rise through this hierarchy, to transcend the influence of the Demiurge and return to the Pleroma. The Gnostic path is a journey of self-discovery, where the seeker gradually becomes aware of their divine nature and learns to see through the illusions that keep them bound. Through this journey, the soul reconnects with the Supreme God, not as a distant ruler but as an intimate presence, a source of light and truth that exists within. The soul's ascent is a return to fullness, a process of reuniting with the divine essence from which it originated.

For the Gnostic, this divine hierarchy is not a barrier but a map, a guide to understanding the nature of existence and the soul's place within it. It is a reminder that the material world, with all its trials and challenges, is only a temporary realm, a stepping stone on the path to spiritual awakening. The Gospel of Judas captures this vision, portraying Judas as a figure who understands the true nature of the cosmos and is willing to embrace the journey that leads beyond the Demiurge's world and into the Pleroma.

The divine hierarchy, with its layers of beings and emanations, represents the Gnostic vision of a universe that is both ordered and transcendent. It is a structure that reflects the Supreme God's infinite nature, a realm of light and unity that calls each soul to remember its divine origin. For those who seek, who dare to look beyond the visible and embrace the hidden truths, the path to the Pleroma opens, offering a way back to the fullness that lies beyond all form, beyond all separation, in the eternal light of the Supreme God.

Chapter 8
The Dual Nature of the Universe

In the depths of Gnostic thought, the universe reveals itself as a landscape divided—a place where the eternal spirit and the transient material are locked in opposition. Gnosticism teaches that the cosmos is composed of two fundamental aspects: the spiritual and the material, the divine and the fallen, each pulling in different directions, each representing a distinct facet of existence. This duality is not merely a division of realms but a reflection of an ongoing tension between two competing forces, each with its own nature, purpose, and destination. The Gnostic journey is, at its heart, an attempt to navigate this divided universe, to understand the true nature of these opposing worlds and to find a path back to the unity that lies beyond the split.

The material world, according to Gnostic belief, is the domain of the Demiurge, the lesser god who creates out of ignorance and arrogance. The Demiurge, blind to the higher realms, fashions a universe that is imperfect, filled with suffering, death, and limitation. This world, though tangible and immediate to our senses, is ultimately a prison—a web of illusion designed to keep souls from seeing the truth of their divine origin. The Demiurge's creation is a place of fragmentation, where unity is lost, and beings are separated from one another and from their divine source. In this world, the spirit, which originates in the realm of the Supreme God, is trapped in physical form, bound to cycles of birth and death, experiencing the dualities of joy and pain, light and darkness.

In stark contrast, the spiritual world is the domain of the Supreme God, a realm known as the Pleroma. This is a place of fullness and unity, a state where all is in perfect harmony, undivided by the illusions of form and matter. The Pleroma is not merely a distant heaven but an entirely different order of existence—a reality where duality dissolves, and all beings exist in oneness with the divine. Here, there is no separation, no suffering, and no death; it is a realm of eternal life and light, untouched by the forces that govern the material world. The Gnostics see the Pleroma as the true home of the soul, the place from which it originates and to which it longs to return.

This fundamental duality between the Pleroma and the material world shapes the Gnostic understanding of existence. For the Gnostic, the physical universe is a place of exile, a realm that pulls the soul away from its divine source, binding it to the Demiurge's creation through desires, fears, and attachments. Yet within each human being lies a fragment of the divine—a spark of the Supreme God, hidden beneath layers of materiality. This spark, or divine essence, is the soul's connection to the Pleroma, a reminder of its origin and a guide that can lead it back to the fullness of the divine. The Gnostic path, then, is a journey of liberation, an ascent from the world of form to the world of spirit, from division to unity.

The dual nature of the universe also shapes the Gnostic understanding of good and evil. In Gnostic thought, good and evil are not simple moral opposites but reflections of the cosmic division between spirit and matter. Goodness is associated with the realm of the Pleroma, where divine light and wisdom flow freely, while evil is linked to the material world, a place governed by ignorance, desire, and separation. Yet the Gnostic view of evil is complex, for it does not arise from malice or malevolence but from the Demiurge's ignorance and blindness. The material world is flawed not because it is intentionally harmful but because it is disconnected from the source of true wisdom. The Demiurge creates without knowledge of the Supreme God, resulting in a world that is inherently limited and incomplete.

This understanding of evil as ignorance rather than malice leads to a unique Gnostic view of salvation. For the Gnostic, salvation is not about atonement for sin but liberation from ignorance. It is the recognition that the material world, with all its allure and suffering, is a distraction from the soul's true purpose. The path to salvation is not one of moral perfection but of knowledge—gnosis—that allows the soul to see beyond the illusions of the Demiurge's world and understand its true nature as a fragment of the divine. This knowledge frees the soul from the grip of the material world, enabling it to ascend to the Pleroma and reunite with the Supreme God.

In the Gospel of Judas, Jesus speaks of this duality, revealing to Judas the nature of the material world and the hidden truth of the divine realm. He explains that the physical universe is not the true creation, but a shadow, a temporary construct that obscures the eternal reality of the Pleroma. To Jesus, the material world is a veil that must be lifted, an illusion that must be seen through for the soul to awaken. Judas, as the chosen disciple, is granted insight into this truth, understanding that the visible world is not the final reality but a place where souls are held captive by ignorance and illusion.

For Gnostics, the body itself is a symbol of this imprisonment. The physical body, with its desires and limitations, represents the material world's hold on the soul. It is a vessel that binds the divine spark to the earthly plane, subjecting it to the influences of the Demiurge and his Archons, who work to keep souls focused on the physical rather than the spiritual. The body, though necessary for life in the material world, is ultimately a hindrance to spiritual awakening. The Gnostic path involves a process of detachment from the body's desires, a turning inward to discover the divine spark within and cultivate a connection to the Pleroma. This detachment is not a rejection of the body but a recognition that the soul's true nature lies beyond physical existence.

The dual nature of the universe creates a tension that shapes every aspect of the Gnostic path. To live in the material world while striving for the spiritual is to live in a constant state of paradox, balancing the demands of the physical realm with the call of the divine. Gnostics see the material world as a place of trials and challenges, where the soul is tested, refined, and ultimately prepared for its return to the Pleroma. This world, though flawed, serves a purpose—it is a crucible in which the soul can learn, grow, and awaken to its divine nature. Yet this process is fraught with obstacles, for the Demiurge and his Archons work tirelessly to keep souls distracted, bound to the cycle of birth and death, unable to see the path that leads beyond.

The Gnostic duality also redefines the role of the teacher. In Gnostic texts, teachers like Jesus do not merely impart knowledge; they serve as guides who help seekers navigate the material world's illusions and find their way back to the Pleroma. Jesus's role in the Gospel of Judas is precisely this: he offers Judas insights that enable him to understand the true nature of the universe, to see beyond the superficial and recognize the hidden truth of his own divine origin. Jesus does not demand worship or obedience; he invites Judas to see, to awaken, and to remember. This approach reflects the Gnostic belief that each individual must undertake their own journey of awakening, that true knowledge cannot be given but must be discovered within.

The dual nature of the universe also challenges the way Gnostics view life, death, and the afterlife. In the Demiurge's world, life and death are part of a cycle that keeps souls bound to the physical realm. Birth leads to death, which leads to rebirth, in a seemingly endless loop that prevents souls from reaching the Pleroma. For the Gnostic, this cycle is a trap, a means by which the Demiurge and his Archons keep souls from awakening. True liberation involves breaking free from this cycle, transcending the material world, and returning to the realm of spirit. Death, in this sense, is not an end but a transition, a moment when the soul has the opportunity to escape the Demiurge's creation and ascend to the Pleroma. Yet this ascent requires gnosis, for without knowledge of the true God, the soul remains bound to the cycle, reincarnating again and again, unable to find its way home.

This duality is also reflected in the Gnostic view of knowledge itself. In the Demiurge's world, knowledge is often confined to the material—knowledge of science, art, history, and philosophy, all of which relate to the world of form. But gnosis, the spiritual knowledge that leads to liberation, is of an entirely different order. It is a knowledge that transcends facts and information, a direct experience of the divine that awakens the soul to its true nature. This gnosis is what the Gnostic seeks, for it is the key to seeing through the illusions of the material world and entering the Pleroma. It is a knowledge that cannot be taught but must be realized, a journey of self-discovery that each soul must undertake for itself.

The Gospel of Judas illuminates this path, showing the dual nature of the universe not as a flaw but as a structure through which the soul can find its way back to the divine. Judas, in his unique role, is not condemned for his actions but elevated as a figure who understands the necessity of transcendence. His betrayal is not a sin but an act that facilitates Jesus's return to the Pleroma, a reminder that the journey to the divine often involves difficult choices and sacrifices. Judas's understanding of this duality allows him to see the material world for what it is—a place of temporary exile—and to embrace the spiritual truth that lies beyond.

For the Gnostic, this dual nature of the universe serves as a guide, a framework that helps the soul navigate the challenges of existence. The material world, though flawed and limited, provides the soul with the experiences and insights needed to grow, to learn, and to awaken. The Pleroma, the ultimate reality, is the soul's true destination, a realm of light and unity that awaits those who dare to seek the truth. The journey from the material to the spiritual, from the world of illusion to the realm of fullness, is the essence of the Gnostic path—a path that leads not away from the world but through it, toward a greater understanding of the divine light that shines within and beyond.

Chapter 9
Creation and the Material World

The Gnostic view of creation is a tale woven with paradox, a story of divine light and dark shadows, of a world brought into being not by the Supreme God but by the Demiurge—a figure of limited vision and flawed understanding. This perspective turns conventional religious views of creation on their head, for in Gnosticism, the material world is not seen as a perfect work of a loving God. Instead, it is the product of ignorance, a construct designed to confine and deceive, to keep souls bound in a realm of illusion and separation from their divine origin. To the Gnostic, creation is not a glorious act but a cosmic misstep, an unintended consequence of separation from the divine fullness of the Pleroma.

At the heart of Gnostic cosmology lies the figure of the Demiurge, a being who fashions the material universe but lacks awareness of the Supreme God. This Demiurge, though powerful, is ultimately a limited creator. He is driven by a false belief in his own supremacy, blind to the higher reality of the Pleroma, where the true God resides. In many Gnostic texts, he is depicted as arrogant and jealous, fiercely protective of his creation and insistent that he is the only god. But he is, in truth, a lesser being, an accidental byproduct of a momentary lapse in the Pleroma's perfect harmony.

The story of the Demiurge's origin begins with the Aeon known as Sophia, the divine personification of Wisdom. Sophia, in her desire to know the Supreme God more fully, acts independently, attempting to create without the consent of the Pleroma. This act of separation results in the birth of the

Demiurge, a being who embodies her lack of complete knowledge and understanding. The Demiurge, born outside the Pleroma, lacks direct access to the divine fullness and is therefore separated from the true source of light and wisdom. Believing himself alone and supreme, he undertakes the act of creation, crafting a world that reflects his own ignorance and limitation.

This world, the material realm in which we live, is a place of imperfection and suffering, a shadowed reflection of the Pleroma's divine light. The Demiurge's creation is governed by cycles of birth, death, and decay—a place where souls are bound to the physical, separated from the spiritual, and kept in ignorance of their divine origin. In this world, everything is fragmented, divided by the boundaries of form and matter. The Gnostics see this fragmentation as a result of the Demiurge's flawed nature; he cannot create a world of unity and wholeness because he himself is cut off from the Supreme God. His creation, therefore, is marked by duality, by the oppositions of light and dark, pleasure and pain, life and death.

According to Gnostic teachings, the Demiurge does not work alone. He is aided by a group of beings known as Archons, rulers who govern different aspects of the material world. These Archons are his agents, enforcers of his order, and they serve to maintain the structure of the Demiurge's creation. In many ways, they embody the forces that keep souls bound to the material world—forces of desire, fear, and ignorance. The Archons create laws and systems that govern the physical realm, influencing human thought, emotions, and behaviors, ensuring that souls remain focused on the material rather than the spiritual. They are the keepers of illusion, manipulating human perception to prevent individuals from awakening to the truth of their divine essence.

The Gnostic view of creation, then, is not one of celebration but of caution. To the Gnostic, the material world is a prison, a place where the soul's divine spark is trapped within the limits of the body and subjected to the cycles of time and change. The body, though necessary for life in the material realm, is seen as a hindrance to spiritual awakening, a vessel that binds the soul to the physical and distracts it from its higher purpose. The Archons, through their influence, encourage attachment to the body and the pleasures of the physical world, reinforcing the illusions that keep souls from recognizing their divine origin.

In the Gospel of Judas, Jesus reveals this hidden reality to Judas, offering him insight into the true nature of creation and the identity of the Demiurge. He explains that the material world is a place of shadows, a realm crafted by a being who does not know the true God and who, in his ignorance, believes himself supreme. Jesus's revelation to Judas serves as an invitation to see beyond the visible, to recognize the prison of the material world and seek the path that leads beyond it. For Judas, this knowledge is both a burden and a liberation, for it sets him apart from the other disciples, granting him a glimpse of truths that they cannot yet understand.

The Gnostics believe that within each human being lies a spark of the divine—a fragment of the Supreme God that the Demiurge cannot control. This divine spark is the soul's connection to the Pleroma, a reminder of its origin and a guide on the journey back to the divine fullness. The Demiurge and his Archons may rule the material world, but they cannot extinguish this spark, for it is a part of the Supreme God, a light that endures even in the darkest of realms. This spark is the soul's true essence, its divine core, and it is through the awakening of this spark that the soul can begin to transcend the material world and find its way back to the Pleroma.

To the Gnostic, the journey of the soul is a journey of awakening, an inner path that leads from ignorance to knowledge, from bondage to freedom. Salvation is not found through obedience to the Demiurge or adherence to his laws, but through gnosis—a deep, personal knowledge of the divine that allows the soul to see beyond the illusions of the material world. This gnosis is not mere intellectual understanding but a transformative insight, a realization that changes the soul's perception of reality. Through gnosis, the soul comes to understand that the material world is not the ultimate reality, but a temporary state, a place of exile that can be transcended.

In this view, creation is not an end in itself but a means—a stage in the soul's journey toward awakening. The material world, with all its beauty and suffering, its joys and sorrows, serves as a testing ground, a place where the soul can learn, grow, and ultimately recognize its true nature. The Gnostic does not deny the value of the material world, but sees it as a realm that must be understood and transcended. The soul's task is to see through the illusions of the Demiurge's creation, to recognize the divine spark within, and to embark on the journey back to the Pleroma.

The concept of creation in Gnosticism also carries implications for the role of the teacher. In the Gospel of Judas, Jesus serves not as a conventional savior but as a revealer of mysteries, a guide who helps Judas understand the true nature of the universe. His role is not to lead his followers in worship of the Demiurge or to teach them how to thrive in the material world, but to open their eyes to the hidden truths that lie beyond it. Jesus's teachings offer a path to liberation, a way out of the cycles of birth and death, of pleasure and pain, that define the Demiurge's creation. His message is one of awakening, an invitation to see beyond the physical and recognize the spiritual reality that lies within.

The material world, though governed by the Demiurge and the Archons, is ultimately a place of potential transformation. For the Gnostic, each experience, each moment of suffering or joy, can serve as a catalyst for awakening, a reminder of the soul's true nature and its connection to the Pleroma. The trials of the material world are not meaningless; they are opportunities for the soul to learn, to grow, and to remember its divine origin. The journey through creation is a process of refinement, a gradual awakening to the truth that lies beyond the visible and the tangible.

In this journey, the Gnostic must confront the illusions of the Demiurge's creation, must see through the desires and fears that bind the soul to the physical. The path to liberation is one of detachment, a letting go of the attachments to wealth, power, and pleasure that keep the soul focused on the material. This detachment is not a rejection of life but a reorientation of perception, a shift from seeing the material world as the ultimate reality to understanding it as a temporary state, a stage in the soul's journey.

The Gnostic concept of creation challenges conventional religious views by suggesting that the physical universe is not the work of a benevolent, all-knowing God, but of a limited, ignorant being. This perspective invites the seeker to question the nature of reality, to look beyond appearances and consider the possibility of a higher truth that lies beyond the material. In this vision, creation is a paradox—a world of beauty and pain, of light and darkness, that both binds and liberates, that confines the soul yet offers a path to freedom.

The Gospel of Judas captures this paradox, portraying Judas as a figure who understands the need to transcend the material world and the limitations of the Demiurge's creation. His actions, though misunderstood by the other disciples, are part of a larger plan, a step on the path to liberation that leads beyond the physical and into the spiritual. Through his understanding of creation, Judas becomes a symbol of the Gnostic seeker, an individual who dares to look beyond the surface and embrace the mysteries of the divine.

For the Gnostic, creation is not a final destination but a gateway, a place where the soul can learn to see, to awaken, and to remember. It is a realm of separation that ultimately calls the soul back to unity, a place of exile that serves as a guide back to the Pleroma. The journey through creation is a journey of awakening, a process of seeing through the illusions of the Demiurge and recognizing the divine spark within. In this vision, the material world is not a curse but a challenge, a test of the soul's ability to remember its true nature and find its way back to the Supreme God.

Through creation, the soul embarks on a journey of self-discovery, a path that leads from ignorance to knowledge, from bondage to freedom. The Demiurge's world, though flawed and imperfect, offers a path to the divine, a way for the soul to awaken and return to the fullness of the Pleroma. This journey is the essence of the Gnostic path—a journey that transcends the visible, that moves beyond the bounds of the material, and that ultimately leads back to the infinite light and unity of the Supreme God.

Chapter 10
Judas and the Sacrifice of the Body

In the Gospel of Judas, Judas Iscariot is no longer just the infamous betrayer but the pivotal figure who understands the necessity of Jesus's path—specifically, the release of his divine essence from the confines of his physical form. To the Gnostics, this act is not one of betrayal but of profound spiritual insight. Judas, as the chosen disciple, is entrusted with a knowledge that transcends the material world, revealing the ultimate purpose behind Jesus's earthly journey and the role of the body as a vessel to be transcended. The body, in the Gnostic perspective, is a temporary prison, and the act of relinquishing it is seen as the ultimate sacrifice, an essential step for the soul to return to the divine Pleroma.

The story of Judas in the Gospel of Judas sheds light on the Gnostic perception of the body and physical existence as a limitation, a binding that must be overcome for the soul to attain freedom. This perspective is at odds with orthodox Christianity, which views the body as a divine creation to be resurrected and redeemed. In contrast, Gnosticism teaches that the physical form is crafted by the Demiurge, the lesser god whose ignorance and limitations are reflected in the material world. This world of flesh and blood, subject to decay, suffering, and death, is an imperfect reflection of the divine light, a shadow cast by the Demiurge's ignorance. In this view, the body is a shackle, an earthly vessel that obscures the soul's true, eternal nature.

In Gnostic tradition, Jesus's mission is not about saving humanity through bodily resurrection but about liberating souls from the material prison of flesh. His teachings guide those who seek liberation, urging them to awaken to the true reality beyond the physical. In the Gospel of Judas, Jesus conveys this understanding to Judas, helping him see that the act of "betrayal" is, in fact, a necessary step for Jesus to shed his earthly form. By handing Jesus over to the authorities, Judas facilitates his release from the physical world, enabling him to return to the divine Pleroma. Judas, in this role, becomes more than just a follower; he is the one who understands the secret, who recognizes that Jesus's death is not a loss but a liberation.

To understand the significance of Judas's role, we must look deeper into the Gnostic conception of the body and its relationship to the soul. For the Gnostic, the body is an impediment, a temporary vehicle that weighs down the divine spark within. Life in the material world is seen as a state of exile, where the soul is trapped in physical form, separated from the divine light of the Supreme God. This separation is not merely physical but spiritual; it creates a sense of alienation, a longing for something beyond the tangible world. The soul yearns to return to the Pleroma, yet it is bound by the body, distracted by physical desires, needs, and attachments. The body, though essential for earthly existence, is ultimately an obstacle to the soul's true purpose.

Judas's role in Jesus's death serves as a powerful symbol of the Gnostic journey toward liberation. In choosing to hand Jesus over, Judas becomes a catalyst for the release of the divine spark from its earthly confines. This act is not a betrayal in the conventional sense, but a sacred duty, a recognition of the higher purpose that transcends human judgment and morality. Judas's willingness to fulfill this role speaks to his spiritual maturity, his understanding of the Gnostic truth that the soul's freedom lies beyond the material, beyond the attachments that bind it to the physical world. He understands that true liberation requires the ultimate sacrifice—the release of the body, the shedding of the material in order to embrace the spiritual.

The Gnostic view of sacrifice is far removed from the traditional understanding of martyrdom or atonement. In orthodox

Christianity, sacrifice is often seen as an act of redemption, a way to purify or cleanse. However, in Gnosticism, sacrifice is the means by which one transcends the physical, a way to return to the Pleroma by shedding the limitations of the body. For Jesus, this act of sacrifice is not about appeasing a deity or atoning for sin but about breaking free from the Demiurge's creation and returning to the divine source. His death, facilitated by Judas, is not an end but a transition, a moment when the soul is freed from the body's prison and allowed to ascend to the true realm of spirit.

This perspective on the body and sacrifice reflects the Gnostic duality between spirit and matter. The physical world, governed by the Demiurge, is a realm of illusion, a place where the soul is bound by the senses and the desires of the flesh. The body, while necessary for life in this realm, is ultimately a limitation, a vehicle that confines the soul to the material. The Gnostic path involves transcending these limitations, awakening to the divine spark within, and moving beyond the illusions of the physical. Sacrifice, in this context, is the act of letting go of the body, of releasing the soul from the bonds of flesh so that it may return to the Pleroma.

In the Gospel of Judas, Jesus's teachings to Judas emphasize this need for liberation. He explains that the other disciples, though devoted, do not understand the true nature of his mission. They see him as a king who will establish a kingdom on earth, a savior who will deliver them from earthly suffering. But Judas understands that Jesus's mission is not about earthly power or redemption; it is about transcending the material world, about guiding souls back to the divine light. Judas's role, then, is one of profound spiritual insight, for he is the only disciple who perceives the necessity of Jesus's death as an act of liberation.

Judas's "betrayal" becomes a symbol of the Gnostic path—a willingness to defy convention, to embrace the mystery of death as a step toward spiritual freedom. In delivering Jesus to the authorities, Judas is not condemning him; he is freeing him. This act becomes a model for the Gnostic understanding of sacrifice, where the release of the body is seen not as a loss but as a gateway to the divine. Judas, as the chosen disciple, embraces this truth, recognizing that the material world's attachments and fears are illusions that must be transcended for the soul to find its way back to the Pleroma.

For the Gnostic, this view of sacrifice is not limited to physical death but extends to a way of life, a practice of letting go of attachments to the material. The body, while necessary, is a temporary vessel, and the soul's journey involves learning to see beyond its confines. Gnostic practices of contemplation and self-knowledge are designed to help the seeker detach from the body's desires, to see through the illusions of the physical world and cultivate an awareness of the divine spark within. This awareness allows the soul to begin its journey back to the Pleroma, a journey that ultimately leads to the shedding of the body and the return to unity with the Supreme God.

In Gnostic thought, this concept of sacrifice also transforms the way one views suffering. In the Demiurge's world, suffering is inescapable; it is part of the fabric of the material realm, a reflection of the ignorance and limitation that define the Demiurge's creation. Yet for the Gnostic, suffering can serve as a catalyst for awakening, a reminder that the material world is not the soul's true home. By embracing this perspective, the Gnostic learns to see suffering not as an end but as a means—a way to transcend the illusions of the Demiurge's world and find the path that leads back to the Pleroma.

The Gospel of Judas portrays Jesus's death as the ultimate act of liberation, an event that allows him to return to the divine realm from which he came. Judas, in understanding this, becomes a symbol of the soul's journey toward freedom, a figure who dares to see beyond the surface and embrace the deeper truth. His actions reflect the Gnostic ideal of sacrifice, where the release of the body is seen as a necessary step for the soul to find its way back to the light. Judas's understanding of this truth sets him apart, marking him as a figure of profound spiritual courage, a disciple who perceives the mystery of life and death beyond the illusions of the material world.

For Gnostics, the story of Judas and the sacrifice of the body serves as a reminder of the path to liberation. It is a call to transcend the physical, to let go of the attachments and fears that keep the soul bound to the material. The Gnostic journey is not about preserving the body but about recognizing the body's role as a temporary vessel, a means by which the soul experiences the material world but ultimately seeks to rise beyond it. The true sacrifice, in this view, is the willingness to release the body, to embrace the journey back to the Pleroma, where the soul is reunited with the divine fullness.

The figure of Judas in the Gospel of Judas thus becomes a powerful symbol of the soul's quest for liberation. His actions reflect a deep understanding of the need to transcend the material, to release the body and return to the source. For the Gnostic, this is the ultimate act of faith—a faith not in the power of the Demiurge or the permanence of the physical, but in the eternal light of the Supreme God. Judas's sacrifice, then, is not an act of betrayal but an expression of love and knowledge, a recognition that true freedom lies beyond the body, in the realm of spirit.

In this vision, the Gnostic path is one of constant letting go, a journey of shedding the layers of attachment and illusion that bind the soul to the material world. The body, while essential for life in the Demiurge's creation, is ultimately a hindrance to the soul's true purpose. Judas's role in Jesus's death serves as a model for this journey, a reminder that the path to the Pleroma involves sacrifice, a willingness to release the body and embrace the divine. The Gospel of Judas invites the reader to see beyond the surface, to understand that the body is but a temporary state, and that true life lies in the eternal light of the Supreme God.

Through the story of Judas, Gnosticism offers a vision of liberation that defies conventional beliefs, a path that leads not to attachment but to freedom, not to preservation but to transcendence. It is a journey that moves beyond the body, beyond the physical, and into the realms of spirit, where the soul finds its true home. Judas's actions in the Gospel of Judas, misunderstood and condemned by the world, serve as a testament to the Gnostic ideal of sacrifice—the ultimate release of the body and the return to the Pleroma, where the soul is once again united with the infinite, boundless light of the Supreme God.

Chapter 11
The Gnostic Path of Salvation

In the Gnostic vision of the universe, salvation is a journey of awakening, an act of recognition rather than redemption. It is not a gift bestowed by a deity nor a reward for obedience, but an inner process—a personal, transformative revelation known as *gnosis*, or divine knowledge. The Gnostic path of salvation is both a rejection of the illusions imposed by the material world and an ascent back to the divine fullness of the Pleroma. In this framework, salvation lies in seeing the world as it truly is, freeing the soul from ignorance and returning to its origin in the Supreme God.

In conventional religious beliefs, salvation is often associated with absolution from sin, adherence to laws, and faith in an external savior. Orthodox Christianity, for instance, teaches that salvation is attained through belief in Christ's atoning sacrifice, through the church's teachings, and through sacraments that cleanse and sanctify. In contrast, Gnosticism proposes a radically different view, one that dismisses the material world as a flawed construct crafted by the Demiurge—a being of ignorance who ensnares souls in cycles of birth, death, and spiritual amnesia. To the Gnostic, the need for salvation arises not from moral failings but from ignorance of the soul's true nature and origin. In the Gnostic view, the act of waking from this ignorance, the recognition of one's inner divinity, is the essence of salvation.

The term *gnosis* is central to this process. Derived from the Greek word for "knowledge," gnosis represents not intellectual knowledge but an intuitive, experiential understanding of divine truth. It is a form of spiritual awakening, a direct apprehension of one's true self as a fragment of the divine. For the Gnostic, gnosis is not something that can be taught or transferred by external means; it is a deep, personal revelation that occurs within the soul. This knowledge is transformative, liberating the soul from the illusions of the Demiurge's world and allowing it to perceive the divine light within.

The Gospel of Judas hints at this Gnostic path of salvation, presenting Jesus as a guide who reveals hidden truths rather than a savior who enforces obedience. In his private conversations with Judas, Jesus explains the nature of the material world and the true purpose of his mission, offering Judas insights that transcend conventional belief. Jesus does not instruct Judas to follow laws or perform rituals; instead, he invites him to see beyond appearances, to perceive the invisible truths that lie beneath the surface. This teaching resonates with the Gnostic belief that salvation is not found in outward acts or devotion to a deity but in the soul's journey inward, where it encounters the divine spark within itself.

The Gnostic path of salvation is also deeply personal, an individual journey that each soul must undertake on its own. Unlike orthodox religions, which often emphasize collective worship and communal rites, Gnosticism values solitude and self-exploration. Each person's experience of gnosis is unique, shaped by their own inner journey and encounters with the divine. The Gnostic path is not one-size-fits-all; it is a path of self-discovery and transformation, where each soul finds its own way back to the Pleroma. This inward journey requires courage, for it involves confronting the illusions of the material world, shedding attachments, and letting go of familiar beliefs. The soul must be willing to stand apart from the world, to question its reality and seek the hidden truth that lies beyond.

In Gnostic thought, the material world is seen as a realm of deception, a place where the Demiurge and his Archons maintain a veil of ignorance that keeps souls trapped in spiritual darkness. The Demiurge creates illusions that bind individuals to the physical, to desires, fears, and attachments that prevent them from seeing the truth of their divine nature. These illusions are reinforced by societal norms, cultural beliefs, and even religious doctrines that emphasize obedience and conformity. For the Gnostic, the first step on the path to salvation is recognizing these illusions for what they are—a false reality designed to keep souls blind to the divine spark within.

The journey toward gnosis is often described as a process of awakening. Just as a person awakens from sleep and leaves dreams behind, the soul awakens from the illusions of the Demiurge's world and begins to perceive the true reality beyond. This awakening is a gradual process, a shedding of layers of ignorance and attachment. It requires the seeker to cultivate an awareness of their inner life, to listen to the subtle voice of the divine spark that calls them back to the Pleroma. Through practices such as meditation, contemplation, and inner reflection, the Gnostic learns to quiet the distractions of the physical world and focus on the divine light within.

In the Gospel of Judas, Jesus's teachings emphasize the importance of this inner journey. He tells Judas that the other disciples, though sincere in their devotion, are blind to the true nature of reality. They follow him with expectations of earthly rewards, unable to see that his mission is not about establishing a kingdom on earth but about liberating souls from the bonds of the material. Judas, however, is different. He alone among the disciples is able to understand the hidden meaning of Jesus's words, to perceive the truths that lie beyond the visible. His role as the chosen disciple is a testament to his spiritual readiness, his ability to see through the illusions of the world and grasp the deeper reality of the Pleroma.

The concept of gnosis as the key to salvation also shapes the Gnostic view of sin and redemption. In orthodox teachings, sin is often defined as a transgression against divine law, an act that separates individuals from God and requires repentance. For the Gnostic, however, sin is not a matter of breaking commandments but of remaining in ignorance. True sin is the failure to recognize one's divine nature, the refusal to seek knowledge of the Supreme God and the Pleroma. In this framework, salvation is not about forgiveness but enlightenment, a shedding of the ignorance that keeps souls bound to the material world. Redemption is found not in confession or penance but in the act of waking up, of remembering who one truly is.

This focus on knowledge and self-discovery makes the Gnostic path one of intense inner work. The journey of salvation is not something that can be achieved through external rituals or through the mediation of a priest or church; it is a process that unfolds within the soul, an intimate encounter with the divine spark. Gnostic texts often describe this process as a journey through darkness, a descent into the depths of the self where one confronts the illusions and attachments that bind the soul to the Demiurge's world. This journey is not for the faint of heart, for it requires the seeker to look beyond comforting beliefs, to question reality itself, and to embrace the unknown.

In Gnosticism, the path of salvation is also a path of transformation. As the soul awakens to its divine nature, it begins to see the world differently, perceiving the material realm not as the ultimate reality but as a temporary stage, a place of learning and growth. The seeker who attains gnosis understands that they are not bound by the laws of the Demiurge, that their true identity lies beyond the physical. This shift in perception is a form of liberation, a freedom from the fears and desires that keep souls attached to the material world. The Gnostic no longer lives as a captive of the physical but as a being of spirit, a soul that remembers its origin in the divine fullness.

The Gospel of Judas reflects this transformative process, portraying Judas as a figure who is willing to embrace the path of gnosis, even at great personal cost. He understands that true salvation requires him to let go of the expectations and attachments of the material world, to see through the illusions that keep souls bound. His willingness to play his role in Jesus's death is an act of profound insight, a recognition that the body must be transcended for the soul to return to the Pleroma. Judas, in his unique role, exemplifies the Gnostic path—a path that is not defined by external loyalty or moral conformity but by the courage to seek knowledge and transcend the material.

For the Gnostic, salvation is not a reward given to the obedient but a state of liberation attained by the awakened. It is the act of breaking free from the cycle of birth and death, from the forces of desire and fear that keep souls bound to the material. This salvation is a return to the Pleroma, where the soul is once again united with the Supreme God, free from the limitations of the Demiurge's world. The Gnostic seeker, in pursuing this path, learns to see the material world as a temporary place, a realm of illusion that must be transcended in order to reach the fullness of divine light.

This understanding of salvation transforms the way the Gnostic views life itself. Each moment, each experience becomes an opportunity for awakening, a step on the path toward gnosis. Challenges and suffering are not seen as punishments but as tests, opportunities to grow and deepen one's understanding. The Gnostic path is one of constant vigilance, a willingness to question, to seek, and to remember. It is a path that requires the seeker to look beyond appearances, to embrace the mystery of the divine, and to walk in the light of their inner knowing.

In this journey, the Gnostic is guided not by doctrines or commandments but by the light of the divine spark within. This inner light, a fragment of the Supreme God, illuminates the path, leading the soul through the darkness of the material world and back to the Pleroma. Salvation, in this vision, is a homecoming, a return to the fullness from which the soul originated. It is a state of union, a merging with the divine that dissolves the illusions of separateness and reveals the soul's true nature as a being of light.

The Gnostic path of salvation, as portrayed in the Gospel of Judas, is a call to remember, to awaken, and to transcend. It is an invitation to see beyond the visible, to embrace the mystery of the divine, and to journey back to the Pleroma. In this journey, the soul finds not only freedom from the material but a profound communion with the Supreme God, a state of eternal peace and joy that lies beyond the reach of the Demiurge's world. This is the

Gnostic promise, the hope of salvation through gnosis—a path that leads from ignorance to enlightenment, from separation to unity, from darkness to light.

Chapter 12
Jesus' Revelations about the Spirit

In the Gospel of Judas, Jesus imparts a vision of the spirit that transcends traditional teachings, reaching into the heart of Gnostic wisdom. Here, the spirit is not merely a passive part of humanity or a reflection of moral virtue; it is the divine spark itself, an eternal fragment of the Supreme God that exists within each soul. This spirit, or divine essence, is the connection between the individual and the Pleroma, the boundless fullness of the Supreme God, and it serves as both guide and goal on the path to spiritual awakening. Jesus's teachings on the spirit are a call to remember, to recognize the divine presence within, and to understand that this spirit is the soul's true nature, hidden beneath the layers of material existence and illusions crafted by the Demiurge.

In orthodox interpretations, the spirit is often understood as a source of morality, obedience, and devotion, a part of the human being that, when properly cultivated, brings one closer to God. Yet in the Gnostic view, the spirit is far more profound. It is the core of the soul, an eternal essence that exists beyond the influence of the Demiurge and his material world. This spirit is not shaped by external teachings or religious practices; it is an unchanging, intrinsic aspect of the self, a silent witness to the illusions of the physical realm and a fragment of the divine light. For the Gnostic, awakening to this spirit is the ultimate goal of spiritual life, for it is through the spirit that one reconnects with the Pleroma and transcends the boundaries of the material world.

Jesus's revelations about the spirit in the Gospel of Judas offer a path to liberation through knowledge of this inner divine presence. He explains to Judas that the body and mind are temporary, created by the Demiurge to keep souls tethered to the material plane. The spirit, however, originates from the Supreme God and is unaffected by the changes and cycles of the physical world. Unlike the body, which is destined to decay, or the mind, which is shaped by desires and fears, the spirit is pure, unchanging, and eternal. It is the light that guides the soul through the darkness of the material world, illuminating the path back to the Pleroma.

In his teachings, Jesus emphasizes that the spirit is distinct from the soul's other faculties, such as emotions, thoughts, and bodily senses. These aspects of the self are influenced by the Demiurge's creation, entangled in the illusions of the physical world. The spirit, however, remains untouched by these distractions; it is the true self, the divine essence that lies beyond human identity and personality. This Gnostic understanding of the spirit contrasts sharply with traditional beliefs, for it sees the spirit not as a part of oneself to be developed or perfected, but as a reality to be discovered, a presence to be awakened. The journey to gnosis is therefore a journey inward, a process of turning away from the external world and focusing on the inner light of the spirit.

Jesus explains to Judas that most people, even his disciples, are unable to perceive the spirit within. They are caught in the web of the Demiurge's creation, focused on the physical and unaware of the divine essence that resides within them. These individuals live according to the dictates of the material world, seeking fulfillment in physical pleasures, social status, and earthly achievements. Their focus remains outward, bound to the shifting desires and fears that define life in the Demiurge's realm. Jesus tells Judas that such people are spiritually asleep, unable to see the truth of their own divinity, blind to the spirit that connects them to the Pleroma.

This revelation sets Judas apart from the other disciples, who see Jesus as a worldly messiah, a figure who will bring freedom and glory to their earthly lives. Judas, however, understands that Jesus's mission is not to establish a kingdom on earth but to reveal the path to the divine kingdom within. Jesus's teachings show Judas that the spirit is the doorway to this kingdom, the bridge between the material world and the divine fullness of the Pleroma. By guiding Judas to recognize the spirit within, Jesus opens the way for him to transcend the illusions of the material world and return to the realm of light and unity.

The spirit, in Gnostic belief, is both the guide and the destination on the path to enlightenment. It is the part of oneself that remembers the Pleroma, that longs for reunion with the divine, and that can lead the soul back to its true home. This spirit, however, is hidden beneath layers of conditioning, desires, and fears, obscured by the mind's attachment to the physical world. The Gnostic path involves a process of uncovering, of peeling away these layers to reveal the pure essence beneath. Through practices such as meditation, contemplation, and self-inquiry, the Gnostic seeker learns to quiet the distractions of the mind and focus on the stillness of the spirit, the silent presence that lies beyond thought and feeling.

Jesus's teachings to Judas about the spirit also highlight the importance of detachment from the material world. The Demiurge's creation is filled with attractions and distractions, designed to keep souls focused on the physical and prevent them from recognizing their true nature. The Gnostic seeker must learn to see these attractions for what they are—illusions that serve only to bind the soul to the material. By practicing detachment, the seeker allows the spirit to come forward, to shine through the layers of illusion and reveal the path to the Pleroma. This detachment is not a rejection of life but a reorientation of perception, a shift from seeing the physical as reality to recognizing it as a temporary state.

In the Gospel of Judas, Jesus tells Judas that the spirit cannot be controlled or manipulated by the Demiurge or his Archons. While the Demiurge may have created the physical body and the mind, the spirit is beyond his reach, an eternal aspect of the Supreme God that exists independently of the material world. This spirit is immune to the limitations of the physical, untouched by suffering, death, or decay. It is a fragment of the Pleroma, a piece of the divine that resides within each soul and calls it back to its source. The Gnostic seeker, by recognizing and cultivating this spirit, gains the power to transcend the Demiurge's world and return to the fullness of the divine.

The spirit, as Jesus reveals to Judas, is also the source of true knowledge, or gnosis. Unlike the knowledge of the physical world, which is limited and fragmented, gnosis is a direct, intuitive understanding of the divine. It is the knowledge of one's own essence, a realization of the spirit's connection to the Supreme God. This knowledge cannot be learned from books or teachings; it is an experience, a moment of awakening in which the soul remembers its true nature and perceives the unity of all existence. For the Gnostic, this gnosis is the key to salvation, the only path that leads beyond the illusions of the Demiurge and into the light of the Pleroma.

In the Gnostic view, Jesus serves as a guide to this gnosis, a revealer of mysteries who helps the seeker recognize the spirit within. His role is not to dictate laws or enforce rituals but to awaken the soul to its own divine nature. Through his teachings, he shows the way to the Pleroma, encouraging his followers to look beyond the material and focus on the spirit that lies within. Jesus's message is not one of obedience but of liberation, a call to remember, to see beyond the illusions of the physical world, and to embrace the truth of one's divine essence.

Judas, in his unique understanding of Jesus's teachings, becomes a model of the Gnostic seeker, an individual who perceives the spirit and is willing to follow it, even at the cost of earthly attachments and recognition. His role in the Gospel of Judas is not that of a betrayer but of a chosen disciple, one who understands the need to transcend the physical, to embrace the spirit, and to follow the path back to the Pleroma. Through his understanding of the spirit, Judas is able to see beyond the desires and fears that bind others to the material world, recognizing the truth of Jesus's mission and the path to salvation that it reveals.

The Gnostic path of salvation, as outlined in the Gospel of Judas, is thus a journey toward the spirit, a return to the divine fullness of the Pleroma through the awakening of the inner light. This path requires the seeker to cultivate awareness of the spirit, to recognize it as the true self, and to allow it to guide the soul back to its origin. The spirit is both the means and the destination, the guide and the goal, a divine spark that remembers the Pleroma and longs to return to it.

For the Gnostic, the realization of the spirit is a profound moment of transformation, a shift from seeing oneself as a mere physical being to understanding one's nature as a fragment of the divine. This realization dissolves the illusions of the material world, freeing the soul from the bonds of desire, fear, and attachment. The seeker who attains gnosis no longer sees the world as a place of separation and division but as a temporary stage, a realm that reflects the Demiurge's limitations yet also offers a path to enlightenment.

The Gospel of Judas invites readers to embark on this journey, to look within and discover the spirit that lies at the core of their being. It is a call to transcend the illusions of the Demiurge, to awaken to the divine light within, and to embrace the path that leads back to the Pleroma. In this journey, the spirit is the guide, the spark of the Supreme God that illuminates the way, reminding the soul of its true nature and its ultimate destination.

Through Jesus's revelations about the spirit, the Gospel of Judas reveals a path to liberation that defies conventional beliefs, a journey that moves beyond the physical and into the realms of spirit. It is

Chapter 13
The Pursuit of Self-Knowledge

In the Gnostic understanding, the journey of the soul is, at its heart, a journey of self-knowledge. This pursuit of self-knowledge is not merely an exploration of one's personal characteristics, nor is it a simple introspective quest; it is a deep and transformative process that seeks to uncover the divine spark within, an essence beyond the reach of personality and identity. For the Gnostic, self-knowledge is the bridge that leads from the illusions of the material world to the truth of the divine realm, the Pleroma. It is the process by which the soul awakens, perceiving its own divinity and recognizing its profound connection to the Supreme God. In this way, self-knowledge becomes the foundation of spiritual enlightenment, the means by which the soul finds its way back to its eternal source.

Unlike the goals of conventional religious faiths, which often emphasize moral obedience, social duty, or ritual, Gnosticism proposes that true enlightenment can only come from an inward journey. This journey requires the seeker to turn away from external distractions, to quiet the mind's restless pursuits, and to delve into the hidden depths of the soul. In the Gospel of Judas, Jesus encourages this search for self-knowledge, revealing to Judas that only by understanding his own divine essence can he transcend the limitations of the physical world and reach the divine fullness of the Pleroma. This journey toward self-knowledge, however, is not simple or straightforward; it is a path that demands both courage and dedication, a willingness to confront difficult truths and leave behind familiar illusions.

In Gnostic thought, self-knowledge is inseparable from the knowledge of God. To know oneself is to know the divine spark within, the fragment of the Supreme God that resides in the soul. This spark, hidden beneath layers of earthly identity and conditioned beliefs, is the true essence of each individual. In discovering it, the soul awakens to its own divinity, realizing that it is not a product of the material world but a piece of the divine, temporarily bound to the physical but destined to return to the Pleroma. This understanding transforms the way the Gnostic perceives themselves and the world around them, for it reveals that the soul's true identity lies beyond the physical body, beyond the mind, beyond the personality.

The pursuit of self-knowledge in Gnosticism is therefore a process of peeling away illusions, of stripping off the layers of identity that have been constructed by the Demiurge's world. The physical world, shaped by the Demiurge and governed by his Archons, encourages individuals to identify with the body, the mind, and the ego. It reinforces desires, fears, and attachments that keep the soul focused outward, bound to the cycles of birth and death, pleasure and pain. For the Gnostic, self-knowledge means moving beyond these distractions, uncovering the divine spark that lies hidden beneath the false self created by the material world.

This process of self-discovery is often described as an inner journey, a descent into the soul's depths where the divine light is hidden. It requires the seeker to confront the attachments, beliefs, and desires that keep them bound to the material world. These attachments are not merely physical or emotional; they are mental constructs, ideas and beliefs that define the self in terms of the material. To know oneself, the Gnostic must question these constructs, letting go of the conditioned identities that obscure the truth of the divine spark within. The Gnostic path is therefore a journey of continual questioning and release, a willingness to move beyond the known self and embrace the mystery of the divine.

The Gospel of Judas hints at this journey toward self-knowledge in its portrayal of Judas as the chosen disciple. Unlike the other disciples, who see Jesus as a worldly savior and who expect him to establish a kingdom on earth, Judas perceives the deeper meaning of Jesus's mission. He understands that Jesus's teachings are not about physical liberation but about spiritual awakening, about recognizing the divine spark within and transcending the limitations of the material world. Judas's unique understanding reflects his readiness for gnosis, his willingness to confront the unknown and seek the truth beyond appearances. In this way, Judas serves as a model of the Gnostic seeker, one who is not satisfied with surface truths but is driven to discover the divine reality within.

For the Gnostic, self-knowledge is not just a means to personal enlightenment but a step toward universal truth. The divine spark within each individual is not separate from the Supreme God; it is a reflection of the Pleroma, a piece of the divine fullness that connects the soul to all of existence. To know oneself is to recognize one's place in the larger cosmic order, to see oneself not as an isolated being but as part of a vast, interconnected reality. This realization dissolves the sense of separation that binds the soul to the Demiurge's world, revealing a unity that exists beyond the physical, beyond the dualities of light and dark, good and evil. The pursuit of self-knowledge, then, is not a solitary journey but a return to the universal, a recognition of one's oneness with the divine.

This path of self-discovery is not without challenges, for the Demiurge's world is filled with distractions and illusions that keep the soul focused on the material. The Gnostic must cultivate a state of inner awareness, a mindfulness that allows them to see through these illusions and focus on the truth within. Practices such as meditation, contemplation, and introspection become essential tools on this path, helping the seeker to quiet the mind and turn inward, to listen to the silent voice of the spirit. Through these practices, the Gnostic learns to distinguish between the temporary self of the material world and the eternal self of the divine spark.

The Gospel of Judas portrays Jesus as a guide on this journey of self-knowledge, a revealer of mysteries who helps Judas see beyond the visible world and recognize the divine truth within. Jesus's role is not to impose beliefs or enforce obedience but to inspire the seeker to look within, to question, and to discover. His teachings emphasize the importance of inner understanding, of recognizing the illusions of the Demiurge and embracing the path that leads back to the Pleroma. In this way, Jesus becomes a model of the enlightened teacher, one who illuminates the way but leaves the journey itself to each individual.

The Gnostic pursuit of self-knowledge also transforms the way one perceives the world. As the seeker gains insight into their own divine nature, they begin to see the material world not as an ultimate reality but as a temporary stage, a place of exile that holds the soul but does not define it. This shift in perception allows the Gnostic to live in the world without being bound by it, to engage with life's experiences without becoming attached. Self-knowledge frees the soul from the need to seek fulfillment in the external, revealing that true peace and joy lie within, in the recognition of the divine spark.

In Gnosticism, self-knowledge is also a path of healing, for it allows the soul to release the wounds and fears imposed by the material world. The Demiurge's creation is a place of conflict, suffering, and death, a realm that often leaves the soul burdened with pain and sorrow. Yet by turning inward, by connecting with the divine spark, the Gnostic finds a source of healing that transcends these wounds, a light that cannot be dimmed by the darkness of the material. This inner light, the essence of the soul, offers a sanctuary of peace, a refuge where the soul can rest in the knowledge of its eternal nature.

Through the journey of self-knowledge, the Gnostic also encounters the ego, the false self that the Demiurge's world has created. The ego, with its attachments, desires, and fears, represents the aspects of the self that are bound to the material. It is the part of the soul that identifies with the body, the mind, and the external, and it is the source of much of the soul's suffering. The Gnostic path involves recognizing the ego for what it is—an illusion that keeps the soul focused on the physical and prevents it from awakening to the divine. By understanding and releasing the ego, the Gnostic frees the soul to move beyond the limitations of the material and enter the realms of spirit.

The Gospel of Judas presents this pursuit of self-knowledge as the key to liberation, the essential step on the path back to the Pleroma. Jesus's teachings to Judas emphasize that the material world, with all its distractions, is a place of illusion, a construct that keeps souls from recognizing their true nature. By turning inward, by seeking knowledge of the divine spark, the soul can break free from these illusions and return to its origin in the Pleroma. Judas, in his understanding of this truth, becomes a symbol of the soul's journey, a figure who dares to see beyond the visible and embrace the divine mystery within.

In the Gnostic tradition, self-knowledge is the first step on the path to gnosis, a journey that leads from ignorance to enlightenment, from separation to unity. It is a path that transforms the way one sees oneself and the world, revealing that the soul's true identity lies not in the physical but in the divine. This understanding allows the Gnostic to live with freedom and clarity, to move through the world with a sense of purpose and peace that transcends the illusions of the material. The pursuit of self-knowledge is therefore not an end in itself but a doorway, an opening that leads to the infinite light of the Pleroma.

The Gospel of Judas calls each seeker to embark on this journey, to look within and discover the truth of their own divine essence. It is a call to remember, to awaken, and to recognize that the self is not defined by the body or the mind but by the spirit within. In this journey, the soul finds its true home, reconnecting with the Supreme God and returning to the fullness of the divine.

Chapter 14
The Role of the Soul and Consciousness

In the Gnostic tradition, the soul is the silent bearer of divine truth, a fragment of the Supreme God encased in the earthly experience, yearning to return to its origin. Unlike conventional perspectives that view the soul as an element within a mortal body awaiting judgment, Gnosticism sees the soul as a luminous, eternal essence entangled in the illusions of the material world. It is not merely a creation within the Demiurge's realm, but an emissary from the Pleroma, the boundless fullness of the divine, and it exists beyond the reach of any temporal power or structure. The journey of the soul, then, is not toward salvation in a distant heaven but toward self-reclamation, a remembering of its true nature and ultimate reunion with the divine. The role of consciousness in this journey is essential, for consciousness is the awareness that illuminates the path and allows the soul to distinguish truth from illusion.

The Gnostic soul begins its journey in a state of spiritual amnesia, its memory of the Pleroma veiled by the attachments, desires, and distractions of the material world. The soul's consciousness, the light of divine awareness within, lies dormant, clouded by the dense fog of the Demiurge's creation. In this state of ignorance, the soul experiences life as a fragmented, dualistic reality, unable to perceive the unity that exists in the Pleroma. The physical body and the mind, influenced by the Archons, keep the soul focused outward, lost in a world of form and matter that conceals its inner divinity. The Gnostic journey, then, is a journey of awakening, a gradual return to consciousness that allows the soul to see beyond the illusions of the material world and reconnect with the divine source.

For the Gnostic, consciousness is more than mere awareness of the self or the outer world; it is a form of divine illumination, a light that reveals the hidden truths of existence. In the Gospel of Judas, Jesus shares with Judas a vision of the soul's purpose, explaining that consciousness is the key to liberation. He emphasizes that the other disciples, while sincere in their devotion, remain bound to the physical because they are unable to perceive the spiritual reality beyond it. They see him as an earthly king, a messiah who will bring freedom within the material world. But Judas, the chosen disciple, is different. He alone is able to understand the mysteries that Jesus reveals, for he possesses the consciousness needed to see through the veils of illusion and grasp the hidden truth.

In Gnostic cosmology, consciousness acts as a bridge between the material and the spiritual. It is the part of the soul that remembers, that carries the faint yet persistent memory of the Pleroma and the Supreme God. This memory is not a collection of facts or experiences but an inner knowing, a sense of belonging to a reality beyond the physical. This consciousness, often described as the "divine spark," lies at the core of the soul, waiting to be awakened. The journey of the soul involves bringing this consciousness to the forefront, allowing it to shine through the layers of illusion imposed by the Demiurge and his Archons.

The role of consciousness in the Gnostic path is one of awakening and transformation. As the soul begins to remember its divine origin, it experiences a shift in perception, a change in the way it sees both itself and the world. The material world, once seen as solid and enduring, is now perceived as a temporary construct, a shadow of the true reality that lies beyond. The soul comes to understand that its identity is not defined by the physical body, the mind, or the ego, but by the divine essence within. This realization frees the soul from the fears, desires, and attachments that keep it bound to the Demiurge's world, allowing it to focus on the path that leads back to the Pleroma.

The concept of the soul as a conscious, divine essence also redefines the Gnostic understanding of life and death. In the Demiurge's realm, life and death are seen as opposites, part of the cycle that keeps souls bound to the material. Yet for the Gnostic, the true life of the soul is not tied to the body or the mind; it is an eternal existence that transcends the physical. Death, therefore, is not an end but a transition, a moment when the soul has the opportunity to break free from the Demiurge's cycle and return to its origin. This return, however, is only possible for those who have awakened to their true nature, for those who have attained the consciousness needed to see through the illusions of the material and recognize the path that leads back to the divine.

In the Gospel of Judas, Jesus emphasizes the importance of consciousness by revealing to Judas the nature of the spiritual and material realms. He explains that the Demiurge's creation is a world of illusion, a place where souls are kept in ignorance by the distractions and desires of the physical. He speaks of the divine spark within each soul, a fragment of the Supreme God that cannot be controlled by the Demiurge. This spark, or divine consciousness, is the key to liberation, for it allows the soul to see beyond the limitations of the material and connect with the light of the Pleroma. By awakening this consciousness, the soul gains the power to transcend the Demiurge's creation and return to the divine fullness.

The awakening of consciousness is often described as a process of inner purification. The soul, entangled in the Demiurge's world, accumulates layers of ignorance, attachment, and fear, which obscure its divine essence. The Gnostic path involves a process of stripping away these layers, of clearing the mind and heart of the influences that keep the soul bound to the material. Through practices such as meditation, contemplation, and self-reflection, the Gnostic learns to quiet the distractions of the physical and focus on the inner light. This purification is not a matter of moral perfection but of spiritual clarity, a return to the soul's original state of divine awareness.

The role of consciousness in this process is to act as a guide, a light that illuminates the path and reveals the illusions that must be overcome. The Gnostic learns to trust this inner light, to follow the silent voice of the divine spark that calls the soul back to the Pleroma. This journey requires a deep commitment, for the Demiurge's world is filled with obstacles and distractions that seek to keep the soul bound to the physical. The Gnostic must cultivate a state of constant awareness, a mindfulness that allows them to see through these distractions and remain focused on the truth within.

In this journey of awakening, the Gnostic soul also confronts the ego, the false self that the Demiurge's world has created. The ego, with its attachments to the body, mind, and identity, is the part of the self that is most deeply entangled in the material. It is the source of desires, fears, and insecurities that keep the soul focused on the physical. The Gnostic path involves recognizing the ego for what it is—an illusion that keeps the soul from awakening to its true nature. By seeing through the ego, the Gnostic frees the soul to focus on the divine spark within, to embrace the consciousness that connects it to the Supreme God.

The Gospel of Judas presents this journey of consciousness as the essential path to liberation, a return to the Pleroma through the recognition of the soul's divine essence. Jesus's teachings emphasize that the soul's true identity lies beyond the physical, beyond the mind, in the eternal light of the spirit. By awakening to this light, the soul is able to see through the illusions of the material world and recognize the divine presence within. Judas, in his unique understanding of Jesus's mission, becomes a symbol of this journey, a figure who perceives the hidden truth and is willing to follow it, even at great personal cost.

For the Gnostic, consciousness is the essence of life itself, a divine awareness that connects the soul to the Supreme God. This consciousness, often described as the divine spark, is the key to liberation, for it reveals the truth of the Pleroma and allows the soul to transcend the Demiurge's world. The journey of the soul is therefore a journey of awakening, a process of remembering its true nature and returning to the divine fullness from which it originated. Through the cultivation of consciousness, the soul finds the path that leads beyond the physical, beyond the illusions of the Demiurge, and into the realms of spirit.

The Gospel of Judas invites each seeker to embark on this journey, to look within and discover the light of consciousness that lies at the heart of their being. It is a call to transcend the material, to move beyond the ego, and to embrace the truth of one's divine essence. In this journey, the soul finds not only freedom from the Demiurge's world but a profound communion with the Supreme God, a state of eternal peace and joy that lies beyond the reach of the material. Through the awakening of consciousness, the soul is able to fulfill its true purpose, to return to the Pleroma and reunite with the divine fullness.

In the Gnostic vision, the role of the soul and consciousness is not merely to experience life in the physical but to transcend it, to awaken to the truth of its divine origin and embrace the journey back to the Supreme God. This is the promise of gnosis, the hope of liberation through self-knowledge, a path that leads from ignorance to enlightenment, from separation to unity, from darkness to light.

Chapter 15
Spiritual Enlightenment

In the Gnostic vision, enlightenment is the soul's awakening to its divine nature, a revelation that lies beyond the limits of the physical, beyond the illusions crafted by the Demiurge, and beyond even the definitions of knowledge as understood by the material world. Spiritual enlightenment is not a sudden flash or a single moment of insight; rather, it is a gradual transformation, a shift in perception where the seeker comes to see the reality behind the veil, the eternal light that resides within and beyond. Enlightenment, in this sense, is the culmination of the Gnostic journey—the point where the soul remembers its divine origin, recognizing itself as a fragment of the Supreme God, and moves to reconnect with the Pleroma.

In the Gospel of Judas, Jesus reveals the nature of enlightenment to Judas, not through conventional teachings or commands but through the awakening of a deeper perception. This enlightenment, or gnosis, is the ability to see the material world as it truly is—a temporary construct designed by the Demiurge to obscure the divine essence within. Jesus explains to Judas that the path to enlightenment involves shedding the illusions imposed by the physical realm, a process of peeling away the layers that keep the soul bound to form and matter. Through this unveiling, the soul comes to recognize its own eternal nature, perceiving itself as a part of the infinite light of the Pleroma, a truth that has been hidden but not destroyed by the forces of the material world.

The process of enlightenment is marked by a profound transformation in consciousness, a reorientation from the external to the internal, from the visible to the hidden. For the Gnostic, this journey begins with a spark of self-recognition, a moment of awakening that allows the soul to glimpse its own divinity. Yet this spark is only the beginning; true enlightenment involves nurturing this inner light, cultivating a state of awareness that transcends the limitations of the physical. The seeker learns to quiet the distractions of the material world, to turn inward and listen to the silent voice of the divine spark. This process is not a single event but a lifelong journey, a commitment to deepening one's connection with the spirit and moving ever closer to the Pleroma.

Enlightenment, in the Gnostic sense, is inseparable from self-knowledge, for it is through the knowledge of the self that the soul comes to know God. This self-knowledge is not an intellectual understanding but an experiential realization, a direct encounter with the divine presence within. The Gnostic seeks to go beyond the mind, beyond concepts and beliefs, and enter into a state of direct communion with the spirit. This state of communion is the essence of gnosis, a knowing that is both deeply personal and universally connected, a recognition of the self as both individual and part of the divine fullness.

In the Gospel of Judas, Jesus encourages Judas to pursue this path, to seek not answers from others but to look within and find the truth that lies beyond words. He reveals to Judas that true enlightenment is not about gaining knowledge of the world but about shedding that which binds the soul to it. The other disciples, though devoted, remain attached to worldly understandings of salvation, unable to perceive the mystery of the spirit that Jesus imparts to Judas. They look for a savior to bring liberation within the material world, yet Judas alone understands that Jesus's mission transcends earthly concerns, offering a path that leads beyond the physical and into the realms of spirit.

The enlightenment that Jesus reveals is a journey away from the ordinary self, the self defined by the body, the mind, and the ego. In Gnostic thought, this lower self is a construct of the Demiurge, a limited identity that binds the soul to the cycles of desire, attachment, and ignorance. True enlightenment involves transcending this self, moving beyond the illusions of personality and identity to discover the higher self, the divine essence that lies within. This higher self is the true self, a part of the Supreme God that remembers the Pleroma and seeks to return to it. The journey to enlightenment, then, is a journey of self-discovery, a process of realizing that one's true nature is not bound by the physical but is infinite, eternal, and divine.

For the Gnostic, the path to enlightenment is a path of purification, an ongoing process of releasing attachments and beliefs that obscure the truth of the self. Each step on this path brings the seeker closer to the divine light, illuminating the inner darkness created by ignorance and desire. The Gnostic learns to see the material world for what it is—a temporary construct, a realm of form and duality that is ultimately an illusion. This understanding allows the seeker to live in the world without being bound by it, to engage with life's experiences without becoming attached. Enlightenment is thus a state of inner freedom, a detachment from the physical that allows the soul to remain focused on its true purpose, its journey back to the Pleroma.

The Gnostic vision of enlightenment also transforms the way one experiences suffering and joy. In the Demiurge's world, these opposites define human existence, creating cycles of pleasure and pain that keep souls attached to the physical. Yet the enlightened soul sees beyond these dualities, recognizing that both pleasure and pain are aspects of the same illusion, a temporary reality that does not affect the true self. This understanding brings a profound sense of peace, a state of equanimity that allows the soul to move through life with a sense of balance and clarity. The Gnostic who attains enlightenment does not reject life but perceives it as a stage, a place of learning and growth where the soul can deepen its understanding and prepare for its return to the Pleroma.

In the Gospel of Judas, Judas's role as the chosen disciple highlights the Gnostic understanding of enlightenment as a path that requires courage, willingness to confront difficult truths, and a deep commitment to self-discovery. Judas alone among the disciples is able to understand Jesus's teachings about the spirit, perceiving the hidden truths that the others cannot see. His actions, though misunderstood, reflect his readiness to embrace the path of enlightenment, to follow the spirit even when it means defying conventional beliefs and expectations. In this way, Judas serves as a model of the Gnostic seeker, a figure who is willing to look beyond appearances and embrace the mystery of the divine.

The enlightened soul, in Gnostic thought, becomes a beacon of light, a presence that radiates peace, wisdom, and compassion. This soul is not detached in a cold or distant way but is deeply engaged with life, moving through the world with a sense of purpose and understanding that transcends ordinary concerns. Enlightenment brings a state of clarity, a direct perception of the divine presence in all things. The Gnostic who attains this state of awareness is able to live fully, experiencing each moment as an expression of the divine, yet remains unattached, knowing that true life lies beyond the physical, in the eternal light of the Pleroma.

The Gospel of Judas presents enlightenment as a process of self-liberation, a journey that involves both inner transformation and an outward detachment from the Demiurge's world. Jesus's teachings reveal that the soul's true destiny is not to remain in the material but to return to the Pleroma, to merge once again with the divine fullness from which it originated. Enlightenment is the fulfillment of this destiny, a state where the soul perceives its own divine nature and embraces the path that leads back to the Supreme God. For Judas, this realization marks him as the chosen disciple, the one who understands that true freedom lies not in the promises of the world but in the journey beyond it.

In Gnosticism, enlightenment is the state of knowing oneself as both individual and divine, a being who is both in the world and beyond it. This realization dissolves the sense of separateness that defines life in the material, revealing the soul's unity with the divine and its connection to all existence. The

Gnostic path, therefore, is a path of awakening, a gradual return to consciousness that allows the soul to recognize its place within the larger cosmic order, to see itself not as a separate being but as a part of the divine fullness.

Through the journey of enlightenment, the Gnostic finds a sense of inner peace, a state of joy that is not dependent on external conditions but arises from the recognition of one's true nature. This peace, often described as a state of divine stillness, allows the soul to move through life with grace and purpose, to engage with the world without being bound by it. The enlightened soul understands that life in the Demiurge's world is temporary, a momentary experience in the soul's journey back to the Pleroma, and this understanding brings a sense of freedom that transcends all fear and desire.

The Gospel of Judas invites each seeker to pursue this path, to seek the light of enlightenment that lies within and to embrace the journey that leads beyond the physical. It is a call to remember, to awaken, and to return to the divine fullness of the Pleroma. In this journey, the soul finds not only liberation from the illusions of the material world but a profound communion with the Supreme God, a state of eternal unity and joy that lies beyond all form and matter.

For the Gnostic, enlightenment is the ultimate goal, the fulfillment of the soul's true purpose. It is the state of complete understanding, where all questions dissolve and the soul rests in the knowledge of its own divinity. This is the promise of gnosis, the hope of liberation through self-knowledge, a journey that leads from ignorance to truth, from separation to unity, from darkness to light. Through enlightenment, the soul finds its way home, returning to the Pleroma and merging once again with the boundless light of the Supreme God.

Chapter 16
The Concept of Spiritual Archetypes

In the Gnostic worldview, the journey of the soul is guided by forces that exist beyond the visible, beyond the tangible. These guiding forces, known as spiritual archetypes, are the embodiments of divine attributes—symbols of wisdom, strength, love, knowledge, and truth—that reside within the soul as inherent potentials. Archetypes, in Gnosticism, are not mere concepts or ideals; they are living aspects of the divine fullness, the Pleroma, that reach into the soul, calling it back to its origin. Through these archetypes, the Supreme God communicates with each soul, encouraging it to awaken, to see beyond the illusions of the material world, and to move toward the divine fullness.

In traditional belief systems, archetypes might be understood as symbols of human ideals or aspects of the psyche. However, in Gnosticism, spiritual archetypes are the emanations of divine attributes that live within each soul as seeds waiting to be awakened. Each archetype represents a path of development, an aspect of the divine that guides the soul in its journey from ignorance to gnosis. The archetypes reflect the qualities of the Aeons—the divine beings within the Pleroma—who embody specific facets of the Supreme God. By aligning with these archetypes, the Gnostic seeker connects with the Pleroma, receiving guidance, wisdom, and inspiration that transcend ordinary perception.

These spiritual archetypes serve as maps of the divine qualities, illuminating aspects of the Supreme God's nature that can be realized within the soul. Through meditation, contemplation, and inner reflection, the Gnostic begins to uncover these qualities, moving from a fragmented sense of self to an awareness of the unified, divine essence. In the Gospel of Judas, Jesus hints at these spiritual archetypes in his teachings to Judas, revealing that the path of gnosis is one of internal transformation—a journey of awakening each archetype within, allowing the soul to reflect the light of the Pleroma. This journey is not one of learning or acquisition but of remembering, a process of uncovering what is already present within each soul.

One of the most significant spiritual archetypes in Gnosticism is Wisdom, or *Sophia*, an Aeon who plays a central role in the creation of the material world. Sophia represents the soul's yearning for divine truth, the desire to know and understand the Supreme God. Her journey, as described in Gnostic texts, is both tragic and redemptive. In her longing to experience the divine, Sophia falls from the Pleroma, creating a separation that gives rise to the material world and the Demiurge. Yet even in her fall, she retains a spark of the divine, an aspect of the Supreme God that remains within her and calls her back to the light. For the Gnostic, Sophia serves as a powerful archetype of the soul's journey, embodying both the longing for truth and the potential for redemption through gnosis.

As the seeker contemplates the archetype of Wisdom, they begin to see their own life as a reflection of Sophia's journey—a path of seeking, falling, and ultimately, returning to the divine. By aligning with this archetype, the Gnostic learns to embrace the qualities of wisdom, discernment, and spiritual insight, allowing these attributes to guide them on the path of self-knowledge. The story of Sophia reminds the soul that even in moments of separation and confusion, the divine spark within remains, and the way back to the Pleroma is always open through the pursuit of gnosis.

Another profound archetype in Gnosticism is Light. The Supreme God is often described as the ultimate source of light, an uncreated, pure radiance that exists beyond the physical. Light in Gnostic symbolism represents clarity, truth, and the power of revelation. The Gnostic seeks to embody this light, to cultivate a state of inner radiance that dispels the darkness of ignorance and illusion. By aligning with the archetype of Light, the soul learns to see beyond appearances, recognizing the divine essence within themselves and others. Light, as an archetype, reveals the path forward, illuminating the truth that lies hidden beneath the surface of the material.

In the Gospel of Judas, Jesus's teachings reflect the qualities of Light, guiding Judas to see beyond the physical and recognize the hidden reality. He encourages Judas to look beyond the limitations of the body, the mind, and the visible world, to perceive the eternal light within. This light is not an external force but an inner knowing, a form of divine awareness that connects the soul to the Supreme God. For the Gnostic, the archetype of Light serves as both a guide and a goal, a quality to be cultivated and an experience to be attained, leading the soul closer to the Pleroma.

Truth is another essential archetype in the Gnostic tradition, an aspect of the Supreme God that represents pure knowledge, free from distortion or illusion. The Gnostic path is a path of truth-seeking, a journey of stripping away false

Chapter 17
The Duality of Good and Evil

In the Gnostic tradition, the forces of good and evil are not merely moral distinctions but cosmic principles, reflections of the deeper duality that underlies the structure of the universe. Unlike orthodox religious perspectives, which often see good and evil as absolute forces in a moral battle over human souls, Gnosticism views these concepts as interwoven aspects of a divided reality—two expressions that emerge from the separation between the spiritual and material realms. This duality is not simply a conflict between right and wrong, but a schism between knowledge and ignorance, unity and fragmentation, the Supreme God and the Demiurge.

Good, in Gnostic thought, is associated with the realm of the Pleroma, the divine fullness where unity, light, and wisdom prevail. It is a force of enlightenment, representing the purity and harmony of the Supreme God. This divine essence is not bound by laws or definitions; it is a boundless state of unity where all beings exist in perfect harmony, beyond the struggles of duality and separation. The Supreme God, who resides in this state, is the source of all that is truly good—qualities such as compassion, wisdom, love, and eternal peace that transcend any worldly definition of morality. Goodness, in the Gnostic sense, is not a set of rules but an inner reality, a state of being that emerges from the awareness of one's divine nature.

Evil, conversely, is linked to the Demiurge, the flawed creator of the material world. This being, often depicted as arrogant and ignorant, believes himself to be the ultimate god, yet he is blind to the Pleroma and the Supreme God. In his ignorance, the Demiurge creates a universe that reflects his own limitations—an imperfect world filled with suffering, illusion, and decay. Evil, in this sense, is not an active malice but a consequence of separation, an inherent flaw that arises from the Demiurge's ignorance and his inability to perceive the divine truth. This evil manifests as a form of spiritual blindness, a state that keeps souls bound to the material, focused on desires and fears that prevent them from recognizing their divine essence.

In Gnosticism, therefore, evil is deeply tied to ignorance. It is the blindness of the Demiurge and the Archons, his servants, who work to keep souls focused on the material realm. The Archons use desire, fear, and attachment to hold human consciousness within the limits of the physical, perpetuating the illusions of separateness and division that define the Demiurge's world. In this way, evil becomes a force that binds, a limitation that restricts the soul's potential to awaken and remember its true nature. For the Gnostic, then, overcoming evil is not about defeating a malicious enemy but about awakening from ignorance, breaking free from the illusions of the material, and embracing the light of gnosis.

The Gospel of Judas offers insight into this complex relationship between good and evil. In his teachings to Judas, Jesus explains that the material world, with its cycles of birth, death, pleasure, and pain, is a construct designed by the Demiurge, a world that keeps souls ensnared in ignorance. Yet he reveals that even within this flawed creation, there exists a path to transcendence. Good and evil, as experienced in the material world, are temporary forces, reflections of the larger spiritual reality. For Judas, the path to enlightenment involves seeing beyond these opposites, understanding that true liberation lies not in conforming to moral codes but in awakening to a reality beyond duality, where the soul exists in unity with the divine.

This duality between good and evil also reveals the Gnostic concept of freedom. For the Gnostic, true freedom is not about choosing between good and evil within the material realm but about moving beyond these forces altogether, returning to the state of unity in the Pleroma. The Gnostic seeks to cultivate an awareness that transcends the dualistic conflicts of the physical world, understanding that good and evil are illusions that arise from separation. By awakening to their divine nature, the soul begins to see that true goodness is not a matter of adherence to external rules but an inner state of harmony, a reflection of the divine light within.

This understanding transforms the Gnostic perspective on morality. While orthodox religious systems often emphasize obedience to divine laws as the path to righteousness, Gnosticism proposes that moral behavior is a natural expression of inner enlightenment. When the soul awakens to its divine essence, it naturally embodies qualities such as compassion, wisdom, and love. These qualities are not imposed from outside but arise from the soul's connection to the Pleroma. In this sense, true goodness is a result of gnosis, a byproduct of self-knowledge that emerges when the soul recognizes its unity with the divine. Evil, on the other hand, is the consequence of ignorance, a state that keeps souls blind to their true nature and entangled in the illusions of the Demiurge's world.

The Gospel of Judas presents Judas as a figure who understands this complex relationship between good and evil. Unlike the other disciples, who see Jesus's mission in terms of worldly liberation, Judas perceives the spiritual dimension of his teachings. He recognizes that the path to enlightenment involves moving beyond conventional morality, seeing through the illusions of the material world, and embracing the divine truth that lies within. His actions, though condemned by others, reflect a deeper understanding of the nature of good and evil, an awareness that true freedom lies beyond the limits of the Demiurge's creation.

For the Gnostic, the journey of the soul is a journey of overcoming duality, a path that leads from ignorance to knowledge, from darkness to light. This journey requires the seeker to confront the illusions of good and evil, to recognize them as aspects of the Demiurge's world and to seek the truth that lies beyond. The soul learns to see beyond the conflicts and oppositions of the material, moving toward a state of unity and peace that reflects the Pleroma's harmony. In this state of enlightenment, good and evil dissolve, revealing the soul's true nature as a being of light and love, a reflection of the Supreme God.

The concept of duality also shapes the Gnostic understanding of suffering. In the Demiurge's world, suffering is an inevitable consequence of the ignorance and limitations that define the material. Pain, loss, and decay are aspects of a reality created by a being who cannot see the divine fullness. Yet for the Gnostic, suffering can also be a teacher, a reminder that the material world is not the soul's true home. By experiencing and transcending suffering, the soul learns to detach from the illusions of the physical, to seek the inner light that offers true peace. In this way, suffering becomes a catalyst for awakening, a force that pushes the soul toward gnosis and liberation.

This understanding of good and evil as aspects of duality also transforms the way the Gnostic relates to the material world. The enlightened soul no longer sees the world as a battleground between opposing forces but as a temporary stage, a realm where the soul can learn, grow, and prepare for its return to the Pleroma. The Gnostic moves through life with a sense of detachment, engaging with experiences without becoming bound by them. This detachment is not a rejection of life but a reorientation of perception, a shift from seeing good and evil as ultimate realities to recognizing them as aspects of a larger, unified truth.

In the Gospel of Judas, Jesus's teachings to Judas emphasize this need to look beyond duality, to understand that true liberation involves moving beyond the conflicts of the material world. He reveals that the soul's true home is in the Pleroma, a realm beyond good and evil, where all beings exist in harmony. Judas, in his unique understanding of this truth, becomes a model of the Gnostic seeker, a figure who dares to see beyond appearances and embrace the mystery of the divine. His willingness to defy conventional beliefs reflects his awareness that true freedom lies not in conformity but in self-knowledge, in the recognition of the soul's divine nature.

The Gnostic path, then, is a journey of transcending good and evil, of seeing through the illusions of the Demiurge's world and awakening to the unity of the Pleroma. This path requires the seeker to cultivate a state of inner awareness, a mindfulness that allows them to see beyond the oppositions of the physical and focus on the divine essence within. By aligning with the qualities of the Supreme God, such as wisdom, compassion, and love, the Gnostic learns to embody true goodness, not as a set of rules but as a state of being that reflects the light of the Pleroma.

In this journey, the soul learns to live with a sense of peace and clarity, to move through life with an understanding that transcends the conflicts of good and evil. The Gnostic finds a state of inner balance, a harmony that reflects the unity of the divine. This state of enlightenment allows the soul to experience life fully, to engage with the material world without becoming attached, to see the beauty and meaning in each moment while remaining focused on the path that leads back to the Pleroma.

The Gospel of Judas calls each seeker to pursue this path, to see beyond the dualities of good and evil and embrace the truth of their divine essence. It is a call to remember, to awaken, and to recognize that the soul's true identity lies beyond the physical, beyond the conflicts and oppositions of the material world. In this journey, the soul finds not only freedom from the Demiurge's creation but a profound communion with the Supreme God, a state of eternal unity and joy that lies beyond all duality, beyond all form, in the boundless light of the Pleroma.

Chapter 18
The Role of Ignorance in Suffering

In Gnostic philosophy, ignorance is the root of all suffering, a dark force that keeps the soul bound to the illusions of the material world and obscures the divine truth within. This ignorance is not merely a lack of information or intellectual understanding; it is a profound spiritual blindness, a condition that prevents the soul from recognizing its true nature as a fragment of the divine, an aspect of the Supreme God. In the Gnostic worldview, to remain ignorant is to remain captive to the Demiurge's realm, a prisoner of the physical senses and desires that distract from the eternal light of the Pleroma. For the Gnostic, the path to liberation lies not in faith or ritual, but in knowledge—*gnosis*—a deep, intuitive awakening that dispels ignorance and reveals the truth of the soul's divine origin.

The Demiurge, in Gnostic cosmology, is the embodiment of this ignorance. Believing himself to be the supreme creator, he constructs a material world based on his limited understanding, a realm filled with suffering, conflict, and decay. He enforces his rule through the Archons, spiritual rulers who keep humanity in a state of ignorance by focusing attention on the physical and temporal, rather than the spiritual and eternal. These Archons manipulate desires, instill fears, and create attachments to the body and the material world, thus ensuring that souls remain trapped in the cycle of birth, death, and rebirth. In the Demiurge's realm, ignorance is woven into the fabric of existence, a pervasive force that keeps souls from perceiving the light within.

In the Gospel of Judas, Jesus's revelations to Judas touch upon this fundamental role of ignorance. He reveals that the world, as most people understand it, is an illusion, a construct of the Demiurge designed to keep souls unaware of their true divine essence. The other disciples, while earnest in their devotion, remain blind to this truth, seeing Jesus only as a figure who will bring redemption within the material world. Judas, however, is granted insight into a deeper truth, understanding that Jesus's mission is not to fulfill worldly expectations but to reveal a path beyond them, a way to transcend ignorance and awaken to the divine light within.

In Gnostic thought, ignorance is closely linked to the illusions of the material world. The physical senses provide a limited and fragmented perception of reality, focusing on forms and appearances while obscuring the deeper, unified truth of the Pleroma. The body and mind, influenced by the Archons, generate desires, fears, and attachments that keep the soul focused outward, bound to the temporal and unable to perceive the eternal. This external focus is the essence of ignorance—a state where the soul identifies with the physical self rather than the divine spark within. To remain in this state is to be lost in a world of shadows, unable to see the light of the Pleroma that lies just beyond the veil of illusion.

For the Gnostic, the journey toward enlightenment begins with the recognition of this ignorance. It is a process of waking up, of seeing through the illusions of the material world and realizing that one's true identity lies beyond the body, beyond the mind, in the divine essence that dwells within. This awakening requires a shift in perception, a willingness to turn inward and question the assumptions that define ordinary existence. By embracing self-inquiry, meditation, and contemplation, the Gnostic learns to quiet the distractions of the physical senses, to focus on the inner light, and to cultivate a state of awareness that transcends the limitations of the material.

The concept of ignorance in Gnosticism is not simply a personal failing but a cosmic condition, a state imposed upon souls by the Demiurge and his Archons. These forces are not merely external; they manifest as internal obstacles—thoughts, emotions, and beliefs that keep the soul focused on the physical. The Archons' influence creates a state of spiritual amnesia, a forgetting of the soul's divine origin that binds it to the cycles of birth and death, pleasure and pain. To free oneself from this ignorance is to reclaim one's true identity, to remember the soul's connection to the Pleroma and its divine purpose.

In the Gospel of Judas, Jesus teaches that liberation from ignorance involves a recognition of the soul's true nature, an awareness that transcends the dualities of good and evil, pleasure and pain. He reveals to Judas that the material world, with its constant changes and conflicts, is a temporary construct, a place of exile that distracts the soul from its true home in the Pleroma. Judas, in understanding this truth, realizes that the soul's journey is not about achieving status, power, or fulfillment in the material realm, but about awakening to the divine reality that exists beyond it. His role as the chosen disciple reflects his willingness to look beyond appearances, to question the illusions that bind others and to seek the hidden truths that lie within.

In Gnostic teachings, suffering is seen as the direct consequence of ignorance. As long as the soul remains unaware of its divine essence, it is bound to the desires, attachments, and fears that characterize the material world. This ignorance creates a sense of separation, a feeling of incompleteness that drives the soul to seek fulfillment in external things—wealth, pleasure, status, and relationships. Yet these pursuits can never satisfy the soul's true longing, for they are temporary, bound to the cycles of change that define the Demiurge's world. The soul, lost in ignorance, experiences life as a series of fleeting pleasures and inevitable losses, a cycle of desire and dissatisfaction that perpetuates suffering.

The path to freedom from suffering, therefore, lies in the dissolution of ignorance. Through gnosis, the soul awakens to its true nature, recognizing that it is not a physical being defined by its desires and attachments but a divine spark of the Supreme God, temporarily bound to the material. This realization brings a profound sense of peace, a freedom from the cycles of pleasure and pain that define ordinary existence. The Gnostic no longer seeks fulfillment in external things, for they understand that true joy lies within, in the recognition of one's unity with the divine.

The dissolution of ignorance also transforms the way the Gnostic relates to the material world. Rather than seeing life as a struggle to achieve or acquire, the enlightened soul perceives it as a place of learning and growth, a temporary stage where the soul can deepen its understanding and prepare for its return to the Pleroma. This shift in perception allows the Gnostic to engage with life's experiences without becoming attached, to move through the world with a sense of detachment and clarity. Suffering, in this perspective, becomes a teacher, a reminder of the soul's true nature and the need to transcend the illusions of the material.

In the Gospel of Judas, Judas's willingness to embrace Jesus's teachings reflects his understanding of the nature of suffering and ignorance. He alone among the disciples perceives the spiritual dimension of Jesus's mission, recognizing that true liberation involves not the fulfillment of worldly expectations but the dissolution of attachment to the material. His role as the chosen disciple represents his readiness to confront the ignorance that binds others, to look beyond the visible and embrace the truth of the divine light within. Judas's path is not one of conventional heroism but of spiritual courage, a willingness to defy appearances and seek the hidden truth.

For the Gnostic, the dissolution of ignorance is a process of inner purification, a gradual clearing away of the beliefs, desires, and fears that keep the soul focused on the physical. Through practices of self-inquiry, meditation, and inner reflection, the Gnostic learns to quiet the distractions of the body and mind, to cultivate a state of awareness that allows them to see beyond the illusions of the material. This purification is not about moral perfection but about spiritual clarity, a return to the soul's original state of unity with the divine.

In the journey of gnosis, ignorance is transformed from an obstacle to an opportunity. Each moment of awareness, each step toward self-knowledge, brings the soul closer to its true nature, dispelling the darkness of ignorance and revealing the light within. The Gnostic path is therefore a path of awakening, a journey that leads from blindness to vision, from suffering to peace, from separation to unity. In this journey, the soul finds its way back to the Pleroma, the realm of divine fullness where all beings exist in perfect harmony, beyond the illusions of the material.

The Gospel of Judas calls each seeker to embark on this path, to confront the ignorance that binds and embrace the light that liberates. It is a call to remember, to awaken, and to recognize that the soul's true nature lies not in the physical but in the eternal. Through the dissolution of ignorance, the Gnostic finds freedom from suffering, a state of inner peace that arises from the knowledge of one's unity with the Supreme God. This is the promise of gnosis, the hope of liberation through self-knowledge, a path that leads from darkness to light, from illusion to truth, from ignorance to enlightenment.

Chapter 19
Judas's Journey

In the Gnostic view, the story of Judas Iscariot in the Gospel of Judas represents more than a historical account; it is a profound spiritual journey that echoes the path each soul must take in its quest for truth and liberation. Judas's role as the "chosen disciple" in this narrative reveals him not as the traitor reviled in orthodox teachings, but as a seeker of hidden knowledge, someone willing to venture beyond conventional beliefs to uncover deeper truths. Judas's journey, marked by revelation, struggle, and sacrifice, symbolizes the Gnostic path—a journey of inner transformation, a quest for gnosis that requires courage, detachment, and a willingness to defy appearances.

In the Gospel of Judas, Jesus calls Judas aside, confiding in him secrets about the nature of the universe, the Demiurge, and the Supreme God. Judas alone among the disciples is entrusted with these revelations, marking him as the bearer of mysteries, the one capable of understanding the spiritual truths that lie beyond the physical. This unique relationship between Judas and Jesus reflects the Gnostic belief in an inner circle of initiates, seekers who are ready to receive the hidden teachings and pursue the path of gnosis. Unlike the other disciples, who cling to their hope of an earthly kingdom, Judas perceives a reality beyond the material, a realm of spirit that calls him to transcend ordinary understanding.

Judas's journey begins with a revelation—a moment of gnosis in which he recognizes that Jesus's mission is not about earthly salvation but spiritual liberation. This insight sets Judas apart, for he realizes that Jesus's teachings challenge the illusions of the material world, calling souls to awaken from the ignorance imposed by the Demiurge. Judas's willingness to embrace this truth, even when it means acting in ways that others would condemn, speaks to his role as the Gnostic seeker, someone willing to break free from conventional beliefs and follow the path of self-knowledge.

In his journey, Judas faces the profound challenge of stepping outside the accepted norms and expectations of his time. The other disciples, unable to grasp the deeper meaning of Jesus's teachings, expect him to lead them to worldly freedom. They envision a messiah who will bring liberation within the physical realm, establishing a kingdom on earth where they will be rewarded for their faith. Judas, however, comes to understand that Jesus's mission transcends these earthly concerns, that his role is to reveal the path that leads beyond the material, to a higher realm where the soul can find unity with the divine.

This realization marks the beginning of Judas's inner journey, a path that requires him to turn inward, to seek answers not from the world around him but from the spirit within. In many ways, Judas's journey mirrors the Gnostic process of self-discovery, a journey of awakening that involves moving beyond appearances and embracing the hidden truths of existence. To undertake this path, Judas must be willing to confront the illusions that bind others, to see through the veil of material reality and recognize the light that lies beyond. His willingness to do so places him on a solitary path, for the truths he discovers are not understood or accepted by those around him.

The path of Judas is not without sacrifice, for his understanding of Jesus's mission sets him apart from the other disciples and leads him to make difficult choices. In the Gospel of Judas, he realizes that his role involves facilitating Jesus's release from the material world, a role that will require him to act in ways that will forever brand him as a betrayer. Yet this act, misunderstood by others, becomes a profound symbol of spiritual courage, an expression of Judas's willingness to transcend conventional morality in pursuit of a higher truth. By helping Jesus shed his physical form, Judas enables him to return to the

Pleroma, completing his mission and freeing him from the cycle of birth and death imposed by the Demiurge.

In this way, Judas's journey becomes a model of the Gnostic path, a journey that requires the seeker to confront not only external obstacles but internal conflicts and doubts. Judas's willingness to play his role, even at the cost of his reputation and legacy, reflects the depth of his understanding and his commitment to the truth. His actions reveal the Gnostic belief that true liberation involves a willingness to question, to defy appearances, and to embrace the inner calling that leads beyond the physical. Judas's journey is not a betrayal in the traditional sense but a surrender to the divine mystery, a recognition that the soul's true purpose lies beyond the reach of earthly judgments.

In Gnostic thought, the journey of the soul is a journey of remembrance, a process of awakening to its divine origin and transcending the illusions of the material world. Judas's journey reflects this process, for he becomes a figure of inner vision, someone who sees beyond the surface and perceives the hidden reality that lies beneath. His path requires him to confront the expectations of others, to reject the idea of salvation within the material and embrace the path that leads back to the Pleroma. Judas's understanding of Jesus's mission reflects his readiness to walk this path, to seek a truth that transcends the visible and leads to a union with the divine.

The isolation Judas experiences on his journey also speaks to the Gnostic concept of the solitary path. The Gnostic seeker, by embracing hidden truths, often finds themselves at odds with the prevailing beliefs of their culture or community. This sense of separation is not a punishment but a sign of spiritual maturity, a recognition that the truths of gnosis cannot be found in the collective but must be discovered within. Judas, in his willingness to accept this role, becomes a symbol of the Gnostic initiate, someone who is ready to walk the solitary path, guided not by the approval of others but by the light of inner knowledge.

For the Gnostic, Judas's journey is also a reminder of the importance of self-knowledge. The knowledge he gains from

Jesus is not an external doctrine but an inner revelation, a gnosis that allows him to see beyond the limitations of the material world and understand the divine reality within. This self-knowledge is the foundation of the Gnostic path, for it allows the soul to transcend the illusions of the Demiurge's realm and return to its true home in the Pleroma. Judas's role as the chosen disciple reflects his readiness to embrace this self-knowledge, to look within and discover the divine spark that connects him to the Supreme God.

Judas's journey is ultimately a journey of transformation, a path that leads from ignorance to enlightenment, from separation to unity. By choosing to follow the inner calling, Judas aligns himself with the divine purpose, allowing his actions to serve a higher truth that transcends the physical. His willingness to release Jesus from the material world is an expression of his understanding of the nature of true freedom, a recognition that liberation lies not in earthly salvation but in the soul's return to the Pleroma. In this way, Judas's journey becomes a powerful symbol of the Gnostic quest, a reminder that true knowledge requires courage, sacrifice, and a willingness to embrace the unknown.

For the Gnostic seeker, Judas's journey is both a challenge and an inspiration. It calls each individual to question, to look beyond appearances, and to seek the truth within. His path reveals that the journey to gnosis is not an easy one; it requires the seeker to confront their own illusions, to let go of attachments, and to embrace a path that often leads away from the familiar and into the mystery of the divine. Judas's journey, with all its struggles and sacrifices, stands as a testament to the transformative power of self-knowledge, the liberation that comes from recognizing the soul's true nature and aligning oneself with the light of the Pleroma.

In the Gospel of Judas, Judas's journey also serves as a critique of conventional views of salvation and discipleship. His willingness to question and to see beyond the surface reflects a Gnostic skepticism toward religious dogma, a belief that true spiritual understanding cannot be imposed from without but must be discovered within. For Judas, following Jesus is not about obedience or conformity but about self-discovery, a journey that allows him to transcend the limits of the material world and perceive the deeper truths that lie beyond. His actions challenge the reader to look beyond the familiar narratives of faith and explore the inner path of gnosis, the journey that leads to true liberation.

The Gospel of Judas invites each seeker to undertake this journey, to follow the path of inner revelation and embrace the calling that leads to the Pleroma. Judas's journey serves as a guide, a model of the Gnostic path that encourages each soul to remember, to awaken, and to return to the divine fullness. It is a call to transcend the illusions of the Demiurge's world, to see through the dualities of good and evil, and to embrace the truth of one's divine essence. Through this journey, the soul finds not only freedom from the material but a profound unity with the Supreme God, a state of eternal peace and joy that lies beyond all form and matter.

Judas's journey is a reminder that the path to gnosis is a path of courage, insight, and self-knowledge. It is a journey that requires the seeker to look within, to trust the divine spark, and to follow the light that leads beyond the visible world. In the Gnostic vision, this journey is not about adhering to external beliefs or conforming to societal expectations but about finding the truth that lies within, a truth that reveals the soul's true identity and its ultimate purpose. Through this journey, the soul returns to its source, merging once again with the boundless light of the Pleroma, the divine fullness that is the essence of all existence.

Chapter 20
The Secret of the Divine Kingdom

In Gnostic cosmology, the "Divine Kingdom" is a concept that goes beyond earthly definitions of power, territory, or rule. It is a realm of pure spirit, a dimension of eternal light and unity that transcends all physical existence. This kingdom, which exists in the Pleroma, the fullness of the divine, represents the soul's true home—a place beyond time, beyond division, and beyond the reach of the Demiurge. The Gospel of Judas reveals this kingdom not as a physical paradise to be entered after death or a promised land on earth, but as a state of being, an inner reality accessible to those who awaken to gnosis. To know the Divine Kingdom is to recognize the divine essence within, to enter a state of unity with the Supreme God.

Jesus speaks of the Divine Kingdom to Judas as something beyond the material, something that cannot be observed or established in earthly terms. While the other disciples look for a kingdom that will be made manifest in their world, Judas comes to understand that this kingdom is not an external realm. Instead, it is a spiritual reality, a place of truth that one can enter only through enlightenment, by seeing through the illusions of the material world. This secret of the Divine Kingdom is revealed not to the masses or to the outwardly faithful, but to those who are prepared to look beyond appearances, to question the structures of the Demiurge's creation, and to seek the truth within.

The Divine Kingdom, in Gnostic thought, is both a goal and a journey. It is a reality that exists beyond the illusions of duality, a place where the soul experiences unity with the divine fullness. This unity is not simply an abstract ideal but a direct experience of oneness, a sense of belonging to a reality that is unchanging and infinite. To enter the Divine Kingdom is to move beyond the cycle of birth and death, beyond the pull of desires and fears that define life in the material world. It is a return to the Pleroma, a reunion with the source of all light and life.

For the Gnostic, the path to the Divine Kingdom requires a transformation of consciousness, a process of awakening that allows the soul to see beyond the illusions of the Demiurge's world. The Demiurge, in his ignorance, creates a reality filled with conflict, desire, and separation, a place where souls are bound by the limitations of the physical. Yet within each soul lies a divine spark, a fragment of the Supreme God that remembers the Pleroma and longs to return. The journey to the Divine Kingdom is a journey of self-discovery, a process of uncovering this divine essence and allowing it to guide the soul back to the light.

The Gospel of Judas presents this journey as a secret path, a way that is hidden from those who remain focused on the physical. Jesus's teachings to Judas emphasize that the Divine Kingdom is not something that can be accessed through outward rituals or obedience to laws; it is a state of inner knowledge, a gnosis that arises when the soul recognizes its own divinity. Judas, in his unique understanding of Jesus's mission, comes to realize that the path to the Divine Kingdom requires him to look within, to see through the illusions that bind others, and to embrace the inner truth that leads beyond the material.

In Gnosticism, entering the Divine Kingdom involves shedding the attachments and identities that keep the soul bound to the physical. This detachment is not a rejection of life but a reorientation of perception, a shift from seeing the material world as ultimate reality to understanding it as a temporary realm. The soul learns to see the physical as a reflection, a shadow of the true light that exists in the Pleroma. By letting go of the desires, fears, and identities that define life in the material, the Gnostic seeker clears the way for the divine essence to emerge, allowing them to enter the kingdom of the spirit.

The concept of the Divine Kingdom also redefines the Gnostic view of salvation. For the Gnostic, salvation is not a reward granted after death but an awakening that can occur within this life, a state of consciousness that allows the soul to perceive its unity with the Supreme God. This salvation is not a promise of future bliss but an immediate experience of liberation, a release from the limitations of the Demiurge's world. To enter the Divine Kingdom is to escape the cycles of suffering and illusion, to recognize the eternal light within and live in harmony with the truth of one's divine nature.

In the Gospel of Judas, Jesus reveals to Judas that the other disciples, though devout, are unable to grasp the secret of the Divine Kingdom because they remain focused on worldly aspirations. They see Jesus as a figure who will bring about a new order on earth, a kingdom where they will find reward and honor. But Judas, through his inner vision and willingness to embrace Jesus's teachings, perceives a reality beyond these desires. He comes to understand that true liberation lies not in earthly power or position, but in the transcendence of the material. His journey becomes a model of the Gnostic path, a reminder that the kingdom of the spirit cannot be found in the external but must be discovered within.

The secret of the Divine Kingdom is a call to awaken, a reminder that the soul's true purpose lies not in the accumulation of wealth, status, or power, but in the realization of its unity with the divine. The Gnostic path involves a process of purification, a gradual shedding of the beliefs, fears, and attachments that keep the soul focused on the physical. Through meditation, contemplation, and inner reflection, the seeker learns to quiet the distractions of the material world and focus on the inner light. This light, the spark of the Supreme God, becomes a guide, leading the soul out of the shadows of the Demiurge's realm and into the radiance of the Pleroma.

The Gnostic understanding of the Divine Kingdom also transforms the way one perceives life and death. In the Demiurge's world, life and death are seen as opposites, part of a cycle that keeps souls bound to the physical. Yet for the Gnostic, true life is not defined by physical existence but by the experience of unity with the divine. Death, therefore, is not an end but a transition, a moment when the soul has the opportunity to leave the Demiurge's realm and return to the Pleroma. For those who have entered the Divine Kingdom, death holds no fear, for they understand that their true self is eternal, untouched by the cycles of the material.

Judas's understanding of the Divine Kingdom reflects his readiness to embrace this truth. He perceives that Jesus's mission is not about establishing an earthly reign but about guiding souls to the spiritual kingdom, a reality that lies beyond the reach of the Demiurge and his Archons. Judas's willingness to fulfill his role, even at the cost of his reputation, reveals his commitment to the path of inner knowledge. His actions, though misunderstood by others, reflect his understanding that true liberation involves transcending the material and embracing the eternal.

For the Gnostic, the Divine Kingdom is the ultimate destination, the fulfillment of the soul's journey. It is a place of perfect harmony, where all beings exist in unity with the Supreme God, beyond the dualities and conflicts of the material world. To enter this kingdom is to return to the fullness of the Pleroma, to experience a state of eternal peace and joy that transcends all form and matter. This state of being is not something to be achieved in the future but can be accessed here and now, through the awakening of gnosis, the recognition of one's divine essence.

The Gospel of Judas invites each seeker to pursue this path, to seek the kingdom of the spirit that lies within. It is a call to remember, to awaken, and to transcend the limitations of the material world. Through the journey to the Divine Kingdom, the soul finds not only liberation from the Demiurge's illusions but a profound communion with the Supreme God, a state of unity that lies beyond all division, beyond all suffering, in the eternal light of the Pleroma.

In the Gnostic vision, the Divine Kingdom is not a reward granted by an external god but an inner reality, a state of consciousness that reveals the soul's true nature. It is the place where all separations dissolve, where the soul experiences the fullness of the divine and finds peace that surpasses all understanding. This kingdom, hidden yet present, is the ultimate goal of the Gnostic journey, the final step in the soul's return to the Pleroma. Through this journey, the Gnostic finds not only freedom from the illusions of the material world but a profound and lasting union with the Supreme God, a return to the source from which all life and light flow.

Chapter 21
Gnostic Mysteries

In the heart of Gnostic spirituality lies a series of mysteries—hidden teachings, sacred symbols, and transformative practices that guide the soul from ignorance to enlightenment. These mysteries are not simple doctrines to be learned or formulas to be followed; they are experiences, moments of revelation, and secret practices that open the way to gnosis, the deep knowledge of the divine. They serve as doorways to self-discovery and spiritual awakening, leading the seeker to see beyond the illusions of the material world and into the infinite light of the Pleroma. For the Gnostic, the mysteries represent a secret path, a journey inward where the divine presence reveals itself within the soul.

Unlike traditional religious teachings, which are often shared openly through scriptures and communal rituals, the Gnostic mysteries are veiled, hidden from those who are not yet ready to receive them. They are mysteries in the truest sense—secrets that must be approached with reverence, for they are not merely to be understood but lived, felt, and experienced. In the Gospel of Judas, Jesus imparts such mysteries to Judas alone, offering him insights that remain concealed from the other disciples. This exclusivity reflects the Gnostic belief that spiritual truths are not for all to see; they are reserved for those who are prepared to seek beyond the surface, those who have begun the journey toward the inner self.

The Gnostic mysteries encompass various aspects of divine knowledge and include teachings on the nature of the Supreme God, the structure of the spiritual realms, and the path of the soul's return to the Pleroma. These teachings are often shared through symbolic language, using metaphors, images, and stories to convey truths that cannot be expressed in literal terms. This symbolic approach protects the mysteries from misinterpretation, allowing them to reveal their meaning only to those who are ready to comprehend the depth of their significance. Symbols such as light, the divine spark, and the journey from darkness to illumination are central to these mysteries, each offering a glimpse of the soul's ultimate destination.

One of the central mysteries in Gnosticism is the mystery of the self. This mystery reveals that the true self is not the body or the mind but a divine spark, a fragment of the Supreme God that exists within each soul. To discover this true self is to awaken to one's divine nature, to recognize that the soul is not bound to the physical but is eternal, a being of light destined to return to the Pleroma. This realization transforms the way the Gnostic perceives themselves and the world, for it reveals that the self is not an isolated entity but a part of the divine fullness. The mystery of the self is the foundation of all Gnostic teachings, for it leads the soul to seek gnosis, the knowledge that liberates and unites it with the divine.

Another profound mystery is the mystery of the divine realms, the spiritual hierarchy that includes the Supreme God, the Pleroma, and the Aeons. These realms represent the structure of divine reality, a vast and interconnected order that exists beyond the limitations of the physical world. In Gnosticism, the Supreme God is not a figure of command or judgment but a source of infinite light and love, a boundless presence that encompasses all things. The Pleroma, the divine fullness, is the realm where all beings exist in unity, where duality dissolves, and where each soul finds its true home. The Aeons, divine emanations within the Pleroma, represent qualities of the Supreme God, aspects of wisdom, love, and truth that guide the soul on its journey.

These divine realms are not physical places but states of being, dimensions of consciousness that the soul can enter through gnosis. The mystery of the divine realms teaches the

Gnostic to look beyond the visible, to recognize that the true kingdom of the spirit is not to be found in the material world but within the depths of their own being. By contemplating these realms and aligning with the qualities of the Aeons, the soul begins to awaken to its divine nature, preparing itself for the journey back to the Pleroma.

One of the most challenging mysteries in Gnosticism is the mystery of the Demiurge and the material world. In orthodox belief, creation is often viewed as a reflection of divine goodness, a world crafted by a benevolent God. Yet in Gnostic thought, the material world is the work of the Demiurge, a lesser creator who, in his ignorance, produces a realm of illusion and limitation. This world, with its suffering and impermanence, is not the true home of the soul but a place of exile. The mystery of the Demiurge teaches that the material is a veil, a shadow cast by the separation from the divine. The Gnostic must learn to see through this veil, to recognize the world as a temporary state that obscures the soul's true purpose.

The Gospel of Judas reveals this mystery to Judas, showing him that the other disciples, though devout, are bound by their attachment to the material. They seek a kingdom on earth, unaware that the true kingdom exists within. Judas, in receiving this revelation, begins to understand the need to detach from the illusions of the physical and seek the divine within. The mystery of the Demiurge encourages the Gnostic to question appearances, to see beyond the forms and cycles of the material world and perceive the spiritual reality that lies beneath.

Integral to the Gnostic mysteries is the concept of initiation, a transformative process that allows the seeker to experience the truths revealed in the teachings. Initiation is not a ritual performed in a single moment but a lifelong journey, a process of inner awakening that unfolds gradually. Through meditation, contemplation, and self-inquiry, the Gnostic undergoes an inner transformation, peeling away the layers of illusion to reveal the divine spark within. Each stage of initiation brings the soul closer to the Pleroma, each revelation deepening their understanding of their true nature and their connection to the Supreme God.

The mysteries also involve practices that guide the seeker along this path, techniques that allow them to cultivate inner awareness and connect with the divine presence. These practices include meditation, where the seeker learns to quiet the mind and focus on the inner light; visualization, where the soul imagines itself ascending to the Pleroma; and prayer, an act of communion with the Supreme God that allows the soul to express its longing for unity. These practices are not merely rituals but tools for transformation, techniques that bring the mysteries to life within the seeker, allowing them to experience the truths that the teachings convey.

In the Gospel of Judas, Jesus's relationship with Judas is itself an initiation into these mysteries. Through his private teachings, Jesus reveals the hidden nature of the universe, guiding Judas toward a deeper understanding of himself and his role in the divine order. This initiation sets Judas apart, marking him as one who has been chosen to receive the mysteries, to see beyond the ordinary and recognize the truth of the divine kingdom. His willingness to embrace these teachings, even when they lead him down a path that others would condemn, reflects his commitment to the Gnostic path, a path that values knowledge and insight over obedience or conformity.

The Gnostic mysteries are both a journey and a destination, a path that leads from ignorance to enlightenment, from separation to unity. They offer a way for the soul to navigate the complexities of existence, to see through the illusions of the material and align with the light of the Pleroma. Each mystery reveals a piece of the larger truth, guiding the seeker toward a deeper understanding of the self, the divine, and the journey of return. For the Gnostic, these mysteries are sacred gifts, insights that provide a map for the soul's journey and a vision of the divine fullness that awaits.

The Gospel of Judas calls each seeker to undertake this journey, to enter the mysteries and seek the light that lies within.

It is a call to remember, to awaken, and to recognize that the truths of the divine cannot be found in the visible but must be discovered in the hidden depths of the self. Through the Gnostic mysteries, the soul finds not only knowledge but transformation, a way to transcend the limitations of the material and enter the kingdom of the spirit. This is the essence of gnosis, the ultimate revelation that leads the soul back to the Pleroma, where it is reunited with the Supreme God in a state of eternal light, peace, and unity.

Chapter 22
Gnostic Meditation Practices

Meditation, in the Gnostic tradition, is not just a practice of calming the mind; it is a journey of the soul, a means of transcending the illusions of the physical world and awakening to the divine spark within. Gnostic meditation is a sacred act, a practice that aligns the soul with the deeper truths of the divine kingdom and opens a pathway toward gnosis—direct knowledge of the divine. Unlike meditative practices that focus merely on mindfulness or mental clarity, Gnostic meditation aims to pierce the veil of the material, to lift the soul beyond the realm of the Demiurge and into communion with the Supreme God. Through these practices, the seeker is guided inward, moving closer to the light of the Pleroma, the boundless realm of divine fullness.

The central aim of Gnostic meditation is to quiet the distractions of the physical senses, to create a stillness in which the soul can hear the voice of the spirit within. In the Gospel of Judas, Jesus invites Judas to look beyond the visible world, to perceive the truths that lie hidden beneath appearances. This inner seeing, a perception beyond ordinary sight, is cultivated through meditation, which allows the soul to withdraw from the external and journey inward. In this state of interior awareness, the Gnostic enters a space of divine silence, a realm where the spirit can guide the soul toward a deeper understanding of its true nature and purpose.

One of the foundational Gnostic meditation practices is *centering*, a method of focusing on the divine spark that exists within each person. To practice centering, the Gnostic begins by sitting quietly, free from external distractions. They then direct their attention to the heart, imagining a small flame or radiant light at its center. This light is not a mere image but a symbol of the divine presence, the fragment of the Supreme God that resides within. By focusing on this inner light, the Gnostic learns to quiet the mind, to let go of thoughts, fears, and desires, and to enter a state of communion with the divine essence. This simple act of centering becomes a doorway to gnosis, a way to align with the eternal truth that lies within.

Another powerful practice in Gnostic meditation is *contemplation of the Pleroma*. In this meditation, the seeker visualizes the Pleroma, the realm of divine fullness that exists beyond all form and matter. They may imagine the Pleroma as an infinite expanse of light, a place where all beings exist in unity, beyond the dualities of the material world. By focusing on this vision, the Gnostic allows themselves to experience a sense of expansion, a feeling of oneness with the divine. This contemplation serves as a reminder of the soul's true home, a way to cultivate a deep yearning for the Pleroma that fuels the journey of return.

Breath awareness is also central to Gnostic meditation. In this practice, the seeker pays attention to the natural rhythm of their breath, observing each inhale and exhale as a movement of life and spirit. Breath, in Gnostic thought, symbolizes the connection between the physical and the divine, the bridge between body and soul. By focusing on the breath, the Gnostic enters a state of presence, a state of awareness that transcends the mind and connects with the spirit. This practice of breath awareness helps to quiet the restless mind, to ground the soul in the present moment, and to create a space where divine insight can arise.

Guided by these practices, the Gnostic seeker learns to cultivate a state of detachment, a quality of inner stillness that allows them to witness the world without becoming entangled in its illusions. Detachment is not an abandonment of life but a clear seeing, a way of perceiving the material world as a temporary construct. Through meditation, the Gnostic learns to release the desires and attachments that bind them to the Demiurge's realm, to focus instead on the eternal light that resides within. This state of detachment allows the soul to live in the world without being of it, to engage with life's experiences while remaining anchored in the divine.

Visualization is another essential aspect of Gnostic meditation, a practice that strengthens the soul's perception of the spiritual realm. One common visualization is the *ascent to the Pleroma*, in which the seeker imagines themselves moving upward, leaving behind the material world and entering the realms of light. As they ascend, they may visualize passing through layers of illusion, moving beyond the influences of the Archons and the Demiurge. Each level of ascent brings the seeker closer to the Pleroma, the realm of divine unity. This visualization reinforces the soul's understanding of its journey, reminding the Gnostic that the path to enlightenment involves a process of rising above the physical, moving ever closer to the divine.

In addition to these practices, Gnostic meditation often involves the use of sacred sounds or *vibrations*. These sounds are not merely words or chants but are believed to resonate with the frequencies of the divine. For instance, the sound "Aum," representing the primordial vibration, can be used to attune the soul to the presence of the Supreme God. By chanting or intoning these sounds, the Gnostic aligns their inner being with the higher realms, creating a resonance that draws the soul closer to the divine. This practice of sacred sound creates a space for inner harmony, a vibration that connects the seeker to the Pleroma and helps to dispel the darkness of ignorance.

The Gospel of Judas suggests that Jesus imparted certain practices to Judas that went beyond what the other disciples could understand. These were not teachings intended for the masses but hidden instructions, methods of meditation and contemplation that allowed Judas to see the truth of Jesus's mission and the nature of the Divine Kingdom. Judas's role as the chosen disciple reflects his readiness to embrace these practices, his willingness to enter the mysteries and seek the divine presence within. Through his devotion to these practices, Judas becomes a model of the Gnostic seeker, someone who is willing to look beyond the visible and pursue the path that leads to the Pleroma.

In the practice of Gnostic meditation, the seeker also learns to cultivate an attitude of *openness and surrender*. This involves letting go of preconceived notions, releasing the desire to control or achieve, and simply allowing the experience to unfold. The Gnostic understands that enlightenment cannot be forced or grasped; it is a gift that arises from within, a revelation that comes when the soul is ready. Through surrender, the seeker creates a space where the divine can reveal itself, allowing the light of the Supreme God to shine through the layers of illusion. This attitude of surrender deepens the practice, transforming meditation from an effort to a state of being, a place where the soul can rest in the presence of the divine.

The Gnostic meditation practices are both a means of transformation and a path of return, a way for the soul to prepare itself for the journey back to the Pleroma. Each practice, whether centering, contemplation, breath awareness, visualization, or sacred sound, serves to deepen the soul's connection to the divine, to strengthen its awareness of the eternal light within. By cultivating these practices, the Gnostic aligns themselves with the Supreme God, creating a resonance that allows the soul to transcend the Demiurge's world and approach the kingdom of spirit.

Through these practices, the Gnostic also learns to overcome the obstacles of the material world, to see through the illusions that keep souls bound to the physical. Meditation becomes a way to break free from the limitations of the Demiurge's realm, to rise above the desires and fears that define life in the material. Each moment spent in meditation is a step on the path to gnosis, a journey inward that brings the soul closer to its true self, its divine essence that waits to be revealed.

In the Gospel of Judas, meditation is suggested as a path not only of self-discovery but of liberation. It is a way to connect with the truths that Jesus reveals to Judas, a means of embracing the inner light that leads to the Divine Kingdom. Through meditation, the Gnostic finds not only knowledge but peace, a state of harmony that transcends the dualities of the physical and allows the soul to rest in the presence of the Supreme God.

The Gnostic meditation practices are a call to remember, to awaken, and to seek the light within. They invite the seeker to embark on the journey of self-knowledge, to cultivate a state of inner stillness and clarity that allows the divine to reveal itself. Through this journey, the soul finds not only freedom from the material but a profound communion with the Supreme God, a state of unity and joy that lies beyond all form and matter, in the eternal fullness of the Pleroma.

Chapter 23
Spiritual Visualizations

In the Gnostic tradition, visualization is a sacred tool, a means by which the soul transcends the confines of the material world and draws closer to the divine. Unlike ordinary imagination or daydreaming, Gnostic visualization is an intentional practice that seeks to reveal spiritual truths, awaken the divine spark within, and connect with the Pleroma, the realm of divine fullness. Through carefully cultivated images and symbols, visualization guides the soul inward, allowing it to bypass the distractions of the physical senses and commune with the hidden light of the Supreme God. These visualizations serve as a bridge to realms beyond the material, helping the seeker to move through the veils of illusion toward a profound awareness of the divine.

In the Gospel of Judas, Jesus imparts truths to Judas that he conceals from the other disciples, guiding Judas toward an understanding that lies beyond physical perception. This hidden knowledge is not a doctrine to be learned, but a vision of reality that can only be perceived through an awakened inner sight. Visualization becomes a tool for cultivating this sight, a practice that allows the Gnostic to see beyond the visible and engage with the mysteries of the spirit. By using spiritual visualizations, the seeker aligns their inner self with the qualities of the divine, creating an inner landscape that mirrors the beauty and harmony of the Pleroma.

One of the most profound visualizations in Gnostic practice is the *Journey to the Pleroma*. In this visualization, the Gnostic imagines themselves ascending through realms of light, moving beyond the physical world and into higher spiritual planes. The journey begins with a moment of grounding, where the seeker becomes fully aware of their breath and the quiet space within. They then visualize a path or staircase leading upward, a path illuminated by a radiant light that calls the soul to ascend. Each step on this journey takes the soul closer to the Pleroma, passing through layers of illusion and moving ever closer to the source of divine light.

As the seeker progresses, they may visualize leaving behind the material world, symbolized by dark clouds or heavy veils that lift and dissolve as they ascend. These veils represent the ignorance imposed by the Demiurge and his Archons, the forces that keep souls bound to the physical. With each step, the soul moves closer to freedom, shedding attachments, desires, and fears, and allowing the divine essence to shine through. Finally, in reaching the Pleroma, the seeker envisions an infinite expanse of light, a space beyond form and time where all beings exist in perfect unity. This visualization serves as a reminder of the soul's true home, a place of peace and fullness that lies beyond the reach of the Demiurge.

Another powerful visualization is the *Unveiling of the Divine Spark*, a practice that focuses on the discovery of the soul's inner light. In this exercise, the seeker sits in a quiet space, focusing inward and becoming aware of a small, radiant flame or spark within the heart. This flame is the divine spark, a fragment of the Supreme God that resides within each soul, waiting to be revealed. The Gnostic then visualizes this flame growing brighter, expanding until it fills their entire being with light. This practice is not just an image but an experience, a way to cultivate a direct awareness of the divine essence within. As the light fills their being, the Gnostic feels a sense of connection to the Pleroma, a reminder that their true identity lies beyond the physical.

The *Light of the Aeons* is another visualization that allows the seeker to connect with the divine qualities embodied by the Aeons. In Gnostic cosmology, the Aeons are emanations of the Supreme God, each representing a specific attribute or aspect of the divine, such as wisdom, love, or truth. Through this visualization, the Gnostic envisions each Aeon as a radiant figure or light, each one shining with a unique color or energy. By focusing on each Aeon in turn, the seeker allows these qualities to resonate within themselves, awakening the corresponding aspects of their own soul. This practice serves as both a form of meditation and a reminder of the divine fullness that exists within.

Visualizations in Gnostic practice also often involve symbols that represent the journey from the material to the spiritual. One such symbol is the *Ladder of Ascent*, which reflects the stages of the soul's journey back to the Pleroma. In this visualization, the seeker imagines themselves climbing a ladder, each rung representing a step toward enlightenment. As they climb, they may encounter various symbols or figures, each offering guidance or insights that help them progress. This ladder represents the Gnostic understanding that the journey to gnosis is gradual, a process that requires persistence, courage, and inner clarity. With each step, the Gnostic rises above the influences of the Demiurge, moving closer to the divine.

The *Temple of the Spirit* is another significant visualization, a practice where the seeker imagines a sacred space within themselves—a temple that represents the soul's connection to the divine. This temple is a place of refuge, a sanctuary where the soul can retreat from the distractions of the physical world and commune with the Supreme God. In this visualization, the Gnostic enters the temple, which is filled with light and peace, and sits quietly, focusing on the silence within. This sacred space serves as a reminder that the Divine Kingdom exists within, a place of unity and harmony that can be accessed at any time through inner reflection.

These visualizations also serve to strengthen the Gnostic's sense of detachment from the material world. By regularly visualizing realms beyond the physical, the soul becomes less bound by the limitations of the Demiurge's creation. The material world, with its cycles of pleasure and pain, begins to lose its hold, allowing the soul to focus on the eternal. Through visualization, the Gnostic learns to see the world as a temporary place, a place of learning and growth that prepares the soul for its journey back to the Pleroma.

In the Gospel of Judas, Jesus's teachings to Judas hint at a similar process of seeing beyond the visible, a way of understanding that transcends ordinary perception. Judas's role as the chosen disciple reflects his ability to perceive hidden truths, to look beyond the surface and grasp the spiritual realities that lie beneath. The visualizations in Gnostic practice cultivate this inner vision, allowing the seeker to experience spiritual truths directly, beyond the confines of logic and intellect.

Visualization, in the Gnostic tradition, is not simply a mental exercise but a spiritual tool, a way to bring the truths of the Pleroma into the seeker's lived experience. Each image, each symbol, serves as a doorway to a deeper understanding, a way for the soul to remember its divine origin and realign with its true nature. The Gnostic does not use visualization to escape the world but to transcend it, to see it from a higher perspective, and to remain focused on the journey back to the divine fullness.

The practice of *Radiance Meditation* is also a central visualization, where the seeker envisions themselves as a vessel of light, a being that reflects the divine radiance of the Pleroma. In this meditation, the Gnostic begins by visualizing a light above them, a light that represents the Supreme God. They then imagine this light descending into their being, filling them with peace, love, and wisdom. As the light fills their entire body, they begin to radiate this divine presence outward, becoming a beacon of light in the world. This visualization reinforces the Gnostic belief that each soul is a reflection of the divine and that by awakening this inner light, they can bring the essence of the Pleroma into the material.

Through these visualizations, the Gnostic learns to cultivate an awareness that bridges the visible and invisible worlds, to perceive both the temporal and the eternal. The Gnostic practices visualization as a path of remembrance, a way to keep the soul aligned with its true purpose. Each image, each symbol, serves to deepen the soul's understanding of its journey, guiding it toward the ultimate goal of union with the Supreme God.

The Gospel of Judas invites the seeker to look within, to cultivate the vision that allows them to see beyond the material and embrace the mystery of the divine. Through spiritual visualizations, the Gnostic finds not only knowledge but transformation, a way to live with an awareness of the divine presence within and around them. These practices lead the soul out of the darkness of the material, helping it rise above the illusions of the Demiurge's realm and move ever closer to the light of the Pleroma.

In this journey, visualization becomes a sacred practice, a means of touching the divine and experiencing the fullness of the Supreme God. Through these visualizations, the Gnostic finds a state of peace, clarity, and joy, a state that reflects the unity of the Pleroma and the boundless love that lies at the heart of all existence. This is the gift of visualization in Gnostic practice—a bridge to the eternal, a reminder of the soul's true home, and a pathway to the divine kingdom that resides within.

Chapter 24
Connection with the Inner Divine

In the heart of Gnostic belief lies the conviction that each soul carries within it a fragment of the divine—a spark, hidden but eternal, that connects it to the Supreme God. This spark, often obscured by the illusions of the material world, is the true essence of the self, a piece of the Pleroma that has journeyed into the physical realm. The quest for gnosis is, at its core, a journey to reconnect with this inner divine presence, to awaken to the soul's true nature and remember its origin beyond the reach of the Demiurge and his imperfect creation. In the Gospel of Judas, Jesus imparts teachings to Judas that speak directly to this connection, guiding him to perceive the divine within and to see beyond the physical world's limitations.

The path to connecting with the inner divine begins with self-awareness, a conscious turning inward. This is not the casual self-reflection of everyday life but a deep and focused introspection that allows the soul to perceive the divine essence within. The Gnostic seeker learns to quiet the mind and senses, to set aside the distractions of the material world, and to enter a state of profound inner stillness. In this silence, the soul finds itself face to face with its own true nature, a divine presence that has remained untouched by the influences of the Demiurge. This is the moment of recognition, an awakening to the truth that the soul is more than a physical being; it is a vessel of the divine, a spark of light that remembers the Pleroma.

One of the primary practices for connecting with the inner divine is *sacred silence*. In this practice, the seeker withdraws from external noise and enters a space of deep quiet. This silence is not merely an absence of sound; it is a state of inner stillness where thoughts, emotions, and desires are set aside. By dwelling in this silence, the soul becomes receptive to the voice of the spirit, a subtle and often wordless guidance that emanates from the divine spark within. The Gnostic learns to listen to this inner voice, to trust its quiet wisdom, and to follow its guidance toward self-discovery and liberation. In this sacred silence, the soul experiences a taste of the divine, a moment of communion that transcends the limitations of the physical.

Meditative visualization also serves as a key to unlocking the connection with the inner divine. The Gnostic often visualizes their soul as a radiant light, a small but intense flame that burns at the center of their being. This flame, though hidden by layers of illusion, shines with the light of the Supreme God, a reminder of the soul's true nature and its ultimate destination. By focusing on this inner flame, the Gnostic strengthens their awareness of the divine presence within, allowing this light to grow and expand. Through this practice, the soul becomes increasingly attuned to its own divinity, perceiving itself as a part of the Pleroma that has been temporarily cast into the material world.

Breathwork, too, becomes a bridge to the inner divine. In Gnostic practice, the breath is seen as a symbol of the spirit, a rhythmic connection between the physical and the spiritual. By focusing on the breath, the seeker enters a state of mindful awareness, a place of balance where the soul can rest and reconnect with the divine spark. Each breath becomes a reminder of the soul's connection to the divine, a movement of life that links the physical body to the eternal spirit. This simple act of awareness becomes a pathway to gnosis, a means of aligning the soul with its true nature and fostering a deeper connection with the Supreme God.

To deepen this connection, the Gnostic practices *inner alignment*—a conscious effort to bring thoughts, emotions, and actions into harmony with the divine presence within. This alignment is not an attempt to impose moral discipline from outside but a natural unfolding, a way of allowing the soul's inherent qualities to shine through. By aligning with the inner divine, the Gnostic finds that qualities such as compassion, wisdom, and peace naturally arise, reflecting the light of the Pleroma. This state of alignment transforms the way the Gnostic moves through the world, allowing them to live with a sense of purpose and clarity that transcends the illusions of the material.

Another essential practice for connecting with the inner divine is *contemplation of divine attributes*. In this exercise, the Gnostic reflects on qualities such as love, wisdom, and unity, qualities that are inherent to the Supreme God and present within the soul as seeds waiting to be awakened. By contemplating these attributes, the seeker allows them to take root, cultivating a state of being that mirrors the Pleroma's harmony. This contemplation is not an intellectual exercise but an act of alignment, a way of tuning the soul to resonate with the divine presence within. Through this practice, the Gnostic learns to embody these divine qualities, to live as a reflection of the Supreme God in the material world.

Prayer, in the Gnostic tradition, is less about petitioning an external deity and more about communing with the divine presence within. This inner prayer is a silent dialogue, a moment of turning inward and acknowledging the soul's connection to the Pleroma. The Gnostic does not ask for material favors or worldly success; instead, they seek guidance, insight, and the strength to align more fully with their true nature. This prayer becomes an act of surrender, a willingness to trust the divine spark within and to follow its wisdom. In this communion, the soul finds peace, a state of inner harmony that arises from the recognition of its own divinity.

In the Gospel of Judas, Judas's unique understanding of Jesus's teachings reflects his ability to connect with this inner divine presence. Unlike the other disciples, who see Jesus as an external savior, Judas perceives a deeper truth—that the path to salvation lies within, in the recognition of the divine spark. This understanding allows him to see beyond the physical, to grasp the spiritual dimension of Jesus's mission, and to embrace the path of inner awakening. Judas's connection to the inner divine becomes the foundation of his gnosis, a knowledge that liberates him from the illusions of the Demiurge and prepares him for the journey back to the Pleroma.

The connection with the inner divine also changes the Gnostic's perspective on the world. No longer does the material realm appear as the ultimate reality; it becomes a temporary place, a realm of shadows that reflect a deeper truth. Through this connection, the Gnostic learns to see the world with a sense of detachment, to engage with life's experiences without becoming bound by them. The material world, with all its pleasures and pains, becomes a backdrop for the soul's journey, a place where the divine essence can be awakened and nurtured in preparation for the return to the Pleroma.

This connection to the inner divine also brings a sense of inner peace, a state of serenity that arises from the recognition of one's eternal nature. The Gnostic understands that they are not defined by the body, mind, or external circumstances but are, in essence, a spark of the Supreme God. This awareness brings freedom from fear, a release from the anxieties that arise from attachment to the material. The soul, anchored in the knowledge of its own divinity, finds a state of equilibrium, a peace that remains unshaken by the changes of the physical world.

As the Gnostic deepens this connection, they also experience a sense of *inner guidance*, an intuitive knowing that comes from the divine spark within. This guidance is not a voice or a vision but a quiet certainty, a sense of alignment that helps the soul navigate the complexities of life. By listening to this inner guidance, the Gnostic learns to make choices that reflect their true nature, to move through the world with clarity and purpose. This guidance becomes a source of strength, a reminder that the soul is never alone, that it is always connected to the divine presence that resides within.

The connection with the inner divine is ultimately a journey of remembrance, a process of awakening to the truth that has always been present within. The Gnostic does not acquire new knowledge from outside but uncovers a hidden reality that has been forgotten. Through meditation, prayer, and contemplation, the soul remembers its own divinity, reawakening the qualities of the Supreme God that lie dormant within. This remembrance is the essence of gnosis, a knowledge that brings freedom from the illusions of the Demiurge and allows the soul to return to the Pleroma.

The Gospel of Judas invites each seeker to undertake this journey, to look within and discover the light that lies at the core of their being. It is a call to transcend the distractions of the material world, to quiet the mind and open the heart to the divine presence that resides within. Through this connection with the inner divine, the soul finds not only knowledge but transformation, a way of living that reflects the harmony and unity of the Pleroma.

In the Gnostic vision, the connection with the inner divine is not a distant goal but a present reality, a truth that can be experienced in every moment. It is a state of being that allows the soul to live in the world while remaining anchored in the eternal, a state of awareness that transforms every experience into an opportunity for growth and awakening. This is the gift of the inner divine—a light that guides the soul back to its true home, a presence that reminds the soul of its unity with the Supreme God, and a path that leads beyond all form and matter into the boundless fullness of the Pleroma.

Chapter 25
Awakening Consciousness

Awakening consciousness, within Gnostic thought, is the profound shift from perceiving the world as a purely material construct to recognizing the divine truth hidden within. It is the journey from spiritual ignorance to gnosis, a revelation that reshapes the soul's understanding of itself and reality. In this awakening, the Gnostic begins to see beyond the illusions crafted by the Demiurge, to penetrate the layers of deception that hold souls captive in the physical realm. This awakening is not an intellectual realization alone; it is a transformative experience that realigns the soul with the divine light of the Supreme God, allowing it to glimpse the boundless fullness of the Pleroma.

The Gospel of Judas illuminates this concept by portraying Judas as the disciple chosen to receive Jesus's hidden teachings. Jesus invites Judas to see beyond the world that the other disciples still cling to, a world they believe will bring earthly redemption. Judas's path represents the journey of awakening consciousness, a journey that defies the expectations of society and the superficial beliefs that obscure the deeper truths of the spirit. In choosing to follow Jesus's revelations, Judas becomes a symbol of the Gnostic seeker—a soul willing to confront the unknown, to let go of conventional illusions, and to awaken to the true nature of reality.

Awakening consciousness in the Gnostic tradition begins with *self-inquiry*, a process of questioning one's own thoughts, beliefs, and attachments. The Gnostic learns to recognize that many of the assumptions they hold about themselves and the world are not based in truth but in the illusions of the Demiurge's creation. By examining these beliefs, the soul begins to discern the difference between the temporary constructs of the material world and the eternal reality of the spirit. This inquiry is not merely intellectual; it is a deep and honest introspection, a willingness to let go of the false identities that bind the soul to the physical.

Central to this awakening is the practice of *mindful observation*, where the Gnostic becomes a witness to their own thoughts, emotions, and actions. Through this practice, the seeker learns to detach from the fleeting desires, fears, and judgments that define the ordinary state of consciousness. By observing these inner movements without attachment, the soul begins to cultivate a space of awareness, a place of stillness where the divine presence can be perceived. This mindful observation allows the Gnostic to recognize the difference between the ego—the constructed self bound to the material—and the divine essence within.

Breathwork and meditation are essential tools in awakening consciousness. Through focused breathing, the Gnostic quiets the mind and anchors themselves in the present moment, creating an inner stillness where the soul can experience its own divinity. The breath serves as a bridge between the body and spirit, a rhythm that harmonizes the physical with the eternal. By concentrating on the breath, the Gnostic learns to move beyond thought, to enter a state of pure awareness that reveals the divine spark within. This practice becomes a doorway to gnosis, a way of experiencing the presence of the Supreme God beyond the distractions of the material.

In the Gospel of Judas, Jesus's guidance to Judas suggests a similar path of awakening, a call to perceive reality through the inner eye rather than the physical senses. Jesus reveals that the kingdom he speaks of is not of this world, a statement that echoes the Gnostic understanding that true reality exists beyond the visible. Judas's willingness to follow Jesus's teachings, even when they lead him away from the path of earthly understanding, reflects his readiness to embrace this awakened consciousness. He becomes an example of the seeker who dares to step beyond convention, to see the world not as it appears but as it truly is—a place of shadows that conceals the light of the Pleroma.

One of the significant aspects of awakening consciousness in Gnosticism is the realization of *interconnectedness*. The Gnostic begins to see that the self is not separate from others or from the divine; instead, it is part of a larger unity, a single light that connects all beings within the Pleroma. This awareness transforms the way the Gnostic relates to the world, fostering a sense of compassion and understanding that transcends individual desires. By awakening to this interconnectedness, the soul begins to live in harmony with the divine will, allowing the qualities of the Supreme God—love, wisdom, and peace—to flow through their being.

Visualization practices also play an essential role in awakening consciousness. Through visualizations such as the *Inner Light* and the *Ascent to the Pleroma*, the Gnostic strengthens their perception of the spiritual realms, allowing the divine spark to shine more brightly within. By imagining themselves surrounded by light, the Gnostic creates a field of awareness that connects them to the Pleroma, reinforcing their sense of unity with the Supreme God. This visualization is not merely an image; it is a shift in consciousness, a way of aligning the soul with its true nature and awakening to the presence of the divine.

Awakening consciousness also involves the practice of *inner alignment*, an effort to bring thoughts, feelings, and actions into harmony with the soul's divine essence. This alignment requires the Gnostic to let go of attachments to the physical and cultivate qualities that reflect the light of the Pleroma. By embodying attributes such as patience, kindness, and humility, the Gnostic aligns themselves with the Supreme God, creating a resonance that deepens their connection to the divine. This inner alignment is not an imposition of external rules but a natural expression of the soul's true nature, a way of living that flows from the awareness of one's divinity.

As the Gnostic awakens, they also come to understand the role of *intention* in shaping consciousness. The Demiurge's world is filled with influences that pull the soul toward the physical, reinforcing desires, fears, and distractions that obscure the divine. By cultivating a clear intention, the Gnostic learns to focus their consciousness on the path of gnosis, to choose thoughts, words, and actions that lead toward enlightenment rather than attachment. This intentionality becomes a tool for liberation, a way of aligning each moment with the soul's highest purpose and moving ever closer to the Pleroma.

Another dimension of awakening consciousness is the realization of *timelessness*. In the Demiurge's world, life is bound by the cycles of birth and death, pleasure and pain, moments passing one after another in an endless stream. Yet in the Pleroma, there exists a state beyond time, a place of eternal presence where the soul can experience the fullness of the divine. By cultivating awareness of this timeless nature, the Gnostic begins to transcend the limitations of the physical, entering a state of consciousness where past and future dissolve and only the eternal now remains. This timeless awareness brings peace, a sense of freedom from the cycles that define ordinary existence, and allows the soul to live with a sense of inner stillness and joy.

In the Gospel of Judas, Judas's journey reflects this awakening to timelessness. By understanding that Jesus's mission is not bound by the expectations of the material, he perceives a truth beyond time, a reality that cannot be measured by earthly standards. His actions, guided by this understanding, become a reflection of his alignment with the divine will, a willingness to see the eternal purpose that lies beyond the visible. Judas's path invites the Gnostic to look beyond the cycles of life and death, to recognize the presence of the divine in every moment and to live with an awareness that transcends the temporal.

For the Gnostic, awakening consciousness is also a path of healing, for it allows the soul to release the wounds and fears imposed by the material world. The Demiurge's creation is a place of separation, a realm that often leaves the soul burdened with pain, guilt, and confusion. Yet by awakening to the divine presence within, the Gnostic finds a source of healing that transcends these wounds, a light that cannot be dimmed by the darkness of the material. This inner light offers a sanctuary of peace, a refuge where the soul can rest in the knowledge of its eternal nature and experience the fullness of the divine.

The journey of awakening consciousness is both a beginning and an end, a process of remembering the truth of one's divine origin and preparing for the return to the Pleroma. Each moment of awareness, each step toward self-knowledge, brings the soul closer to this goal, dispelling the darkness of ignorance and revealing the light within. The Gospel of Judas calls each seeker to undertake this journey, to awaken to the light that lies hidden within and to embrace the path that leads to true liberation. Through this journey, the Gnostic finds not only freedom from the illusions of the material but a profound communion with the Supreme God, a state of unity that lies beyond all separation.

In the Gnostic vision, awakening consciousness is the essence of life itself, the means by which the soul fulfills its purpose and returns to its source. This awakening brings a clarity that allows the Gnostic to see the world as it truly is, to move through life with an understanding that transcends duality and reveals the oneness of all existence. Through this journey, the soul finds its way home, returning to the Pleroma and merging once again with the infinite light of the Supreme God, a state of eternal peace and joy that lies beyond all form and matter.

Chapter 26
Exploring the Aeons

In the intricate and luminous cosmology of Gnosticism, the Aeons are divine emanations, spiritual entities that exist within the fullness of the Pleroma. These beings, or rather energies, are not gods in the traditional sense but expressions of the Supreme God's essence, each embodying a unique attribute or aspect of divine reality. They are the building blocks of existence, the very principles that structure both the invisible realms of the Pleroma and the pathway of spiritual ascent that leads souls back to unity with the divine. Through the Aeons, the Supreme God manifests attributes such as wisdom, truth, love, and harmony—qualities that the soul must cultivate and align with on its journey of return.

For the Gnostic, understanding the Aeons is not a mere intellectual exercise; it is a deeply experiential exploration of these divine qualities as they exist both within and beyond. The Aeons act as spiritual archetypes that mirror the true nature of the soul, representing what each being must become to move closer to the divine. The Gospel of Judas hints at these mysteries through the unique relationship between Jesus and Judas, as Jesus reveals truths that transcend the physical world and guide Judas toward a realm of greater understanding. This exploration of the Aeons, then, is an invitation to embrace the divine attributes and ascend through the layers of consciousness that lead back to the Pleroma.

One of the most profound Aeons in Gnostic cosmology is *Sophia*, who embodies divine wisdom. Sophia's story is one of longing, a desire to know the Supreme God that leads her to stray from the Pleroma, resulting in her fall. In her separation, she becomes the catalyst for the creation of the material world, sparking a chain of events that ultimately leads to the emergence of the Demiurge. Yet even in her fall, Sophia retains a fragment of divine light, a reminder of her origin. For the Gnostic, Sophia's journey is a reflection of the soul's own story—a descent into ignorance and separation followed by a gradual return to wisdom and divine unity. By contemplating Sophia, the seeker connects with the quality of wisdom within, learning to discern truth from illusion and to embrace the inner knowing that guides them back to the divine.

Another essential Aeon is *Logos*, or divine reason. The Logos represents clarity, order, and harmony—the rational structure that governs the universe and aligns it with the divine will. Logos is the force that brings coherence to creation, a guiding principle that ensures that each part reflects the whole. In the Gospel of Judas, Judas's unique insight into Jesus's mission reflects an understanding of Logos, an ability to see beyond earthly appearances and perceive the underlying truth. For the Gnostic, cultivating the quality of Logos within means developing a balanced mind, a state of clarity that allows them to perceive the unity of all things and to live in harmony with the divine order. The seeker learns to bring this harmony into their own life, allowing the clarity of Logos to dispel the chaos of the Demiurge's world.

Love, or Agape, is another Aeon that holds a central place in Gnostic thought. Unlike the limited, conditional love often experienced in the material world, Agape represents an unconditional, boundless love that flows directly from the Supreme God. This love is not based on desire or attachment; it is a pure expression of divine essence, a force that unites all beings within the Pleroma. In seeking to embody Agape, the Gnostic learns to let go of personal desires and embrace a love that is universal, a love that connects them with the divine spark within all souls. This love transcends the individual self and opens the soul to the fullness of the divine, transforming every interaction into an opportunity for spiritual growth and unity.

The Aeon known as *Truth*, or Aletheia, is also pivotal in the Gnostic journey. Aletheia represents the unveiling of reality, the stripping away of illusions that reveal the true nature of existence. In Gnosticism, truth is not simply a matter of factual knowledge but a deeper understanding of the soul's divine nature and its connection to the Pleroma. By aligning with the Aeon of Truth, the Gnostic undertakes a process of inner purification, removing the false identities and attachments that bind them to the Demiurge's realm. This alignment with Aletheia allows the seeker to see the world as it truly is, to recognize the divine spark within themselves and others, and to embrace the path of gnosis.

Life, or Zoe, is another Aeon that speaks to the soul's essence. Zoe is not merely physical life but the eternal life of the spirit, the vitality that flows from the Pleroma and animates all creation. To connect with Zoe is to awaken to one's eternal nature, to recognize that true life is not bound by the cycles of birth and death imposed by the Demiurge. This Aeon invites the Gnostic to cultivate a sense of inner aliveness, a joy that arises from the recognition of one's connection to the divine. By aligning with Zoe, the soul experiences a state of vitality and purpose, a sense of being fully present in each moment while remaining anchored in the eternal.

In Gnostic meditation and contemplation, the seeker may call upon these Aeons as guides, envisioning them as sources of light that illuminate the path of return. Through visualizations and inner reflection, the Gnostic attunes themselves to the qualities of each Aeon, allowing these divine attributes to resonate within. For instance, in contemplating Sophia, the seeker might visualize themselves surrounded by a warm, golden light, symbolizing wisdom. In this light, they allow themselves to absorb Sophia's essence, to feel a sense of inner knowing that transcends intellectual understanding. This practice transforms the Aeons from abstract concepts into living presences within the soul, energies that shape the Gnostic's journey toward enlightenment.

The hierarchy of the Aeons also represents the structure of spiritual ascent. Each Aeon embodies a step on the ladder that leads back to the Supreme God, a quality that must be realized and integrated for the soul to progress. The Gnostic does not see these Aeons as distant or unattainable; rather, they are aspects of the divine already present within, qualities that can be awakened and embodied through devotion and inner work. By ascending through the Aeons, the soul gradually transforms itself, shedding the limitations of the physical and moving closer to the light of the Pleroma.

In the Gospel of Judas, Jesus's teachings to Judas imply an understanding of these divine qualities and the path they outline. By guiding Judas beyond the illusions of the material world, Jesus prepares him to embrace the qualities of the Aeons, to see beyond duality and experience the fullness of the Pleroma. Judas's journey reflects the path of the Gnostic, a soul ready to undertake the ascent through the Aeons, to recognize their own divinity and the interconnectedness of all beings within the divine order.

The Aeons also serve as a reminder that the Gnostic journey is not a solitary pursuit. Each Aeon represents a part of the greater whole, a facet of the Supreme God that exists in unity with all others. This interconnectedness reflects the Pleroma's harmony, a state where each being shines with its own light while remaining united in the divine fullness. By aligning with the Aeons, the Gnostic learns to see themselves as part of this cosmic order, a reflection of the Supreme God who moves through life with a sense of purpose and connection to all.

For the Gnostic, exploring the Aeons is an invitation to remember their divine origin and to embrace the qualities that lead to enlightenment. Each Aeon becomes a guide, a reminder of the soul's true nature and the path that leads beyond the material. Through the qualities of wisdom, love, truth, life, and reason, the Gnostic begins to embody the fullness of the Pleroma, allowing these divine energies to shape their life and actions. This alignment is not only the soul's path to freedom from the

Demiurge's world but a return to wholeness, a state of being that reflects the harmony of the Supreme God.

In the practice of Gnosticism, the Aeons are not simply divine figures to be revered but aspects of the self to be realized. The journey through the Aeons is a journey into the depths of one's own soul, an exploration of the divine qualities that lie within and the path that leads back to unity with the Supreme God. Through meditation, contemplation, and the cultivation of these qualities in daily life, the Gnostic experiences the Aeons as living presences, guides that illuminate the way to the Pleroma.

The Gospel of Judas calls each seeker to embark on this journey, to explore the Aeons and recognize the divine attributes that already reside within. It is a call to transcend the material, to embrace the qualities of wisdom, truth, and love, and to remember the soul's true purpose. In this journey, the Gnostic finds not only liberation from the illusions of the Demiurge but a profound communion with the Supreme God, a return to the boundless light and unity of the Pleroma. Through the Aeons, the Gnostic reconnects with the source of all life and light, finding their way back to the eternal fullness that lies at the heart of all existence.

Chapter 27
The Journey of the Soul After Death

In Gnostic thought, the journey of the soul does not end with physical death; rather, it is a transition, a release from the limitations of the material realm and an opportunity for the soul to seek return to its true home in the Pleroma. This journey is a return to the divine source, a path that leads the soul beyond the realms of illusion crafted by the Demiurge and his Archons and into the fullness of divine unity. For the Gnostic, death is not a final end but a moment of potential liberation, a passage in which the soul may finally leave behind the cycles of rebirth and suffering that define the material world and awaken to its eternal nature.

The Gospel of Judas offers hints at this understanding through Jesus's teachings to Judas, revealing a path that defies conventional views of salvation and life after death. While the other disciples seek a kingdom that will be established on earth, Jesus invites Judas to see beyond earthly expectations, to embrace a truth that transcends the physical. In Gnostic belief, this vision is not limited to a single disciple but serves as a guide for all who seek liberation—a promise that the soul's true destiny lies beyond the material, in a realm of light and divine fullness.

The journey of the soul after death begins with a process of release, a shedding of attachments to the material world and the identities that bind it to the cycles of birth and death. This release is not automatic but requires a deep awareness of the illusions that have defined the soul's existence in the Demiurge's realm. For the unawakened soul, death may lead to another cycle of rebirth, a return to the material world in an endless loop of suffering and ignorance. Yet for the soul that has embraced gnosis, that has awakened to its divine origin, death becomes a doorway—a way back to the Pleroma, to the fullness of the Supreme God.

In Gnostic cosmology, the soul's journey after death is shaped by its level of consciousness and spiritual understanding. The Gnostic teachings hold that the Demiurge and his Archons rule over the lower realms, governing the cycles of life and death and enforcing the illusions that keep souls bound to the physical. These forces, which seek to trap the soul in ignorance, act as gatekeepers, creating obstacles that the soul must overcome to move beyond the material. However, the soul that has attained gnosis—true knowledge of the divine—can see through these illusions, recognize the Archons for what they are, and pass beyond their reach.

The journey beyond death is often described as an ascent, a process of rising through various realms or layers of existence that separate the material world from the Pleroma. Each of these realms is guarded by Archons who test the soul, challenging its understanding and attempting to pull it back into the cycle of rebirth. These Archons embody the illusions of desire, fear, and attachment—forces that have bound the soul to the material world throughout its life. The soul that has awakened to gnosis, however, is able to see through these tests, to recognize the true nature of the Archons, and to pass beyond them.

In Gnostic meditation and visualization practices, the journey of the soul after death is often rehearsed as a form of spiritual preparation. The seeker imagines themselves ascending through realms of light, encountering and transcending the influences of the Archons. By practicing this journey, the Gnostic strengthens their understanding of the path that lies beyond death, cultivating the awareness and clarity needed to navigate the realms of illusion and move closer to the divine. This preparation is not merely symbolic; it is a way of aligning the soul with its ultimate destination, creating a resonance that draws it toward the Pleroma and away from the forces that would bind it to the material.

One of the most significant aspects of the soul's journey after death is the encounter with *Sophia*, the divine Aeon of wisdom. Sophia, who fell from the Pleroma out of her desire to know the Supreme God, embodies the soul's journey from ignorance to wisdom. In her fall, she becomes trapped in the lower realms, yet she retains her connection to the divine light. For the soul that has attained gnosis, encountering Sophia is a moment of profound recognition, a reminder of its own divine origin and its connection to the Pleroma. Sophia serves as a guide, a presence that helps the soul to remember its true nature and continue its ascent beyond the illusions of the Demiurge's creation.

The Gnostic teachings also suggest that the soul's journey after death includes a process of purification, a shedding of the layers of ego and attachment that have obscured its divine essence. This purification is not punitive but transformative, a process that allows the soul to release the identities and desires that have bound it to the physical. The soul moves through these layers of purification, letting go of the false self that has defined its existence in the material world, until it reaches a state of pure awareness, a state in which it is ready to merge with the divine light of the Pleroma.

In the Gospel of Judas, Jesus's revelation to Judas points toward this ultimate merging with the divine. He explains that true liberation lies not in earthly salvation but in the return to a realm beyond the physical, a state of being where the soul is free from the limitations of form and matter. Judas's willingness to embrace this path, even when it sets him apart from the other disciples, reflects his readiness to transcend the material, to undertake the journey that leads beyond death and into the eternal.

As the soul ascends, it may also encounter the Aeons, divine beings that embody the qualities of the Supreme God. These Aeons are not obstacles but guides, presences that welcome the soul and help it to integrate the divine attributes that will prepare it for the final union with the Pleroma. By aligning with these qualities, the soul deepens its understanding of the divine, allowing the attributes of wisdom, truth, love, and unity to become fully realized within. This alignment is essential for the soul's ultimate return, for only by embodying these qualities can it merge with the divine fullness of the Pleroma.

The final stage of the soul's journey is the return to the Pleroma, the divine fullness from which it originated. This is the moment of true liberation, a state of eternal unity with the Supreme God where all separations dissolve, and the soul experiences the fullness of divine light. In this state, the soul is no longer an individual entity bound by the limitations of form; it becomes one with the infinite, a part of the divine fullness that transcends all duality. This return is the fulfillment of the Gnostic path, the culmination of the soul's journey from ignorance to knowledge, from separation to unity.

In Gnostic thought, this return to the Pleroma is not the annihilation of the self but the realization of the soul's true nature. The soul, in merging with the Supreme God, becomes what it has always been—a being of light, a fragment of the divine that has journeyed through the realms of illusion and returned to its source. This realization is the essence of gnosis, a knowledge that brings peace, freedom, and eternal joy. The soul that has completed this journey experiences a state of boundless love and unity, a state that reflects the harmony and beauty of the Pleroma.

The Gospel of Judas calls each seeker to prepare for this journey, to seek the knowledge that will guide them beyond death and into the Pleroma. It is a call to remember, to awaken to the divine spark within, and to recognize that true life lies not in the material but in the eternal. Through this journey, the Gnostic finds not only freedom from the cycles of birth and death but a profound communion with the Supreme God, a state of unity that transcends all suffering and all separation.

The journey of the soul after death is, therefore, a journey of return, a path that leads from the shadows of the material world to the eternal light of the Pleroma. It is a path that requires courage, clarity, and a deep commitment to self-knowledge. For the Gnostic, death is not to be feared but embraced as a transition, a passage that opens the way to the divine. Through gnosis, the soul learns to see beyond the illusions of the Demiurge's realm, to recognize the eternal truth that lies within, and to follow the path that leads home.

In the Gnostic vision, the journey of the soul is the fulfillment of its true purpose, a return to the state of divine fullness that lies beyond all form and matter. Through this journey, the Gnostic finds peace, a state of unity with the Supreme God that brings an end to all suffering and reveals the boundless joy of existence in the Pleroma. This is the promise of gnosis, the hope of liberation, a path that leads from death to eternal life, from separation to unity, and from darkness to the infinite light that lies at the heart of all creation.

Chapter 28
Rituals of Spiritual Liberation

In Gnostic practice, rituals of spiritual liberation are not mere formalities; they are transformative acts, carefully structured to lift the soul from the entanglements of the material world and guide it toward its divine origin. These rituals, designed to awaken gnosis within, serve as sacred passages through which the seeker sheds illusions, confronts inner darkness, and reconnects with the Supreme God. Unlike traditional rituals that may focus on outward acts of worship, Gnostic rituals are deeply inward, aiming to illuminate the hidden divine within and sever the soul's attachments to the Demiurge's creation. These rituals become moments of spiritual alchemy, where the ordinary self dissolves and the true divine essence emerges.

In the Gospel of Judas, Judas's private encounters with Jesus suggest a kind of initiatory process, a preparation that sets him apart from the other disciples. Jesus shares with Judas insights and mysteries that reveal a path of liberation beyond the physical. This intimate revelation mirrors the purpose of Gnostic rituals, which aim to initiate the seeker into higher truths and provide a spiritual toolkit for transcending the constraints of the material world. Each ritual becomes a step toward liberation, a practice that guides the soul closer to the Pleroma, the realm of divine unity.

One of the fundamental rituals of spiritual liberation in Gnosticism is the *Rite of Detachment*, a ritual designed to break the bonds of attachment to material desires, possessions, and even identities. The Gnostic recognizes that attachment to the material is a powerful force that keeps the soul bound within the

Demiurge's realm, constantly drawing it away from the divine. In this ritual, the seeker meditates on the impermanence of the physical world, envisioning all material things as passing illusions. They may place symbolic objects—representing personal attachments—upon an altar, then consciously release them, letting go of the need to possess or control. This act of detachment purifies the soul, freeing it from distractions and making space for the divine light within to shine more clearly.

Another essential ritual is the *Rite of Inner Illumination*, a practice of invoking the divine spark within and allowing it to expand, filling the entire being with light. In this ritual, the seeker enters a quiet, sacred space, free from distraction, and centers their awareness on the heart, where the divine spark resides. They imagine this spark growing into a flame, a radiant light that dispels all darkness, ignorance, and fear. As the light fills their body, they repeat sacred words or sounds that resonate with the vibration of the Pleroma, anchoring this connection to the divine within. This ritual strengthens the soul's awareness of its true nature, allowing the seeker to feel their unity with the Supreme God and to carry this illumination into daily life.

The *Ritual of Renunciation* is another practice that brings the Gnostic closer to liberation. In this ritual, the seeker symbolically renounces the illusions and false identities that have defined their existence in the material world. They may write down personal fears, desires, or limitations on a piece of paper, then burn it in a flame, watching as these attachments turn to ash. This act represents a willingness to release the ego and its identifications, to let go of the layers of false self that obscure the divine spark. The ritual of renunciation is not about rejecting life but about recognizing and dissolving the illusions that keep the soul bound. Through this ritual, the Gnostic prepares to step into a more authentic, liberated state of being.

The *Ritual of Silence* is a practice that focuses on the power of stillness, creating a space where the seeker can listen for the voice of the divine. In this ritual, the Gnostic enters a state of complete silence, both externally and internally, allowing thoughts, emotions, and distractions to fade away. This silence becomes a sanctuary, a place where the divine can be experienced directly. The Gnostic believes that in this profound silence, the soul can connect with the voice of the Supreme God, receiving guidance, insight, and peace. The ritual of silence teaches the Gnostic to cultivate inner stillness in daily life, to create an openness that allows the divine presence to emerge and illuminate the path forward.

A deeply symbolic ritual of spiritual liberation is the *Crossing of the Realms*, a ritual that enacts the soul's journey beyond the material and into the realms of the spirit. In this ritual, the Gnostic visualizes themselves moving through various planes or realms, leaving behind the influence of the Archons who seek to hold them in the material. Each realm crossed represents a layer of illusion—desire, fear, pride, or attachment—that must be transcended. As the soul moves upward, the Gnostic feels the presence of the Aeons, divine guides who assist in this ascent. This ritual serves as both a meditation and a practice of spiritual strength, reinforcing the soul's commitment to the journey of return and preparing it to overcome the obstacles encountered beyond the physical.

The *Anointing of Light* is a ritual that serves as an affirmation of the soul's divine nature. In this practice, the Gnostic anoints themselves with oil, water, or another symbolic element, marking the body as a vessel of the divine spark. The anointing is performed with intention, recognizing that each touch represents a quality of the Supreme God—wisdom, truth, love, or peace. This ritual serves as a reminder of the divine essence within, a declaration that the body, mind, and spirit are all aspects of a greater unity with the divine. Through the anointing of light, the Gnostic experiences a sense of wholeness and prepares the soul for its eventual return to the Pleroma.

In the Gospel of Judas, Jesus's revelations to Judas can be seen as a form of initiation, a series of teachings that prepare Judas for a path of liberation that goes beyond the material. This type of initiation reflects the purpose of Gnostic rituals, which are designed to initiate the soul into the mysteries of existence and provide it with the tools necessary for spiritual ascent. Each ritual becomes a doorway, a moment where the boundaries between the material and spiritual dissolve, allowing the soul to experience a glimpse of the Pleroma and its own divine origin.

The *Rite of Sacred Breath* is another key ritual in Gnostic practice, symbolizing the life-force that connects the soul to the divine. In this ritual, the seeker focuses on their breath, becoming fully present with each inhale and exhale, and visualizes the breath as a flow of light moving through the body. This breath, representing the spirit, nourishes the divine spark within and serves as a reminder of the soul's connection to the Supreme God. By attuning to the sacred breath, the Gnostic learns to draw strength from this connection, creating a space where the spirit can flourish, unbound by the limits of the physical.

The *Invocation of Aeons* is another significant ritual that allows the seeker to call upon the divine qualities embodied by the Aeons. In this ritual, the Gnostic names each Aeon, visualizing them as presences or lights that surround and guide them. By calling upon the wisdom of Sophia, the truth of Aletheia, or the life of Zoe, the Gnostic strengthens their connection to these divine attributes, allowing these qualities to awaken within. This ritual not only aligns the soul with the Pleroma but also serves as a reminder of the soul's own potential to embody these qualities, to live as a reflection of the divine.

For the Gnostic, these rituals of spiritual liberation are transformative acts that prepare the soul for its return to the Pleroma. Each ritual serves as a step on the path to gnosis, a way of strengthening the soul's awareness of its true nature and loosening the ties that bind it to the Demiurge's world. Through these practices, the Gnostic learns to cultivate a state of inner freedom, a way of being that reflects the harmony and unity of the Pleroma even while living within the material realm.

The Gospel of Judas invites each seeker to embrace this journey, to participate in rituals that transcend the physical and guide the soul toward the light. In this journey, the Gnostic finds not only freedom from the illusions of the material world but a profound communion with the Supreme God. Through these rituals, the soul is purified, strengthened, and prepared for the final journey back to the divine fullness. Each ritual is an expression of the soul's longing for union, a moment where the divine spark within reconnects with its source, reflecting the boundless light and love of the Pleroma.

In the Gnostic vision, rituals of spiritual liberation are essential milestones, acts of dedication that transform the soul's understanding and open the way to enlightenment. They are moments of awakening, where the boundaries between the material and spiritual dissolve, revealing the true nature of existence. Through these rituals, the Gnostic prepares for the ultimate liberation, a return to the state of divine fullness, peace, and unity that lies beyond all form and matter, in the eternal embrace of the Supreme God.

Chapter 29
Practices of Reflection and Contemplation

In the Gnostic tradition, reflection and contemplation are not passive states of thought; they are transformative practices that guide the seeker toward self-discovery and spiritual liberation. Reflection allows the soul to pierce the veils of illusion that the Demiurge has cast over the material world, while contemplation draws the soul deeper into the mysteries of divine truth and unity with the Pleroma. Through these practices, the Gnostic cultivates a heightened awareness of their divine nature, unraveling layers of false identity and stepping closer to the light within.

For the Gnostic, reflection is a form of inner inquiry, a process of examining thoughts, actions, and attachments to reveal the truth of the soul. In the Gospel of Judas, Jesus encourages Judas to look beyond appearances, challenging him to perceive hidden realities that others cannot see. This invitation to "see beyond" is central to the practice of reflection, as the Gnostic learns to question the physical and mental constructs that have defined their existence. Through honest and probing self-reflection, the seeker dismantles the illusions of ego, desires, and fears, uncovering the divine spark that lies beneath these surface identities.

One of the foundational practices of reflection in Gnosticism is the *Examination of Desires and Attachments*. In this practice, the seeker takes time to reflect on the desires, ambitions, and fears that drive their life in the material world. This is not merely an exercise in introspection but a journey of discovery, as the Gnostic observes how each attachment binds them to the physical realm, clouding their awareness of the divine. By identifying and releasing these attachments, the seeker clears a path for the divine essence within to shine more brightly. This practice of examination is a process of spiritual purification, allowing the soul to detach from the illusions of the material and realign with the Supreme God.

Another core aspect of reflection is the *Recognition of the Divine Spark*. The Gnostic reflects on their own true nature, moving beyond the body and mind to recognize the divine spark within. This inner light, a fragment of the Supreme God, serves as a compass for the soul, guiding it through the challenges of the physical world. By contemplating this divine spark, the Gnostic deepens their awareness of their divine origin and purpose, fostering a sense of inner peace and purpose that transcends the illusions of the Demiurge's creation. This practice strengthens the soul's resolve, grounding it in the reality of the spirit rather than the shifting circumstances of the material world.

Contemplation, in Gnostic practice, is a journey into the mysteries of existence, a state where the soul seeks direct communion with the divine. Unlike reflection, which often focuses on self-examination, contemplation is a process of merging with the greater truth that lies beyond the self. It is a movement from the individual to the universal, a state of awareness where the Gnostic opens to the presence of the Supreme God. Through contemplation, the seeker transcends the confines of the physical mind, allowing the soul to touch the divine fullness of the Pleroma, even if only briefly. This experience of unity with the divine is a glimpse of the soul's true home, a reminder of the eternal peace that awaits beyond the material.

The *Contemplation of the Aeons* is a significant practice in this journey. In this practice, the Gnostic reflects on the divine qualities embodied by the Aeons—wisdom, truth, love, and unity. By contemplating these qualities, the seeker aligns their inner being with the attributes of the Pleroma, allowing these divine energies to take root within. This contemplation is not simply a mental exercise; it is a process of inner alignment, a way of cultivating the qualities that will prepare the soul for its return to the divine realm. By meditating on each Aeon, the Gnostic allows these attributes to awaken within themselves, creating a resonance that strengthens their connection to the Supreme God.

Another contemplative practice is the *Meditation on Divine Light*. In this meditation, the Gnostic imagines themselves bathed in a radiant, all-encompassing light, a symbol of the Supreme God's presence. This light fills the soul, dissolving all boundaries between the individual and the divine. In this state of illumination, the Gnostic experiences a sense of unity, a feeling of oneness that reflects the harmony of the Pleroma. By regularly immersing themselves in this divine light, the seeker strengthens their awareness of the Supreme God, cultivating a state of peace and clarity that transcends the fluctuations of the material world.

The practice of *Inner Silence* is another vital form of contemplation, one that allows the Gnostic to move beyond thought and enter a state of pure being. In this silence, the mind becomes still, the distractions of the physical world fade, and the soul rests in the presence of the divine. This silence is not merely the absence of noise; it is an active awareness, a space where the soul can listen to the voice of the spirit within. Through inner silence, the Gnostic learns to quiet the mental chatter, to create a sanctuary where the divine can speak and guide them on their journey. This silence becomes a refuge, a place where the soul can return to whenever it seeks connection with the Supreme God.

In the Gospel of Judas, Jesus's teachings to Judas often take the form of contemplative dialogue, urging Judas to question, to see beyond the visible, and to embrace a deeper understanding of reality. This form of teaching reflects the essence of Gnostic contemplation, a process where the soul is invited to move beyond conventional thought and experience the truths that lie beyond words. Through contemplation, the Gnostic learns to live with an awareness that transcends ordinary perception, a state of inner knowing that aligns them with the divine presence.

The *Contemplation of Death and Liberation* is a unique practice that encourages the Gnostic to reflect on the transient nature of the material world and the eternal reality of the spirit. In this contemplation, the seeker meditates on the impermanence of physical life, recognizing that all things in the material world are subject to change and decay. This awareness of impermanence serves as a reminder that the soul's true home lies beyond the physical, in a realm of eternal light and peace. By embracing this perspective, the Gnostic cultivates a sense of detachment from the physical, a freedom that allows them to face life's challenges with equanimity and to prepare for the journey that lies beyond death.

Reflection on the nature of *Suffering and Ignorance* is another important practice. The Gnostic understands that suffering in the material world often arises from ignorance, a state of spiritual blindness imposed by the Demiurge. By reflecting on the nature of suffering, the Gnostic learns to see it as a teacher, a force that reveals the illusions of the physical and pushes the soul toward gnosis. This reflection transforms the seeker's perspective on suffering, allowing them to view it not as a punishment but as an opportunity for growth and liberation. Through this practice, the Gnostic gains the strength to transcend suffering, to see beyond the pain of the material and recognize the divine presence that lies beneath all experience.

In Gnostic practice, *Gratitude for Divine Guidance* is also an essential contemplative exercise. By reflecting on moments of insight, inner peace, or connection with the divine, the Gnostic cultivates a sense of gratitude, a recognition of the Supreme God's presence in their life. This gratitude is not directed toward a distant deity but is an acknowledgment of the divine spark within, a celebration of the soul's journey toward enlightenment. This practice of gratitude strengthens the soul's connection to the divine, creating a resonance that brings the seeker closer to the Pleroma.

These practices of reflection and contemplation become a way of life for the Gnostic, a continuous journey of self-discovery and inner alignment. Through daily reflection, the soul learns to navigate the complexities of the material world without becoming ensnared by its illusions. Through contemplation, the soul touches the divine, experiencing moments of unity that serve as glimpses of the Pleroma. Together, these practices guide the Gnostic on the path of liberation, helping them to cultivate the awareness and strength needed to return to the divine fullness.

The Gospel of Judas invites each seeker to embrace this journey, to look within and discover the truths that lie hidden beneath the surface of the material. Through reflection and contemplation, the Gnostic moves beyond appearances, recognizing the divine essence within themselves and others. In this journey, the soul finds not only knowledge but transformation, a state of inner peace that arises from the awareness of its own divinity.

For the Gnostic, reflection and contemplation are not ends in themselves but paths that lead to liberation. They are practices that dissolve the illusions of the Demiurge's world, that free the soul from the limitations of the material, and that prepare it for its return to the Pleroma. Through these practices, the Gnostic finds a state of inner clarity, a peace that reflects the harmony of the Supreme God. This is the essence of the Gnostic path—a journey of remembering, a process of awakening to the light within, and a preparation for the ultimate return to the divine fullness.

Chapter 30
The Mystery of the Cross

In Gnostic spirituality, the cross is not merely a symbol of suffering or redemption as it is commonly understood in traditional Christian thought; rather, it embodies a profound mystery, one that reveals the nature of divine liberation and the path of transcending the material world. The cross is a symbol of transformation, an image that represents the soul's journey from limitation to freedom, from the illusions of the Demiurge to the eternal light of the Pleroma. For the Gnostic, the mystery of the cross is an invitation to confront the self, to transcend the ego, and to awaken to a deeper reality hidden beyond the physical realm.

The Gospel of Judas offers a distinct perspective on the cross. Here, Jesus's words to Judas reveal a path that defies conventional interpretations, suggesting that the crucifixion is not merely a tragic event but a deliberate act of liberation from the material world. Jesus speaks to Judas of a realm beyond death, a place where the soul is freed from the Demiurge's control, suggesting that the cross is a portal to this divine reality. Through the cross, Jesus demonstrates the path of self-sacrifice, not as an end, but as a means to transcend the limitations of the physical, to cast aside the prison of the body, and to return to the true home in the Pleroma.

The cross, in Gnostic thought, represents the intersection of two worlds—the material and the spiritual. The vertical line symbolizes the soul's connection to the divine, an axis that reaches from the depths of the material realm up to the heights of the Pleroma. The horizontal line, by contrast, represents the spread of material existence, the world of forms and dualities created by the Demiurge. The point where these lines meet, the center of the cross, is a point of transformation, a place where the soul must confront the illusions of the material world and recognize its divine nature. In this way, the cross becomes a symbol of the Gnostic journey, a path that leads from separation to unity, from ignorance to gnosis.

For the Gnostic, the mystery of the cross is also a mystery of *sacrifice*, but not in the sense of mere physical suffering or martyrdom. Instead, it is a call to sacrifice the ego, to release the attachments, desires, and fears that bind the soul to the Demiurge's realm. This sacrifice is an act of inner purification, a process of shedding the false identities that obscure the divine spark within. By embracing the cross, the Gnostic confronts the shadow aspects of the self, recognizing that true liberation lies in surrendering these illusions and allowing the divine light to emerge.

The cross can also be seen as a representation of *dualities*—light and darkness, spirit and matter, freedom and bondage. For the soul to transcend the material, it must first understand and overcome these dualities, seeing them as illusions imposed by the Demiurge to keep it bound. By contemplating the cross, the Gnostic reflects on these dualities and learns to recognize them as temporary constructs that do not define the soul's true essence. This understanding allows the seeker to rise above duality, to see beyond good and evil, pleasure and pain, and to embrace the unity of the Pleroma.

The *Crucifixion* in the Gospel of Judas carries a symbolic significance for Gnostics, as it represents the soul's journey through suffering toward enlightenment. The crucifixion is not merely a physical event but a spiritual process, a moment where the soul undergoes a profound transformation. Jesus's willingness to undergo crucifixion reflects his understanding that liberation requires moving beyond the physical, embracing death not as an end but as a threshold to the eternal. This understanding transforms the crucifixion from an act of defeat to a moment of victory, a declaration that the soul is not bound by the material world but is, in essence, an eternal being destined to return to the Pleroma.

The *Mystical Death*, symbolized by the cross, is a key concept in Gnostic spirituality. This mystical death is not a literal death but a profound inner transformation, a process of dying to the false self and awakening to the divine self within. Through this mystical death, the Gnostic releases the illusions that bind them to the Demiurge's world, allowing the true self, the divine spark, to shine forth. This experience of mystical death is a rebirth, a resurrection into a higher state of consciousness that transcends the limitations of the material and aligns the soul with the Supreme God. By embracing this inner death, the Gnostic undergoes a personal crucifixion, a sacrifice of ego and illusion that brings them closer to the light.

The *Resurrection* in Gnostic thought is also deeply symbolic, representing the soul's awakening to its divine nature and its liberation from the cycle of birth and death. Unlike traditional views of resurrection as a return to physical life, Gnostic resurrection is a spiritual rebirth, a state of enlightenment in which the soul recognizes its eternal essence. This resurrection is the culmination of the Gnostic path, the moment when the soul, having overcome the illusions of the material, rises into the light of the Pleroma. The cross, therefore, is not an end but a passage, a transformative process that leads to a state of divine unity.

In Gnostic ritual, the cross may be used as a symbol in meditative practice, a focal point for contemplating the journey from ignorance to gnosis. The seeker may visualize themselves at the center of the cross, holding the intersection of spirit and matter, and meditate on the release of attachments that bind them to the physical. This practice allows the Gnostic to experience a moment of surrender, a letting go of the material self in order to embrace the spiritual. Through this meditation on the cross, the Gnostic draws closer to the Supreme God, aligning themselves with the divine and preparing for the journey beyond the physical.

The *Contemplation of the Suffering* associated with the cross is also significant in Gnostic practice. By reflecting on the suffering that Jesus endured, the Gnostic learns to understand their own suffering as a path to self-knowledge. In the material world, suffering is often seen as a punishment or an injustice, but in Gnostic thought, it is a catalyst for growth. The Gnostic learns to see suffering as a tool for breaking through illusions, a way of shedding the attachments that keep them bound to the material. Through this contemplation, the Gnostic gains the strength to face life's challenges with clarity, recognizing that each trial can be transformed into an opportunity for awakening.

In the Gospel of Judas, Jesus's acceptance of the cross serves as a model of spiritual courage, a willingness to confront the limitations of the material and to embrace the truth of the divine. His path offers a template for the Gnostic, a reminder that liberation requires a willingness to look beyond the physical and to embrace the deeper realities of spirit. Judas, too, plays a role in this mystery, as his journey reflects the path of the seeker who is called to see beyond appearances, to understand the cross as a portal to the divine, and to embrace a vision of liberation that transcends the material.

The cross also represents a *union of opposites*, a reconciliation of dualities that leads to wholeness. For the Gnostic, embracing the cross is an act of integration, a way of bringing together the different aspects of the self—light and shadow, spirit and matter—into a harmonious whole. This integration is essential for the soul's journey, as it prepares the Gnostic to experience the unity of the Pleroma. By bringing together these opposites, the Gnostic learns to see beyond duality, to recognize the oneness that underlies all existence, and to move closer to the divine fullness.

The mystery of the cross, therefore, is an invitation to transcend the ordinary, to move beyond the constraints of the physical and to embrace the eternal. It is a reminder that the soul's true purpose is not bound to the material world but lies in the realms of light and unity. Through the cross, the Gnostic finds a symbol of hope, a path that leads not to suffering but to liberation, a promise that the soul can overcome the shadows of the Demiurge and return to the infinite light of the Pleroma.

In the Gnostic journey, the cross is both a challenge and a gift, a call to surrender the self and to embrace the divine. Through this mystery, the Gnostic learns that true freedom lies not in clinging to life but in transcending it, in recognizing that the soul's true life is eternal, untouched by the cycles of birth and death. The cross becomes a beacon of this truth, a signpost that points the way to the divine, guiding the soul through the darkness of the material and into the boundless light of the Pleroma.

The Gospel of Judas invites each seeker to embrace this path, to see the cross not as a burden but as a doorway to the divine. In this journey, the Gnostic finds a liberation that lies beyond suffering, a peace that transcends the trials of the physical, and a unity that reflects the Supreme God's love. This is the promise of the cross in Gnostic thought—a path that leads from death to life, from separation to union, from the material to the eternal, in the divine fullness of the Pleroma.

Chapter 31
Development of Spiritual Love

In the Gnostic journey, spiritual love is a force that transcends the limitations and illusions of the material world. It is not the conditional, possessive love often associated with human relationships, but an expansive, boundless love that reflects the unity of the Pleroma and the divine essence of all beings. This love, known as Agape, exists as an attribute of the Supreme God, a pure and unconditional love that flows through all of creation. For the Gnostic, developing spiritual love means opening the heart to this divine quality, allowing it to dissolve the layers of ego and self-interest that have been shaped by the Demiurge's world and that obscure the soul's true nature.

Spiritual love, in the Gnostic view, begins with the understanding that all souls are interconnected through the divine light, each one a fragment of the Supreme God. This interconnectedness is not merely a philosophical concept but a lived experience, one that transforms how the Gnostic perceives others and the world. Through practices that cultivate spiritual love, the seeker learns to transcend attachments to the material, developing a love that is not bound by personal desire or physical attraction but that resonates with the essence of the Pleroma itself. In the Gospel of Judas, the unique bond between Jesus and Judas can be seen as an expression of this spiritual love, a connection rooted in shared knowledge and divine purpose, rather than earthly expectations.

One of the foundational practices for developing spiritual love in Gnosticism is *Meditative Compassion*. This practice involves focusing on the divine spark within oneself and then extending this awareness to others. In a quiet, reflective state, the Gnostic visualizes the light of the divine spark within, allowing it to fill their entire being. From this inner light, they imagine a wave of love radiating outward, encompassing family, friends, and eventually all beings, regardless of whether they are known personally or even visible. This act of extending compassion cultivates an awareness of the interconnectedness of all souls and strengthens the Gnostic's ability to perceive others as reflections of the divine.

Another essential practice is *Forgiveness as Liberation*. In the material world, resentment, anger, and judgment often entangle the soul, creating barriers that prevent it from experiencing true spiritual love. Through the act of forgiveness, the Gnostic releases these burdens, understanding that they are rooted in the illusions and conflicts of the Demiurge's creation. Forgiveness, in this sense, is not about excusing harm but about freeing oneself from attachment to the pain caused by others. By forgiving, the Gnostic lets go of the ties that bind them to the physical, allowing the heart to remain open to the flow of divine love. This release of resentment becomes a practice of liberation, a way of creating space within the soul for the presence of the Supreme God.

In developing spiritual love, the Gnostic also practices *Self-Compassion*, an acknowledgment of the divine within themselves. This compassion is not an indulgence but a recognition of one's own struggles and imperfections, viewed from the perspective of divine understanding. The Gnostic does not judge themselves harshly for being trapped in the illusions of the material world; instead, they extend love inward, honoring the divine spark within even as they work to dissolve the layers of ego and ignorance. This self-compassion becomes a source of inner strength, a way of fostering the resilience needed to navigate the spiritual path and return to the Pleroma.

The concept of *Non-Attachment* is also central to spiritual love in Gnosticism. In the Demiurge's realm, love is often experienced as possessive and conditional, tied to desires, expectations, and fears. For the Gnostic, however, spiritual love requires the release of these attachments, an openness that allows love to flow freely without the need to control or possess. Non-attachment does not mean indifference; it means loving from a place of inner freedom, where one's love is a reflection of the divine rather than a response to personal need. By cultivating non-attachment, the Gnostic learns to love without clinging, creating relationships that honor the autonomy and divine nature of all beings.

The *Practice of Inner Alignment with Divine Love* is another essential aspect of Gnostic spirituality. In this practice, the Gnostic focuses on the qualities of the Supreme God—unconditional love, compassion, wisdom—and meditates on embodying these qualities in their own life. This alignment with divine love becomes a form of inner transformation, a way of allowing the divine essence within to guide thoughts, actions, and emotions. The Gnostic seeks to live as a reflection of the Supreme God, allowing their love to be a channel through which divine energy flows into the world. This practice strengthens the connection to the Pleroma, helping the soul remain anchored in its true nature even amid the distractions of the physical world.

Reflective Compassion is a contemplative exercise where the Gnostic imagines themselves in the place of others, seeking to understand their struggles, hopes, and fears. This practice is not about judgment but about empathy, a way of breaking down the barriers between self and other. Through reflective compassion, the Gnostic begins to see beyond surface differences, recognizing that all beings share the same journey, the same longing to return to the Pleroma. This understanding fosters a love that is universal, a love that encompasses all beings as part of the divine whole.

In the Gospel of Judas, Judas's relationship with Jesus reflects an understanding of spiritual love that defies conventional expectations. Jesus's connection to Judas is based not on loyalty or obedience but on mutual recognition of the mysteries of the divine. This bond suggests that true spiritual love transcends traditional roles and societal expectations, rooted instead in shared knowledge and purpose. For the Gnostic, this relationship becomes a model of love based on gnosis, a love that flows from the recognition of the divine in oneself and others.

The *Contemplation of Divine Unity* is another practice that fosters spiritual love. In this contemplation, the Gnostic reflects on the Pleroma as a state of perfect unity, a realm where all beings exist in harmony with the Supreme God. By meditating on this unity, the seeker strengthens their sense of interconnectedness, understanding that the true nature of love is an experience of oneness with the divine and with all creation. This contemplation allows the Gnostic to bring the peace and harmony of the Pleroma into their own life, transforming relationships and interactions through a love that transcends separation.

In Gnostic thought, the *Healing Power of Love* is also recognized as a transformative force. Spiritual love has the power to heal the wounds of the soul, to dissolve the scars left by fear, anger, and sorrow. The Gnostic understands that love is not a weakness but a strength, a divine quality that brings the soul closer to its true nature. By embracing spiritual love, the seeker creates a space within themselves where the divine can heal, restoring the soul to a state of harmony and preparing it for its journey back to the Pleroma.

The *Practice of Blessing Others* is another form of expressing spiritual love. In this practice, the Gnostic consciously extends goodwill to others, offering a blessing for their growth, peace, and happiness. This act of blessing is not about seeking favor or reward but about fostering a spirit of generosity, a way of sharing the divine light within. By blessing others, the Gnostic acknowledges the divine spark in each being, creating a bond that reflects the unity of the Pleroma.

Spiritual love, in the Gnostic tradition, becomes a transformative journey, a path that leads the soul closer to the Supreme God. Through these practices, the Gnostic learns to release the bonds of ego, to transcend the illusions of the Demiurge's world, and to experience a love that is boundless and eternal. This love, rooted in the recognition of the divine within all beings, becomes a source of inner strength, a guiding light that leads the soul through the trials of the material and into the harmony of the Pleroma.

The Gospel of Judas invites the seeker to embrace this path of love, to cultivate a love that is not limited by desire or possession but that reflects the true essence of the divine. Through spiritual love, the Gnostic finds not only freedom from the illusions of the material world but a profound connection to the Supreme God. This love becomes a bridge, a way of bringing the peace and unity of the Pleroma into every moment of life, transforming each experience into an opportunity for growth and awakening.

In the Gnostic journey, spiritual love is the soul's highest expression, a state of being that transcends all dualities and reveals the unity that lies at the heart of existence. Through this love, the soul experiences the joy of divine communion, a state of bliss that reflects the boundless light of the Pleroma. This is the gift of spiritual love—a love that heals, a love that liberates, and a love that guides the soul back to its true home in the divine fullness of the Supreme God.

Chapter 32
Transformation of the Ego

In Gnostic spirituality, the transformation of the ego is a crucial step on the path to enlightenment, a necessary shift from a limited, false self to the realization of the soul's divine essence. The ego, in Gnostic understanding, is more than just a personal identity; it is a construct shaped by the Demiurge, a mask that binds the soul to the material world, obscuring its divine light and deeper purpose. To move toward gnosis, the Gnostic must confront and dissolve the illusions of the ego, uncovering the true self that lies hidden beneath. This journey is not an erasure of identity but a profound transformation, a reorientation from the shadows of the Demiurge to the light of the Supreme God.

In the Gospel of Judas, Judas's unique role reflects the path of transformation, as he stands apart from the other disciples, daring to look beyond the ordinary and to question the nature of reality. Jesus's teachings to Judas encourage him to see through appearances, to recognize the limitations of ego-driven perspectives, and to seek the divine essence within. This path, symbolized in Judas's journey, serves as a model for the Gnostic: a path of inner work and surrender that leads beyond the ego's illusions and into true spiritual awareness.

One of the primary practices for transforming the ego in Gnosticism is *Self-Inquiry*, an exploration of the thoughts, beliefs, and attachments that define the personal self. Through self-inquiry, the Gnostic questions the motives behind actions, the fears that limit choices, and the desires that keep the soul bound to the material. By observing these aspects of the self, the seeker begins to see the ego for what it is—a construct created by identification with the physical, an illusion that distorts perception and limits the soul's true potential. This practice of self-inquiry is not merely psychological; it is a spiritual unveiling, a way of stripping away the layers that obscure the divine spark.

Another significant practice in ego transformation is *Non-Identification*, a technique where the Gnostic learns to observe thoughts and emotions without becoming attached to them. In non-identification, the seeker practices being a witness, watching the rise and fall of thoughts, desires, and fears without allowing them to define the self. This witnessing creates a space of freedom, where the Gnostic can experience their consciousness as distinct from the contents of the mind. Through non-identification, the ego's grip weakens, allowing the soul to glimpse its true nature as an expression of the divine, untethered by the limitations of personality or physical form.

Mindful Detachment is another essential practice for transforming the ego. This involves recognizing the impermanence of the material world and releasing attachment to outcomes, status, and possessions. The Gnostic understands that the ego is built on attachment, on the desire for control and validation within the Demiurge's realm. By cultivating mindful detachment, the Gnostic learns to accept life's unfolding without clinging to personal gains or losses. This detachment is not indifference but a deep-rooted inner freedom, a way of living in harmony with the divine flow rather than being bound by the ego's needs.

The *Practice of Humility* also plays a significant role in the transformation of the ego. For the Gnostic, humility is not self-denial but a clear seeing of one's place within the greater whole. The ego seeks to elevate the individual, to distinguish and separate; humility, by contrast, brings the soul into alignment with the Supreme God, fostering a recognition of the interconnectedness of all beings. In humility, the Gnostic lets go of the need to be superior, opening to a state of equality with all life. This humility dissolves the ego's rigid boundaries, allowing the divine essence within to flow more freely and fully into the world.

The Gnostic also engages in *Meditation on Emptiness*, a contemplative practice that invites the seeker to experience a state beyond identity. In this meditation, the Gnostic focuses on releasing all thoughts, images, and self-concepts, entering a state of pure awareness without attachment to form or idea. This experience of emptiness becomes a mirror, reflecting the formless essence of the soul that lies beyond the ego. Through this practice, the Gnostic learns to recognize their true nature as an expression of the divine, untouched by the ego's constructs, and free from the illusions of the Demiurge.

The *Embrace of Inner Silence* is another vital practice in transforming the ego. Silence, in Gnostic thought, is not merely the absence of sound but a profound state of receptivity, a space where the soul can listen to the voice of the divine. The ego thrives on noise—thoughts, opinions, judgments—and silence disrupts its hold. By cultivating inner silence, the Gnostic creates a sanctuary where the divine spark can emerge, a place where the soul can experience itself as separate from the ego. This silence becomes a healing balm, a way of softening the ego's boundaries and opening the soul to the vastness of the Pleroma.

In the Gospel of Judas, Jesus's teachings to Judas reflect this process of transformation, as Judas is encouraged to look beyond the surface and to see the truth that lies within. Judas's path, in Gnostic interpretation, represents the journey of the soul that dares to question, to release attachment to conventional beliefs, and to embrace the unknown. This journey is one of courage, as the Gnostic must confront the illusions that have shaped their sense of self and be willing to step into a new understanding. The transformation of the ego, then, is not a passive process; it requires a commitment to self-exploration and a willingness to release all that is false.

The *Dissolution of Pride* is another key aspect of ego transformation. Pride, in Gnosticism, is seen as one of the most binding illusions of the ego, a force that creates separation and fosters attachment to the material. The Gnostic learns to recognize pride as a barrier to spiritual growth, understanding that it is rooted in the need to assert oneself within the Demiurge's realm. By dissolving pride, the Gnostic moves closer to unity, allowing the soul to flow with the harmony of the divine. This dissolution is a process of surrender, a release of the need to control or dominate, and an opening to the humility that reveals the interconnectedness of all life.

Compassion for Others is also integral to the transformation of the ego. The ego tends to focus on the self, creating barriers that isolate the individual from others. Through compassion, the Gnostic transcends these barriers, recognizing the divine spark within all beings. This compassion transforms relationships, allowing the Gnostic to engage with others from a place of unity rather than division. By cultivating compassion, the Gnostic dissolves the ego's boundaries, fostering a state of openness that aligns with the Pleroma's unity.

The *Practice of Surrender* is perhaps the most profound step in ego transformation. Surrender, in Gnosticism, is not about resignation but about releasing the need to control one's path and trusting in the divine presence within. This surrender is a recognition that the ego's plans and desires are limited, while the Supreme God holds a wisdom that transcends the individual self. In surrendering, the Gnostic allows the divine will to guide their life, moving from a state of personal striving to one of spiritual flow. This surrender is the ultimate release, a letting go that allows the soul to return to its true nature and to experience the peace of divine alignment.

Through these practices, the Gnostic gradually transforms the ego, moving from a limited, self-centered perspective to a state of expanded awareness that reflects the unity of the Pleroma. This transformation is not a loss of self but an awakening to a deeper, truer self—an essence that is connected to the Supreme God and free from the illusions of the Demiurge. The ego, once a source of limitation, becomes a tool for expression, a way for the divine spark within to shine into the world.

The Gospel of Judas suggests this journey of transformation, as Judas moves beyond the conventional views of the other disciples to embrace a path of gnosis. In Gnostic thought, this path requires a willingness to release the ego's hold, to move beyond surface identities and to step into the unknown. By transforming the ego, the Gnostic prepares for the ultimate return to the Pleroma, a state of unity where the soul is no longer bound by individuality but experiences itself as part of the divine fullness.

The transformation of the ego, therefore, is both a liberation and a reunion, a process of shedding falsehoods and awakening to truth. Through this journey, the Gnostic finds not only freedom from the limitations of the material world but a profound connection to the Supreme God. In this transformation, the soul discovers its true nature as a being of light, a fragment of the divine that has journeyed through illusion and returned to its source. This is the essence of Gnostic spirituality—a path of remembering, a journey of awakening, and a transformation that brings the soul home to the boundless peace and unity of the Pleroma.

Chapter 33
The Quest for Absolute Truth

The Gnostic's journey is a search for Absolute Truth, a path that goes beyond conventional knowledge and belief systems. This truth, which lies beyond the material and within the heart of the divine, is not a set of doctrines or ideas, but a state of being, a revelation that transforms the seeker's entire perspective. It is the essence of gnosis—a direct, inner knowing that frees the soul from the constraints of the Demiurge's world and aligns it with the Supreme God, who is the source of all truth. In seeking Absolute Truth, the Gnostic undertakes a profound exploration of self, spirit, and reality, recognizing that true liberation lies in uncovering the divine essence that resides within.

The Gospel of Judas illuminates this quest through the relationship between Jesus and Judas, who is singled out for his willingness to question and seek deeper knowledge. Jesus guides Judas beyond appearances, urging him to see beyond the surface and seek the hidden truths of existence. In this dynamic, Judas embodies the role of the Gnostic seeker, one who is willing to challenge established beliefs and delve into mysteries that others fear or dismiss. This quest for truth is central to the Gnostic path, for only through a relentless pursuit of knowledge can the soul escape the illusions of the Demiurge and return to its origin in the Pleroma.

One of the first steps in the quest for Absolute Truth is the practice of *Inner Questioning*. This practice involves turning inward, examining one's own beliefs, motivations, and assumptions about the world. The Gnostic understands that much of what they have been taught is shaped by the limitations of the

Demiurge's creation—society, culture, and even religious doctrines that reinforce separation from the divine. Through inner questioning, the seeker learns to discern between inherited beliefs and deeper, self-realized truths. This process is both liberating and humbling, for it requires the Gnostic to let go of familiar ideas and to open themselves to new insights that often challenge deeply rooted assumptions.

Another critical practice is *Intuitive Perception*, which involves trusting the insights that arise from the soul rather than relying solely on intellectual reasoning. In Gnostic thought, intuition is a form of knowledge that transcends the limitations of the physical mind, a way of accessing deeper truths that lie beyond ordinary perception. By cultivating intuitive perception, the Gnostic learns to recognize the subtle voice of the divine within, to trust the inner guidance that arises from their connection to the Supreme God. This intuition becomes a compass, a way of navigating the spiritual path that often defies conventional logic and understanding.

The *Contemplation of Divine Unity* is also essential to the quest for Absolute Truth. In this contemplation, the Gnostic reflects on the Pleroma, the fullness of the divine, as a state of perfect unity and harmony. This unity is not merely a concept but an experience, a feeling of connection that transcends the separation imposed by the material world. By contemplating divine unity, the seeker aligns their consciousness with the Supreme God, allowing them to perceive truth as it exists in the spiritual realm, beyond the distortions of the Demiurge's creation. This practice cultivates an awareness of the interconnectedness of all things, revealing a truth that is not fragmented but whole.

Seeking the Hidden Meanings within religious texts and symbols is another aspect of the Gnostic quest for truth. For the Gnostic, scriptures and teachings are not taken at face value but are seen as symbolic narratives that point toward deeper realities. The Gospel of Judas, for example, is not viewed merely as a historical account but as a revelation of hidden truths about Jesus, Judas, and the divine. The Gnostic learns to read between the lines, to uncover the allegorical meanings within spiritual texts, and to perceive the messages that lie beneath the surface. This approach transforms study into a spiritual practice, where each reading becomes an act of revelation, a way of uncovering truths that have been concealed from the unenlightened.

The *Practice of Silence and Stillness* also plays a significant role in the search for Absolute Truth. In silence, the Gnostic can enter a state of inner clarity, free from the distractions and distortions of the material mind. This silence is not merely the absence of noise; it is a state of receptivity, a quietness that allows the divine to speak directly to the soul. In stillness, the Gnostic becomes a vessel for truth, creating a space where insights can arise without interference. This practice of silence is essential for cultivating the discernment needed to recognize truth, as it allows the seeker to separate the voice of the divine from the illusions of the ego.

In the Gospel of Judas, Jesus's teachings encourage Judas to pursue truth in this way, guiding him to a perspective that transcends the other disciples' understanding. This pursuit requires courage and a willingness to move beyond established boundaries, to question even the most sacred beliefs in the search for deeper knowledge. Judas's journey, then, reflects the Gnostic path, where the quest for truth becomes a path of transformation, a process that not only liberates the soul from illusion but also realigns it with the divine.

Another essential aspect of the quest for Absolute Truth is the *Rejection of Deception*, particularly the deceptions imposed by the Demiurge and his Archons. These forces, which rule over the material world, work to obscure the soul's perception of truth, creating illusions of pleasure, power, and identity that bind it to the physical. The Gnostic learns to recognize these deceptions, to see through the false promises of the material, and to cultivate a truth-centered way of being. This rejection of deception requires vigilance, a continuous commitment to truth that protects the soul from becoming ensnared in the illusions of the physical.

The *Embrace of Divine Knowledge* is another practice that aligns the Gnostic with Absolute Truth. In Gnostic thought, divine knowledge, or gnosis, is a form of direct experience that reveals the true nature of the self and the universe. This knowledge is not intellectual but experiential, a knowing that arises from the soul's direct contact with the divine. The Gnostic cultivates this knowledge through practices such as meditation, contemplation, and prayer, opening themselves to insights that go beyond the mind. This embrace of divine knowledge becomes a source of strength and clarity, a way of grounding the soul in truth that cannot be shaken by external forces.

Living with Integrity is also fundamental to the Gnostic quest for truth. Integrity, in this sense, means aligning one's actions, thoughts, and words with the inner truth that has been revealed through gnosis. This alignment is not a matter of moral rules but a commitment to authenticity, a dedication to living as an expression of the divine. For the Gnostic, integrity is a form of spiritual discipline, a way of ensuring that the search for truth is not confined to inner reflection but is manifested in every aspect of life. This practice of integrity becomes a testament to the Gnostic's dedication, a way of embodying the truth they seek and demonstrating it through their actions.

The *Quest for Absolute Truth* also involves a willingness to confront the unknown. In the search for truth, the Gnostic must often venture beyond the familiar, exploring mysteries that challenge their understanding and force them to let go of certainties. This journey into the unknown is a test of faith, a process that requires the Gnostic to trust in the Supreme God and to be open to revelations that cannot be anticipated or controlled. This openness to mystery is essential, for the divine truth cannot be fully known or contained; it is a living, dynamic reality that continually unfolds, inviting the seeker to deeper and deeper understanding.

In the Gospel of Judas, Judas's willingness to embrace this unknown reflects his commitment to truth, even when it sets him apart from others. He embodies the courage required to pursue a path that defies conventional expectations, a path that leads not to earthly power or recognition but to spiritual liberation. His journey serves as a reminder that the quest for Absolute Truth is not about conforming to accepted beliefs but about daring to see beyond them, to discover a reality that is hidden from ordinary sight.

For the Gnostic, the quest for Absolute Truth is a sacred duty, a journey that leads the soul from the darkness of ignorance into the light of divine knowledge. Through practices of inner questioning, intuitive perception, contemplation, silence, and integrity, the seeker cultivates a state of awareness that allows them to perceive truth directly, beyond the distortions of the Demiurge's world. This quest transforms the soul, freeing it from the illusions of the physical and realigning it with the Supreme God.

In the end, the quest for Absolute Truth is a journey of return, a process of remembering and awakening to the divine essence within. This truth is not an external object to be grasped but an inner reality to be realized, a state of unity with the Supreme God that brings peace, clarity, and liberation. Through this quest, the Gnostic finds a path back to the Pleroma, a way of transcending the limitations of the material and embracing the eternal. This is the promise of gnosis—the revelation of a truth that is infinite, boundless, and forever beyond the reach of illusion, a truth that guides the soul home to the fullness of divine light.

Chapter 34
Releasing Material Attachments

In Gnostic practice, releasing material attachments is a vital step on the path to spiritual liberation. The Gnostic recognizes that the material world, ruled by the Demiurge, is filled with illusions that ensnare the soul, pulling it away from its divine origin and binding it to the cycles of birth and death. These attachments—to wealth, status, identity, and the physical body—act as anchors, keeping the soul immersed in the temporal and distant from the eternal. For the Gnostic, freedom lies in detachment, in letting go of the desires and dependencies that tether the soul to the physical realm, allowing it to return to its true nature and ascend to the Pleroma.

The Gospel of Judas hints at this journey of detachment through the teachings Jesus imparts to Judas, inviting him to see beyond the material and understand a reality that lies beyond appearances. Judas's journey exemplifies the Gnostic path: a process of releasing all that is false and embracing the truth that lies within. This release is not a rejection of life but a transformation of perspective, a shift from seeing oneself as bound to the world to recognizing oneself as a soul seeking return to divine unity.

A foundational practice for releasing material attachments is *Reflective Awareness of Desire*. This practice involves observing one's desires and understanding the motivations behind them. The Gnostic reflects on each attachment—whether to possessions, relationships, or identity—and contemplates why these attachments hold significance. Are they rooted in a need for security, control, or validation? By examining these attachments, the Gnostic begins to see that they are all temporary, bound by the limitations of the material world. This awareness allows the seeker to understand the illusionary nature of desire, to recognize that true fulfillment lies not in external things but within the soul's connection to the divine.

Another powerful practice is *Non-Ownership Meditation*, where the Gnostic visualizes releasing everything they "own" or believe they control. In a meditative state, the seeker imagines letting go of each possession, responsibility, or relationship, not as a loss but as a freeing of the soul from entanglements. The practice of non-ownership reinforces the understanding that the soul's essence is not defined by what it holds onto but by its intrinsic connection to the divine. This meditation helps cultivate a sense of inner freedom, a recognition that nothing in the material world truly belongs to the soul and that all it needs is already within.

The *Release of Personal Identity* is another significant practice in this journey. The ego often forms attachments to roles, titles, and labels—father, mother, artist, leader—creating a sense of identity tied to these roles. For the Gnostic, releasing attachment to personal identity involves seeing oneself beyond these labels, recognizing that the true self is not confined by social roles or titles. By letting go of the ego's need to define itself, the seeker finds a sense of wholeness that is rooted in the divine rather than in temporary identities. This release allows the soul to move through the world without clinging to a constructed self, experiencing each role as a fluid expression rather than a fixed identity.

Embracing Impermanence is also key to releasing attachments. The Gnostic reflects on the transient nature of all things in the Demiurge's realm—relationships, possessions, and even life itself. By contemplating impermanence, the seeker learns to value the present moment without becoming ensnared by it. This awareness fosters a sense of appreciation without attachment, a state where one can experience life fully while remaining free from the need to hold onto it. Embracing impermanence becomes a daily practice, a way of moving through the world with grace, knowing that all things are temporary reflections of a deeper, eternal reality.

In the Gospel of Judas, Jesus's invitation to Judas to look beyond the physical world reflects this understanding of impermanence. Jesus encourages Judas to recognize that the kingdom he speaks of is not one of earthly power or permanence but a spiritual reality that transcends the material. This guidance serves as a reminder to the Gnostic that true freedom does not come from accumulating or clinging to physical things but from releasing them and turning toward the divine.

The Practice of Generosity is another essential tool for breaking attachments. When the Gnostic gives freely, without expectation of return, they counter the ego's tendency to hoard and control. Acts of generosity create a flow of energy, a way of participating in the world without being owned by it. Through generosity, the seeker learns that giving is a way of embodying divine love, a way of living from abundance rather than scarcity. This practice helps dissolve attachment to possessions, fostering a sense of inner richness that does not depend on material wealth but on the soul's connection to the Supreme God.

The *Acceptance of Loss* is another profound practice in releasing attachment. Loss—whether of loved ones, status, or health—is a natural part of the material world, yet the ego resists it, fearing change and clinging to the familiar. The Gnostic learns to see loss not as a punishment but as a teacher, an opportunity to practice detachment and to turn inward for strength. By accepting loss, the seeker finds resilience in the face of change, a strength that is rooted in the soul rather than in external circumstances. This acceptance is a form of surrender, a willingness to release control and to trust in the divine flow.

The *Practice of Inner Contentment* also aids in releasing attachment. The Gnostic learns to cultivate a sense of peace that does not depend on external factors, a state of inner fulfillment that arises from connection with the divine. By fostering inner contentment, the seeker becomes less dependent on the physical world for happiness, finding joy in the simple awareness of being. This contentment is a reflection of the Pleroma, a state of fullness that exists beyond material desires. Through this practice, the Gnostic learns to carry the peace of the divine within, regardless of the fluctuations of the material world.

Mindful Presence is another essential aspect of releasing attachment, as it encourages the Gnostic to engage with life fully while remaining free from clinging. By focusing on the present moment, the seeker learns to appreciate experiences without attempting to hold onto them. This mindful presence fosters a sense of detachment, allowing the Gnostic to move through life with openness and curiosity rather than a need to possess or control. This presence is a form of spiritual freedom, a way of living that honors each moment without becoming bound by it.

In the Gospel of Judas, Judas's willingness to follow a path that defies traditional expectations reflects this mindful presence. Unlike the other disciples, who seek positions of authority in the material world, Judas is called to a deeper understanding, a vision that requires him to release attachment to earthly goals. This journey mirrors the Gnostic's own path of detachment, where the soul learns to let go of material concerns and to focus on the quest for divine truth.

The Visualization of Divine Light is another practice that helps the Gnostic release attachments. In this visualization, the seeker imagines themselves surrounded by a radiant, all-encompassing light that dissolves all attachments and fears. This light, a symbol of the Supreme God's presence, fills the soul with a sense of unity and completeness, reminding it that all it needs lies within. By returning to this visualization regularly, the Gnostic strengthens their connection to the divine, finding a source of inner peace that transcends the material.

Finally, *Living in Service to the Divine* becomes a way of releasing attachment. The Gnostic dedicates their actions to the Supreme God, aligning their life with a purpose that goes beyond personal gain. By serving the divine, the seeker finds freedom from the ego's desires, living not for recognition or reward but as an expression of divine love. This service is a form of surrender, a way of letting go of the need to control and allowing the divine to guide one's path.

Through these practices, the Gnostic learns to live with an open heart, fully engaged with the world yet free from the need to possess or control it. This detachment is not a withdrawal from life but a liberation within it, a way of being that allows the soul to experience the beauty of existence without becoming bound by it. In releasing attachments, the Gnostic discovers a profound inner freedom, a state of peace that reflects the harmony of the Pleroma.

The Gospel of Judas calls each seeker to undertake this journey, to release the attachments that bind them to the Demiurge's world and to embrace the path of liberation. By letting go of material concerns, the soul aligns itself with the Supreme God, finding strength, clarity, and joy in the awareness of its divine essence. This release is not a loss but a return—a return to the soul's true nature, a state of wholeness that exists beyond the illusions of the material.

In the Gnostic journey, releasing material attachments becomes a doorway to the divine, a step toward the ultimate goal of reunion with the Pleroma. This detachment reveals the soul's inner light, a boundless love and peace that reflects the Supreme God's essence. Through this release, the Gnostic finds freedom, not in rejecting life but in embracing it with a clear, unbound heart, a heart that is open to the infinite and that knows its place within the divine fullness. This is the gift of detachment: a life lived in harmony with the eternal, free from the illusions of possession, and anchored in the timeless reality of the soul's connection to the Supreme God.

Chapter 35
The Role of Intuition

In Gnostic spirituality, intuition is regarded as a sacred gift, a bridge between the soul and the divine realms that lie beyond the physical senses and intellect. While intellect serves to navigate the external world, intuition guides the soul inward, allowing it to perceive truths hidden from ordinary sight. For the Gnostic, intuition is the voice of the inner divine, an unfiltered and immediate knowledge that arises from the soul's connection to the Supreme God. It is a light that illuminates the path of gnosis, helping the seeker transcend the illusions of the Demiurge's world and recognize the divine essence within.

In the Gospel of Judas, Jesus's teachings to Judas suggest a path guided not by outward authority or conventional beliefs but by a deeper understanding—a knowing that does not come from adherence to doctrine but from direct experience of the divine. Judas's unique role illustrates the journey of the Gnostic, one who must rely on inner guidance rather than the validation of external structures. This path requires trust in the intuitive voice, a willingness to follow insights that often challenge societal expectations. In this way, intuition becomes not only a source of knowledge but a means of liberation, freeing the soul to discover its true essence.

One of the foundational practices for cultivating intuition in Gnosticism is *Inner Listening*, a practice of becoming quiet and receptive to the subtle messages that arise from within. The Gnostic learns to set aside the noise of thoughts, fears, and desires, entering a state of inner stillness where intuition can be perceived. This quietness is not simply silence but a state of heightened awareness, a place where the soul can listen to the voice of the divine spark within. Through inner listening, the Gnostic cultivates a sensitivity to subtle insights, a way of hearing the guidance that comes not from the mind but from the heart, where the connection to the divine resides.

Dream Interpretation is another powerful way to engage with intuition. In Gnostic practice, dreams are viewed as portals to the soul's inner landscape, a realm where the conscious mind's filters are lifted, allowing the deeper self to communicate through symbols and images. The Gnostic learns to record and interpret dreams, seeking patterns and messages that offer guidance for their spiritual path. This practice is not about literal interpretations but about seeing the soul's symbols, the language of the unconscious, and recognizing the deeper truths they reveal. Through dream interpretation, the Gnostic strengthens their intuitive insight, understanding that dreams are a form of divine communication.

Trust in Spontaneous Knowing is essential to cultivating intuition. Unlike rational thought, which unfolds through steps and logic, intuition often arrives as a complete understanding, a sudden clarity that needs no further explanation. The Gnostic learns to trust these moments of spontaneous knowing, recognizing them as insights from the soul rather than thoughts shaped by external influences. This trust in intuition is a form of surrender, an openness to the guidance of the Supreme God that allows the soul to be led beyond the limits of the intellect. By trusting in spontaneous knowing, the Gnostic embraces a state of inner freedom, allowing the divine to reveal itself without interference.

Contemplation of Symbols and Archetypes is another key practice in developing intuition. In Gnostic thought, symbols and archetypes are seen as bridges to the divine, expressions of the deeper truths that cannot be fully captured by language. The Gnostic contemplates these symbols—not as objects of analysis but as portals to inner wisdom, images that reveal aspects of the divine. By meditating on symbols such as light, the Pleroma, or the Aeons, the seeker allows their intuitive mind to perceive layers of meaning that the rational mind might miss. This contemplation opens the soul to a realm of understanding where truths are felt rather than explained, a place where intuition can flourish.

In the Gospel of Judas, Judas's path reflects the role of intuition as he seeks answers beyond what the other disciples can comprehend. His willingness to look beyond conventional teachings, to trust in the revelations shared by Jesus, exemplifies the Gnostic's reliance on inner wisdom. Judas's journey shows that intuition is not merely a passive gift but an active choice, a commitment to following the soul's guidance even when it leads into unfamiliar territory. For the Gnostic, intuition becomes both a guide and a test, a call to trust in the soul's deeper knowing rather than the comfort of established beliefs.

Visualizing the Inner Light is a practice that enhances intuition by strengthening the soul's connection to the divine. In this visualization, the Gnostic focuses on the heart or the center of the chest, imagining a radiant light within—a representation of the divine spark. This light is visualized growing brighter, illuminating the inner being and expanding outward. By focusing on this inner light, the Gnostic tunes into the presence of the Supreme God within, opening themselves to the guidance that flows from this source. This visualization creates a direct line to the soul's intuitive wisdom, a way of aligning the mind with the heart and allowing intuition to rise naturally.

The practice of *Asking for Inner Guidance* is also significant in Gnostic spirituality. The Gnostic may begin each day by asking for clarity and wisdom, opening themselves to insights that can guide them through the challenges and decisions they encounter. This practice is a form of dialogue with the divine, a moment of surrender that acknowledges the limits of the intellect and seeks assistance from a higher source. By asking for guidance, the Gnostic creates a state of receptivity, a willingness to be led by intuition rather than by self-will. This openness to guidance becomes a way of living in harmony with the divine, a trust that the soul's path is being directed by the Supreme God.

Synchronicity Awareness is another practice that fosters intuition, as the Gnostic learns to recognize meaningful coincidences in daily life. Synchronicities are viewed as signs from the divine, messages that reflect the alignment of the inner and outer worlds. By paying attention to these synchronicities, the Gnostic strengthens their intuition, learning to see beyond chance and to perceive the interconnectedness of all things. This awareness of synchronicity becomes a way of seeing the divine at work in the world, a reminder that the material is a reflection of the spiritual, and that the soul's journey is guided by forces beyond the visible.

The Gnostic also engages in the *Practice of Intuitive Writing*, a form of free expression where the seeker allows words to flow without overthinking. In this practice, the Gnostic writes down thoughts, insights, or questions, allowing the pen to move freely without the constraints of rational structure. This intuitive writing serves as a mirror, a way of revealing hidden aspects of the self and receiving insights that might otherwise remain inaccessible. By engaging in this practice, the Gnostic creates a dialogue with the soul, allowing intuition to express itself through words that arise from the depths of the inner self.

Non-Judgmental Observation is another essential aspect of cultivating intuition. In the material world, the mind is often quick to judge, categorize, and analyze, creating barriers that prevent the soul from perceiving subtle truths. The Gnostic practices observing without judgment, allowing experiences, thoughts, and emotions to arise without categorizing them as good or bad. This non-judgmental observation creates a space of openness, where intuition can emerge without interference from preconceived ideas. Through this practice, the Gnostic learns to see with clarity, to perceive the world not through the ego's filters but through the pure lens of the soul.

In the Gospel of Judas, Judas's path highlights the importance of seeing beyond judgment and appearances. By encouraging Judas to question and to perceive deeper truths, Jesus invites him to rely on his inner guidance rather than on external validation. This guidance is central to the Gnostic path, for intuition leads the seeker to insights that cannot be found through ordinary means. Judas's journey serves as a reminder that the path to truth is often solitary and requires the courage to trust one's inner vision.

For the Gnostic, intuition is not only a means of personal insight but a way of connecting with the divine. It is a pathway to gnosis, a direct knowing that reveals the soul's unity with the Supreme God. Through practices of inner listening, dream interpretation, visualization, and non-judgmental observation, the Gnostic strengthens this connection, allowing intuition to become a guiding force in daily life. This intuitive guidance leads the soul beyond the limitations of intellect and into the mysteries of the Pleroma, the realm of divine fullness and unity.

The role of intuition, therefore, is both practical and mystical. It is a way of navigating the world with inner clarity, making choices that reflect the soul's highest purpose, and a means of glimpsing the eternal truths that lie within. By following intuition, the Gnostic discovers a path that transcends the illusions of the Demiurge's world, a journey that brings them ever closer to the divine. This is the gift of intuition—a light that shines from within, a voice that speaks from the heart of the Supreme God, guiding the soul toward its ultimate liberation.

Through intuition, the Gnostic finds a way to live in alignment with their true nature, embracing each moment as an opportunity for spiritual awakening and growth. This intuitive knowing is the soul's compass, pointing the way home to the Pleroma, a place where the soul experiences its fullest expression, free from the illusions of separation and limitation, and in communion with the infinite and eternal truth of the divine.

Chapter 36
Purification of the Soul

In the Gnostic path, the purification of the soul is an essential journey, one that prepares the seeker for union with the Supreme God by stripping away the shadows and impurities that obscure the divine light within. This process of purification involves shedding the layers of illusion and attachment crafted by the Demiurge and his world, cleansing the soul of influences that keep it bound to the material. For the Gnostic, purification is not about external rites but an inward transformation, a deep cleansing of mind, heart, and spirit that allows the soul to remember its origin in the Pleroma and prepare for its return.

The Gospel of Judas illustrates this call to purification through Jesus's teachings to Judas, where Judas is encouraged to see beyond the physical world and recognize the illusions that entrap the soul. Jesus speaks to Judas of a reality that exists beyond the material, a state of purity that transcends earthly desires and identities. This guidance reflects the Gnostic understanding that the soul, in its essence, is pure, but it has been clouded by attachments, judgments, and fears that bind it to the physical realm. The purification journey, then, is about unveiling this inherent purity, allowing the soul to shine with the light of the Supreme God.

One of the foundational practices for purification in Gnosticism is *Mental Cleansing*, a practice of releasing thoughts, judgments, and beliefs that create barriers to divine perception. The Gnostic engages in mental cleansing by observing their thoughts and gently letting go of those that are rooted in fear, desire, or attachment. This practice is not about repressing thoughts but about creating a space of inner clarity, a mind that is free from the influences of the Demiurge's world. By cleansing the mind, the Gnostic opens a pathway for divine insights to flow, allowing the soul to experience truth untainted by illusion.

Emotional Purification is another essential practice, as emotions often carry the weight of attachment and ego, binding the soul to the material. In emotional purification, the Gnostic works to release resentments, fears, and desires, recognizing that these emotions are often tied to the ego's needs rather than the soul's essence. By processing and letting go of these emotions, the Gnostic moves toward a state of inner peace, a heart unburdened by the disturbances of the physical world. This emotional clarity allows the soul to feel the presence of the Supreme God more deeply, creating a state of openness where love, compassion, and peace can flourish.

The practice of *Fasting from Material Distractions* is also central to purification in Gnostic thought. The Gnostic consciously limits their engagement with physical pleasures, luxuries, or distractions that pull the soul's focus outward. This fasting is not about rejection but about moderation, a way of redirecting the soul's attention from the transient to the eternal. By fasting from excess, the Gnostic creates a space of stillness, an inner sanctuary where the divine presence can be felt without interference. This practice helps the seeker to strengthen their inner resolve, cultivating a sense of contentment and self-control that anchors them in the spiritual rather than the material.

Sacred Breathwork is another powerful tool for purification, as it allows the Gnostic to center themselves in the present moment and cleanse both body and spirit. In this practice, the Gnostic focuses on their breath, using deep and intentional breathing to release tension, stress, and impurities that have accumulated in the physical form. The breath becomes a bridge between body and spirit, a rhythm that aligns the soul with the flow of divine energy. Through sacred breathwork, the seeker experiences a sense of renewal, a fresh awareness that clears away the burdens of the material and reconnects the soul with the light within.

Silence and Solitude are also essential for the purification process. In the Gnostic journey, silence is not merely the absence of sound but a sacred state where the soul can listen to the divine without distraction. By entering periods of solitude and silence, the Gnostic creates a sanctuary for the spirit, a place where the illusions of the external world fade and the inner voice of the divine can be heard. This silence becomes a balm, a way of purifying the mind and heart, allowing the soul to experience a state of peace that is untouched by the outside world.

In the Gospel of Judas, Judas's willingness to stand apart from the other disciples can be seen as a form of purification, a step toward inner clarity and alignment with truth. His path reflects the Gnostic understanding that purification often requires a journey away from the familiar, a willingness to step into solitude and to embrace the silence that reveals hidden truths. This solitude becomes a place of transformation, where the soul releases the distractions and attachments of the physical and turns inward to the divine.

Another vital practice in the purification of the soul is *Mindful Repentance*, where the Gnostic reflects on actions or attitudes that have created separation from the divine. Repentance, in Gnostic practice, is not about guilt or shame but about recognition and release. The Gnostic acknowledges patterns of thought or behavior that reinforce the ego, then consciously lets them go, seeking to realign with the divine presence within. This repentance becomes a form of inner alchemy, transforming the soul's focus from the self-centered to the sacred, allowing it to move closer to the purity of the Pleroma.

Visualization of Light is also essential in the purification process. In this practice, the Gnostic imagines a radiant light descending from the Pleroma, filling their body, mind, and spirit. This light is seen as a purifying force, a divine presence that dissolves impurities, cleanses attachments, and renews the soul's connection to the Supreme God. Through this visualization, the

Gnostic experiences a sense of inner illumination, a feeling of being enveloped in divine love and protection. This light serves as a reminder of the soul's true nature, reinforcing the understanding that purity is its original state.

The *Practice of Forgiveness* also plays a significant role in purification. Holding onto resentment or judgment creates barriers in the soul, walls that separate it from the divine. By practicing forgiveness, the Gnostic releases these barriers, allowing the heart to return to a state of openness and peace. This forgiveness is extended not only to others but also to oneself, acknowledging that all beings are subject to the illusions of the material world. Through forgiveness, the Gnostic experiences a sense of liberation, a freedom that lightens the soul's burden and allows it to move closer to divine harmony.

The Gnostic may also engage in *Purification Rituals* that symbolize the release of impurities and attachments. These rituals can be simple acts, such as washing the hands or face with intention, envisioning the water as a symbol of divine cleansing. The Gnostic might also light incense, allowing the fragrance to carry away negative thoughts or emotions. These rituals serve as physical reminders of the soul's intention to purify, to return to a state of inner clarity and peace that reflects the divine fullness of the Pleroma.

Daily Reflection is another practice that supports purification, as the Gnostic takes time each day to examine their thoughts, actions, and intentions. This reflection is not about judgment but about awareness, a moment to recognize any attachments or illusions that may have taken root. By reflecting daily, the Gnostic keeps their focus aligned with the spiritual, continually renewing their commitment to purification. This daily practice reinforces the understanding that purification is an ongoing journey, a process of continual release and realignment with the divine.

In the Gospel of Judas, Jesus's guidance to Judas serves as a call to this kind of reflection, encouraging Judas to look beyond the material and to seek a higher understanding. Judas's path reflects the necessity of inner awareness, a dedication to purifying one's perception and releasing anything that clouds the vision of truth. This inner clarity becomes a foundation for the Gnostic journey, a state of mind and heart that allows the soul to perceive the divine presence in all things.

For the Gnostic, purification of the soul is not a one-time event but a continuous practice, a journey that deepens as the soul grows closer to the divine. Through mental cleansing, emotional release, solitude, silence, and acts of forgiveness, the Gnostic sheds the layers that separate the soul from the Supreme God. This purification is a process of remembering, a return to the soul's original state of purity and unity with the divine.

In the Gnostic path, purification is a way of life, a commitment to living in harmony with the divine and to letting go of all that binds the soul to the material. Through this purification, the Gnostic prepares for the ultimate return to the Pleroma, the realm of divine fullness where all illusions dissolve and only truth remains. This is the gift of purification—a journey that reveals the soul's light, an inner transformation that aligns the seeker with the infinite, and a return to the peace and unity that lies at the heart of all creation.

Chapter 37
The Meaning of Suffering and Trials

In Gnostic thought, suffering and trials are not arbitrary or meaningless; they are woven into the journey of the soul as transformative experiences that guide it toward awakening and liberation. While the material world is ruled by the Demiurge, who enforces illusions that bind the soul, the challenges that arise within this realm serve as catalysts for growth, pushing the soul to see beyond appearances and recognize its divine essence. For the Gnostic, suffering is a teacher, a force that reveals the limitations of the physical and urges the soul to seek the higher truths of the Pleroma, where unity and peace exist beyond the reach of the Demiurge's illusions.

In the Gospel of Judas, Judas's unique path, set apart from the other disciples, is marked by a willingness to embrace difficult truths and to step into unknown territory. His journey is a reflection of the Gnostic understanding of trials as necessary steps on the path to gnosis. Through hardship and struggle, the soul learns to see beyond the immediate pain and to recognize the lessons that lie hidden within. Judas's relationship with Jesus becomes a model for the Gnostic seeker, a reminder that even in suffering, there is a purpose, a hidden wisdom that calls the soul to higher understanding.

A foundational practice for understanding suffering in Gnosticism is *Contemplation of the Dual Nature of Existence*. The Gnostic reflects on the fact that the material world, as the creation of the Demiurge, is inherently flawed, a place where dualities such as pleasure and pain, joy and sorrow, continually pull the soul between opposites. By contemplating these dualities, the Gnostic begins to see suffering as part of the Demiurge's design, a force that is meant to trap the soul in cycles of desire and aversion. This reflection encourages the seeker to view suffering not as an ultimate reality but as an illusion that loses its power when the soul focuses on its divine origin.

The *Acceptance of Trials* is also central to the Gnostic path. The Gnostic learns to accept that challenges and obstacles are an inevitable part of the material world and sees them as opportunities to deepen their understanding and strengthen their connection to the divine. This acceptance is not passive resignation but an active embracing of experience as a means of growth. By accepting trials, the Gnostic transforms suffering into a tool for spiritual development, allowing each hardship to reveal aspects of the self that need to be healed, understood, or released.

Inner Reflection on Causes of Suffering allows the Gnostic to explore the roots of their pain, recognizing that much suffering arises from attachment to the ego, desires, or illusions imposed by the material world. By reflecting on these causes, the Gnostic gains insight into the patterns that keep the soul bound to the physical, learning to identify and release the attachments that fuel suffering. This reflection is a path of self-knowledge, an exploration that reveals how the Demiurge's illusions have shaped the soul's experience, and it helps the seeker to step into a state of liberation from these false sources of pain.

The *Practice of Compassionate Endurance* is another essential approach to suffering in Gnosticism. Compassionate endurance is the ability to face suffering without bitterness or resentment, to move through pain with a sense of grace and inner strength. This practice allows the Gnostic to remain centered in the face of trials, seeing each challenge as a part of the journey rather than an obstacle to it. Through compassionate endurance, the Gnostic learns to view suffering as a temporary state, a test that refines the soul and brings it closer to the divine. This endurance is a source of resilience, a way of standing strong in the face of the Demiurge's world without being defeated by it.

In the Gospel of Judas, Judas's willingness to accept his unique role, even when it leads to isolation and misunderstanding, reflects this compassionate endurance. His path is marked by a commitment to truth, even when that truth isolates him from others. For the Gnostic, this willingness to endure with patience and strength becomes a model for handling suffering, a reminder that the soul's journey is not about external approval but about remaining true to one's inner path.

Transcending the Self in Suffering is another transformative practice in Gnostic thought. When faced with hardship, the Gnostic seeks to move beyond the ego's perspective, to view suffering not as something that defines the self but as an experience that reveals a deeper truth. By transcending the self, the Gnostic sees their pain as part of the larger cosmic process, a reminder that the soul is connected to a reality beyond the physical. This practice shifts the focus from personal suffering to spiritual growth, transforming the pain into a step on the journey back to the Pleroma.

The *Embrace of Inner Silence* is another practice that aids the Gnostic in navigating suffering. In silence, the soul finds a refuge from the noise of pain, a place where the mind can rest and the spirit can reconnect with the divine. This silence becomes a sanctuary, a space where the soul can observe its suffering without becoming overwhelmed by it. Through inner silence, the Gnostic creates a distance from the pain, allowing them to see it with clarity and detachment. This silence is a healing balm, a way of entering a state of peace that transcends the temporary nature of the material world.

The *Practice of Letting Go of Resistance* is also central to understanding suffering in Gnosticism. Resistance to suffering often intensifies pain, creating an inner conflict that deepens the sense of separation. By letting go of resistance, the Gnostic learns to flow with the experience, to accept it as a part of the journey rather than fighting against it. This acceptance does not mean surrendering to suffering but releasing the struggle against it, allowing the soul to find peace even amid challenges. Through this practice, the Gnostic learns that suffering, like all things in the Demiurge's world, is temporary and ultimately illusory.

In the Gospel of Judas, Jesus's guidance to Judas suggests a path that defies traditional expectations, urging him to look beyond the apparent and to accept the difficulties of his role. This guidance reflects the Gnostic understanding that suffering is a tool of enlightenment, a force that pushes the soul toward truth. Judas's willingness to embrace this path becomes a reminder to the Gnostic that suffering is not the end but a passage, a step that brings the soul closer to divine wisdom.

Purification Through Suffering is another important concept in the Gnostic path. Suffering, in this sense, is seen as a means of purification, a way of burning away impurities that cloud the soul. The Gnostic views suffering as a process that strips away false identities, attachments, and fears, leaving the soul in a state of inner clarity. Through this purification, the soul becomes more attuned to the divine, more aligned with the Supreme God. This purification is not a punishment but a transformative fire that reveals the soul's true essence, preparing it for reunion with the divine.

Seeing the Divine Purpose in Suffering allows the Gnostic to find meaning in hardship, recognizing that each trial serves a purpose in the journey toward gnosis. This understanding does not deny the reality of pain but provides a perspective that transforms it into a meaningful experience. By seeing suffering as part of the soul's evolution, the Gnostic cultivates a sense of peace and trust, a belief that even the darkest moments serve a purpose in the grand design of the divine. This trust in the divine purpose becomes a source of strength, a way of embracing life with courage and hope.

Service and Compassion for Others is also essential in the Gnostic's relationship to suffering. By recognizing their own suffering, the Gnostic becomes more attuned to the suffering of others, developing a sense of compassion that transcends personal pain. Through acts of service, the Gnostic expresses their understanding of shared humanity, creating a connection that reflects the unity of the Pleroma. This compassion transforms suffering from a purely personal experience to a bridge that connects the soul with others, a way of living in alignment with the Supreme God's love.

For the Gnostic, suffering and trials are not obstacles but opportunities for spiritual growth and purification. Through practices of inner silence, letting go of resistance, seeing divine purpose, and embracing compassionate endurance, the Gnostic learns to view suffering as a catalyst for transformation. This approach to suffering shifts the focus from escape to acceptance, from fear to understanding, allowing the soul to embrace its journey with strength and clarity.

The Gospel of Judas serves as a reminder that the path to gnosis is not free from hardship but that each trial holds within it a hidden blessing, a step toward the divine. By navigating suffering with wisdom and inner strength, the Gnostic prepares the soul for the ultimate liberation from the Demiurge's world, a return to the peace and unity of the Pleroma. Through this journey, suffering becomes not a curse but a call to transcendence, a force that guides the soul back to its true home in the light of the Supreme God.

This is the Gnostic understanding of suffering—a path that leads from ignorance to knowledge, from separation to unity, and from darkness to the infinite light of the divine. Through the transformation of suffering, the soul finds its way back to the Pleroma, experiencing the ultimate peace and fulfillment that lies beyond the illusions of the material world.

Chapter 38
Communion with the Supreme God

In Gnostic thought, communion with the Supreme God represents the pinnacle of spiritual experience, a state where the soul transcends the illusions of the material world and touches the divine essence that lies beyond it. This communion is not a relationship mediated by external rituals or doctrines but a profound and direct experience, a merging with the source of all existence that brings the soul into harmony with the eternal fullness of the Pleroma. Through communion, the Gnostic finds the ultimate peace, unity, and understanding—a state of pure awareness that liberates the soul from the confines of the Demiurge's realm.

The Gospel of Judas offers a glimpse into this possibility through Jesus's intimate teachings to Judas, revealing mysteries that point beyond the material toward a higher, transcendent reality. Jesus speaks of a divine kingdom that exists beyond the physical, an inner realm of light and unity where the soul's true home lies. This invitation to look beyond the visible world and to seek communion with the divine mirrors the essence of the Gnostic journey—a path that leads the soul away from external forms and into a direct, transformative experience of the Supreme God.

A foundational practice for cultivating communion with the Supreme God in Gnosticism is *Inner Silence*, a state where the soul quiets the noise of thoughts, desires, and fears, creating an inner stillness that allows the divine presence to emerge. In this silence, the Gnostic lets go of the distractions of the material world, entering a space where the mind becomes a vessel for the divine. This silence is not an emptiness but a fullness, a place where the soul can feel the presence of the Supreme God without interference. Through inner silence, the Gnostic prepares the soul to receive the divine, opening themselves to a communion that transcends words and concepts.

Another essential practice is *Prayer of the Heart*, a form of prayer that is not about asking or petitioning but about attuning to the divine within. In this prayer, the Gnostic focuses on the heart, imagining it as a place of light and warmth, a sanctuary where the divine spark resides. The seeker enters this space with reverence, resting in the awareness of the Supreme God's presence within. This prayer becomes an experience of unity, a moment where the boundaries of the self dissolve, and the soul feels its oneness with the divine. Through the prayer of the heart, the Gnostic learns to live in continual communion, carrying the awareness of the divine presence into every aspect of life.

The *Contemplation of the Divine Light* is another powerful practice for deepening communion. In this meditation, the Gnostic visualizes a brilliant light descending from the Pleroma, filling their entire being with warmth and radiance. This light is the presence of the Supreme God, a symbol of purity, wisdom, and love that transcends the material. By allowing this light to permeate their consciousness, the Gnostic feels themselves merging with the divine essence, experiencing a taste of the unity that awaits beyond the physical. This visualization becomes a doorway, a means of entering the divine presence and experiencing communion with the infinite.

In the Gospel of Judas, Judas's journey reflects this call to communion. His willingness to see beyond appearances, to seek knowledge that defies conventional beliefs, mirrors the Gnostic's path toward union with the Supreme God. Judas's path is not about external validation but about a direct experience of truth, a communion with the divine that transcends the limits of the physical world. For the Gnostic, this journey serves as a reminder that true communion requires courage, a willingness to step beyond the ordinary and to trust in the presence of the divine within.

Purification of Intentions is another practice that helps the Gnostic prepare for communion with the Supreme God. The seeker examines their motives, releasing attachments, desires, and fears that cloud the purity of their intent. This purification is an act of devotion, a way of approaching the divine with a heart that is free from selfishness and open to receiving truth. By aligning their intentions with the desire for unity, the Gnostic creates a state of receptivity, a readiness to experience the divine presence without interference. This purified intent allows communion to unfold naturally, as the soul becomes a mirror that reflects the light of the Supreme God.

The *Practice of Surrender* is also essential in the path to communion. Surrender, in this sense, is not a passive resignation but an active trust, a willingness to release control and allow the divine to guide the soul. In surrender, the Gnostic lets go of personal agendas, fears, and expectations, entering a state of openness where the divine presence can emerge. This surrender is a way of making space for the Supreme God, a letting go that invites the fullness of the divine into the soul's experience. Through surrender, the Gnostic transcends the ego, allowing the boundaries of the self to dissolve in the light of divine unity.

Engaging in Sacred Rituals of Devotion also aids in communion. Although Gnosticism often emphasizes direct experience over ritual, certain acts of devotion can serve as reminders of the divine, helping to focus the soul's attention on the Supreme God. Lighting a candle, reciting sacred words, or creating a personal altar can become acts of devotion that reflect the Gnostic's dedication to the path. These rituals are not meant to create distance between the soul and the divine but to foster a sense of reverence, a mindfulness that keeps the Gnostic centered in their intention to experience communion.

Living with Awareness of the Divine in All Things is a practice that allows the Gnostic to see the Supreme God reflected in the world around them. By perceiving each moment, person, and experience as an expression of the divine, the seeker cultivates a state of continual communion, an awareness that transcends separation. This practice of seeing the divine in all things transforms ordinary life into a spiritual journey, where each encounter becomes an opportunity to experience the Supreme God's presence. Through this awareness, the Gnostic lives in a state of unity, a communion that flows from the heart into the world.

In the Gospel of Judas, Jesus's invitation to Judas to see beyond the material reflects this call to divine awareness. Jesus speaks of a kingdom that is not of this world, a realm where the soul experiences oneness with the divine. This guidance encourages the Gnostic to look past appearances and to recognize the Supreme God's presence within themselves and beyond the physical. For the seeker, this awareness becomes a way of moving through life with a sense of inner peace, a communion that is not limited to specific practices but is woven into every aspect of existence.

The Embrace of Divine Love is also integral to communion with the Supreme God. Divine love, in Gnostic thought, is not a conditional or possessive love but an all-encompassing presence that transcends dualities. By opening to this love, the Gnostic allows their heart to be filled with the peace and unity of the divine. This love becomes a path to communion, a way of experiencing the Supreme God not as an external force but as the very essence of the soul. Through divine love, the boundaries between self and other dissolve, creating a state of unity that reflects the harmony of the Pleroma.

The *Practice of Inner Gratitude* also strengthens communion, as the Gnostic cultivates a sense of appreciation for the presence of the divine within and around them. Gratitude becomes a form of prayer, a way of acknowledging the Supreme God's gifts and expressing devotion. By focusing on gratitude, the Gnostic keeps their heart open, fostering a state of receptivity that invites communion. This gratitude is not limited to specific moments but becomes a continual awareness, a way of living in alignment with the divine and honoring the blessings of each experience.

For the Gnostic, communion with the Supreme God is not an occasional event but an ongoing state of connection, a way of being that reflects the soul's alignment with the Pleroma. Through practices of inner silence, prayer of the heart, purification, surrender, and divine love, the Gnostic cultivates this communion, allowing the divine presence to flow into every aspect of life. This communion becomes the soul's greatest fulfillment, a state of peace and unity that transcends the illusions of the Demiurge's world.

In the Gospel of Judas, Judas's journey serves as a reminder that this communion is not about conforming to external beliefs but about an inner experience that brings the soul closer to its true nature. For the Gnostic, this path of communion is a return to the source, a movement from separation to unity, from illusion to truth. In this communion, the soul finds its ultimate liberation, a peace that is not dependent on circumstances but is rooted in the eternal presence of the Supreme God.

This is the essence of Gnostic communion—a direct and transformative experience of the divine that brings the soul into harmony with the infinite. Through this communion, the Gnostic fulfills their deepest purpose, awakening to the truth of their being and returning to the boundless light of the Pleroma. This is the path to which the Gospel of Judas points, a journey that leads not to doctrines or external rituals but to a direct encounter with the Supreme God, where the soul finds its true home in the eternal.

Chapter 39
Rejection of the Demiurge

In Gnostic tradition, the rejection of the Demiurge is a critical step on the soul's journey back to the Pleroma, a step that frees the seeker from the illusions that bind them to the material world. The Demiurge, considered the flawed creator of the physical universe, is often depicted as a false god—a being that imposes limits and distractions to keep the soul entrapped in ignorance. For the Gnostic, to reject the Demiurge is to awaken to the truth beyond appearances, to recognize the illusory nature of the material world, and to seek the higher reality that lies in union with the Supreme God.

In the Gospel of Judas, Jesus's private conversations with Judas reveal a view of the world that is distinct from conventional teachings, pointing to a reality beyond the control of the Demiurge. Jesus speaks of a divine kingdom beyond the material, urging Judas to understand the true nature of creation and the forces that govern it. This perspective challenges the power of the Demiurge, casting him not as a beneficent creator but as a barrier that must be overcome. Judas's willingness to question and explore these teachings reflects the Gnostic's path of rejecting the false world of the Demiurge and seeking the hidden truths of the divine.

A primary practice for rejecting the Demiurge is *Cultivating Inner Discernment*. This practice involves sharpening the soul's ability to see beyond the surface, to question the assumptions and appearances that uphold the material world. The Gnostic learns to view each situation, attachment, or desire with clarity, understanding how these aspects are often designed to bind the soul to the physical. Through discernment, the seeker begins to see the Demiurge's influence in all that creates division, limitation, or distraction. This discernment is an act of liberation, a way of reclaiming the mind from the illusions imposed by the Demiurge's creation.

Conscious Detachment from Material Desires is also crucial for rejecting the Demiurge's influence. The Demiurge operates through the material, drawing the soul into cycles of desire and fulfillment that reinforce attachment to the physical. By consciously detaching from these desires, the Gnostic weakens the Demiurge's hold, freeing the soul to focus on spiritual truths. This detachment does not mean renouncing life but rather cultivating a perspective that places spiritual values above material ones. By choosing the eternal over the transient, the Gnostic aligns with the Supreme God, fostering a state of inner freedom that defies the control of the Demiurge.

The *Practice of Inner Sovereignty* is another essential aspect of rejecting the Demiurge. In this practice, the Gnostic asserts their spiritual autonomy, refusing to allow external forces, beliefs, or authorities to define their truth. The Demiurge seeks to control the soul by imposing limitations and creating dependency on the material. By cultivating inner sovereignty, the Gnostic claims their right to seek truth directly, to experience the divine without the interference of false authorities. This practice of sovereignty is an expression of the soul's alignment with the Supreme God, a declaration that its source of guidance lies within and beyond the reach of the Demiurge.

Recognizing False Narratives and Beliefs is also a vital practice in rejecting the Demiurge's influence. The Gnostic examines cultural, societal, and even religious narratives, discerning which are rooted in divine truth and which serve to reinforce attachment to the physical world. Many systems of belief, while appearing benevolent, uphold the illusion of the Demiurge by promoting obedience, conformity, or fear. By recognizing and releasing these false narratives, the Gnostic clears the way for true understanding, opening themselves to a perspective that is aligned with the Supreme God. This discernment allows the seeker to see through illusions, breaking the power of beliefs that bind them to the material.

The *Invocation of Divine Light* is another essential practice in overcoming the influence of the Demiurge. In this meditation, the Gnostic envisions a light descending from the Pleroma, filling them with clarity and truth. This light is seen as a force that dissolves the shadows cast by the Demiurge, revealing the soul's true nature and the reality of the Supreme God. By regularly invoking this divine light, the Gnostic strengthens their connection to the Pleroma, creating a state of inner illumination that makes the Demiurge's illusions lose their power. This practice serves as both a shield and a compass, guiding the soul through the illusions of the material and toward the light of the divine.

In the Gospel of Judas, Judas's ability to question conventional beliefs and seek direct answers from Jesus reflects this journey of rejecting the Demiurge. His path is marked by a willingness to see beyond the accepted norms, to seek a truth that lies outside the realm of ordinary understanding. For the Gnostic, this questioning becomes a form of liberation, a way of breaking free from the influence of the Demiurge and aligning with the divine essence. Judas's journey serves as a reminder that to reject the Demiurge is to reject complacency, to embark on a path of courage and self-discovery that leads beyond the familiar.

Silencing the Voice of the Ego is also an important step in rejecting the Demiurge. The ego, in Gnostic thought, is often seen as an extension of the Demiurge, a false self that reinforces attachment to the physical. The Gnostic practices quieting the ego's demands for validation, success, and control, recognizing that these desires keep the soul bound to the illusions of the material world. By silencing the ego, the seeker creates a space where the true self, the divine spark within, can emerge. This quieting of the ego is an act of devotion to the Supreme God, a rejection of the false self imposed by the Demiurge's world.

Seeing Through the Illusion of Separation is another key practice. The Demiurge's world is built on the illusion of separation—between self and other, spirit and matter, human and divine. The Gnostic learns to see beyond this separation, understanding that it is an illusion designed to maintain control. By recognizing the unity that underlies all existence, the seeker transcends the limitations of the Demiurge's creation, experiencing a state of oneness that aligns with the Supreme God. This understanding transforms the Gnostic's perception, allowing them to live from a place of divine connection rather than isolation.

The *Cultivation of Inner Peace* is another means of rejecting the Demiurge's influence. The Demiurge thrives on turmoil, chaos, and conflict, all of which keep the soul distracted and focused on the external. By cultivating inner peace, the Gnostic resists this influence, creating a stable foundation that cannot be easily shaken. This peace is rooted in the understanding that the soul's true nature is beyond the reach of the material, a part of the eternal light of the Pleroma. Through inner peace, the Gnostic embodies a state of freedom that reflects their rejection of the Demiurge and their alignment with the Supreme God.

In the Gospel of Judas, the teachings Jesus shares with Judas suggest a way of being that is free from the constraints of the Demiurge's world. Jesus invites Judas to see beyond appearances, to seek the kingdom of the divine that is not of this earth. This guidance becomes a call to the Gnostic to reject the material illusions, to trust in the inner light, and to remember the soul's true home in the Pleroma. Judas's willingness to follow this path, even at great personal cost, reflects the courage required to reject the Demiurge and to pursue the higher truths of the divine.

Living in Alignment with the Supreme God is the culmination of rejecting the Demiurge. The Gnostic seeks to live as an expression of divine truth, embodying qualities such as love, wisdom, and compassion that reflect the nature of the Supreme God. This alignment is not about perfection but about intention, a daily commitment to honor the divine within and to see the divine in others. By living in this way, the Gnostic creates a life that is a reflection of the Pleroma, a state of being that transcends the limitations of the material and embodies the peace, unity, and light of the divine.

For the Gnostic, rejecting the Demiurge is not an act of defiance but an act of remembrance, a return to the soul's original nature before it became entangled in the material. Through practices of discernment, detachment, inner sovereignty, and divine alignment, the Gnostic frees themselves from the illusions that hold the soul captive, creating a space for the Supreme God to emerge within. This rejection is an affirmation of the soul's true essence, a declaration that the seeker's allegiance is to the divine, not to the forces that seek to limit and control.

The Gospel of Judas serves as a guide on this path, inviting the Gnostic to question, to seek, and ultimately to reject the false world of the Demiurge. In this rejection, the soul finds liberation, a freedom that allows it to rise above the material and to reconnect with the eternal fullness of the Pleroma. This is the journey of the Gnostic—to release the illusions of the Demiurge, to trust in the divine spark within, and to return to the light and love of the Supreme God. Through this path, the soul discovers a peace that is not dependent on the physical, a unity that reflects its true nature, and a liberation that brings it home to the divine.

Chapter 40
Integration of Spiritual Knowledge

In Gnostic spirituality, the integration of spiritual knowledge, or *gnosis*, is not merely an intellectual endeavor but a transformative process that bridges the gap between insight and action. Gnosis is knowledge that goes beyond the mind, a direct experience of the divine that illuminates the soul's path to liberation. However, this knowledge must be lived, embodied, and practiced if it is to bring about real change in the seeker's life. For the Gnostic, integration means allowing divine wisdom to permeate every aspect of existence, harmonizing thought, feeling, and action to reflect the soul's inner truth.

In the Gospel of Judas, Jesus's revelations to Judas are profound, leading him to question the nature of the material world and to see beyond accepted beliefs. Yet these revelations are not meant for theoretical understanding alone; they are a call to transformation, a challenge to align one's life with the knowledge received. Judas's journey reflects the path of integration, where the seeker moves beyond intellectual understanding and allows gnosis to reshape how they perceive, act, and relate to others. This integration is the Gnostic's way of embodying truth, a process that allows them to live as an expression of the divine.

A foundational practice for integrating spiritual knowledge is *Daily Reflection on Gnosis*. Each day, the Gnostic takes time to contemplate the insights and truths they have received, reflecting on how these insights apply to their life. This reflection is not passive but an active questioning: How can this truth be applied? How does it change the way I interact with others, view myself, or make decisions? Through daily reflection, the Gnostic keeps their knowledge fresh and alive, ensuring that it is not forgotten or relegated to abstraction but woven into the fabric of their day-to-day existence.

Aligning Thoughts and Actions is another crucial practice in the integration of gnosis. The Gnostic recognizes that true knowledge cannot remain confined to the mind; it must influence behavior and shape choices. This alignment requires self-awareness, a willingness to observe when one's actions diverge from inner truth. When the Gnostic notices a gap between their knowledge and their actions, they consciously work to bring these into harmony, understanding that alignment is essential for true spiritual integrity. Through this alignment, the Gnostic creates a life that is a reflection of their inner convictions, a way of living in unity with the divine.

The *Practice of Mindful Living* supports this process, as it encourages the Gnostic to bring full awareness to each moment, allowing them to act with intention rather than habit. By living mindfully, the Gnostic becomes more attuned to the subtle guidance of the soul, noticing when they are moving away from or toward the truth within. This mindful presence serves as a compass, a way of continually realigning thoughts and actions with the insights of gnosis. Mindful living transforms ordinary activities into spiritual practices, allowing the Gnostic to live with a sense of reverence and purpose in every interaction.

In the Gospel of Judas, Judas's willingness to question, to look deeper, and to engage directly with Jesus's teachings exemplifies the spirit of mindful living. Judas does not accept teachings at face value but explores them, testing them against his own understanding and experience. This approach mirrors the Gnostic's commitment to authenticity, a dedication to living from an inner place of truth rather than conforming to external expectations. For the Gnostic, this commitment to personal understanding is a foundation for integration, a way of ensuring that spiritual knowledge is not superficial but deeply rooted in one's own inner life.

Cultivating Compassion and Empathy is also essential in the integration of spiritual knowledge. The Gnostic understands that true wisdom calls for compassion, an understanding that transcends the self and embraces all beings as part of the divine. By cultivating empathy, the Gnostic allows their knowledge to transform relationships, creating connections that reflect the unity of the Pleroma. This compassion is not merely a feeling but an active practice, a way of extending the insights of gnosis into the world through acts of kindness, understanding, and support. In this way, the Gnostic lives as a reflection of the Supreme God's love, creating a bridge between the inner and outer worlds.

Practicing Non-Attachment is another key aspect of integration. Gnosis reveals that the material world is transient and that attachment to it creates suffering. By practicing non-attachment, the Gnostic learns to hold experiences, possessions, and even relationships with an open hand, valuing them without becoming ensnared by them. This non-attachment creates a state of inner freedom, allowing the Gnostic to live fully in the world without being bound by it. Through non-attachment, the Gnostic lives in alignment with the truth of the Pleroma, a reality where all things are interconnected yet free from possessiveness.

Self-Awareness and Inner Honesty are also essential for integrating spiritual knowledge. The Gnostic practices self-observation, cultivating a willingness to see their own shadows and areas where ego or attachment may still be at play. This self-honesty is not about judgment but about clarity, a desire to remove any barriers that cloud the soul's connection to the divine. By being honest with themselves, the Gnostic allows gnosis to work as a purifying force, clearing away illusions and bringing them ever closer to their true essence. This practice of self-awareness is a continual refining process, a dedication to living in truth.

In the Gospel of Judas, Jesus's guidance encourages Judas to see beyond appearances, to look into his own motivations and to confront the illusions that bind him. This invitation to inner honesty reflects the Gnostic path, where self-awareness becomes a tool for liberation, a way of seeing through the ego's illusions and aligning with the divine spark within. Judas's journey serves as a reminder to the Gnostic that true understanding requires courage, a willingness to see oneself clearly and to let go of anything that is not in harmony with the divine.

Engaging in Rituals of Renewal also supports integration by creating moments of reconnection with the divine. Rituals, whether simple or elaborate, serve as reminders of the soul's commitment to truth, offering a space where the Gnostic can reaffirm their dedication to living in alignment with gnosis. Lighting a candle, meditating in silence, or reciting sacred words are acts that help the Gnostic reconnect with their inner purpose. These rituals are not about external validation but are personal acts of devotion, expressions of the soul's desire to stay aligned with the Supreme God.

Serving as a Channel for Divine Knowledge allows the Gnostic to extend their insights beyond the self, sharing wisdom with others through example, words, or acts of kindness. This service is not about teaching doctrine but about embodying the qualities of the Supreme God—love, compassion, wisdom, and peace—in daily life. By living as a channel for the divine, the Gnostic allows their knowledge to be a blessing for others, creating a ripple effect that spreads light into the world. This service transforms spiritual knowledge from a personal journey into a communal gift, a way of contributing to the awakening of all beings.

For the Gnostic, the integration of spiritual knowledge is a process of continual realignment, a daily commitment to bring inner insights into outer expression. Through practices of reflection, mindfulness, compassion, non-attachment, and self awareness, the Gnostic weaves the truth of gnosis into every aspect of their life. This integration becomes a way of living in harmony with the divine, allowing the soul's inner light to shine through every thought, action, and interaction.

The Gospel of Judas serves as a guide on this path, illustrating the importance of inner understanding and authenticity. Judas's willingness to explore truth beyond the conventional mirrors the Gnostic's dedication to living a life that reflects their own direct experience of the divine. This path requires courage, as the seeker must continually choose truth over comfort, self-awareness over ego, and alignment with the Supreme God over conformity to the material world.

In the end, the integration of spiritual knowledge is the fulfillment of the Gnostic path, a way of bringing the peace, love, and unity of the Pleroma into the world. Through this integration, the Gnostic becomes a living expression of divine truth, a soul that reflects the light of the Supreme God in every aspect of their being. This is the essence of Gnostic wisdom—not knowledge that is confined to the mind but truth that is embodied, lived, and shared. This integration completes the circle, bringing the soul from the outer world of illusion to the inner reality of gnosis and then back into the world as a source of light for others.

Through this journey of integration, the Gnostic fulfills their purpose, living in a way that honors the divine within and the divine around them. This is the path of true gnosis—a life that bridges heaven and earth, a soul that is grounded in eternal truth and that shines with the boundless light of the Supreme God.

Chapter 41
The Return to the Pleroma

In Gnostic spirituality, the ultimate aim of the soul's journey is the return to the Pleroma—the divine fullness, the original source from which all existence flows. The Pleroma represents the boundless, timeless unity of the Supreme God, a realm beyond duality, beyond the material, and beyond the limitations of individual identity. To return to the Pleroma is to achieve the soul's highest state of liberation and reintegration, dissolving back into the essence of pure, infinite light. For the Gnostic, this return is not a simple escape from the physical world but a fulfillment of the soul's purpose, an ascent from ignorance to knowledge, from separation to unity, and from illusion to truth.

The Gospel of Judas hints at this divine origin, suggesting that Judas holds a unique place in Jesus's teachings, a perspective that transcends the earthly and touches the eternal. Through his connection with Jesus, Judas glimpses a reality that lies beyond the physical, a realm of truth and wisdom that calls to the soul. This hidden knowledge guides Judas toward a path that is not about earthly reward or honor but about understanding the soul's divine purpose. Judas's journey reflects the Gnostic understanding that to return to the Pleroma, one must look beyond appearances and follow a path of inner revelation, surrendering the illusions of the Demiurge's world and embracing the eternal.

One of the first steps on the path to the Pleroma is the *Awakening to Divine Origin*. The Gnostic begins by contemplating the soul's true nature, understanding that the physical self is a temporary manifestation, while the divine spark within is an expression of the Supreme God. This awakening shifts the Gnostic's focus from external identity to inner truth, recognizing that the soul's ultimate destiny is a reunion with the Pleroma. Through this awakening, the seeker becomes aware that their life is a journey of remembrance, a gradual return to the divine fullness from which they originated. This shift in perspective helps dissolve attachments and fears that bind the soul to the material, freeing it to pursue higher truths.

Transcending Dualities is also essential in the return to the Pleroma. The material world, shaped by the Demiurge, is built on oppositions—light and dark, good and evil, pleasure and pain. These dualities create tension and separation, keeping the soul focused on external differences rather than the unity that lies beneath. For the Gnostic, transcending these dualities involves seeing beyond apparent contradictions, understanding that they are part of the illusory structure of the physical world. By embracing the unity of all things, the Gnostic aligns with the essence of the Pleroma, where such oppositions dissolve into harmony and completeness.

The *Practice of Divine Surrender* also plays a central role in the journey back to the Pleroma. To return to the Pleroma, the Gnostic must relinquish the ego, the sense of individuality that clings to identity and control. Surrender, in this context, is not a loss but a liberation, a release of the boundaries that separate the self from the divine. By surrendering personal will and desires, the Gnostic opens to the guidance of the Supreme God, allowing the divine essence to lead the soul. This surrender is an act of trust, a recognition that the path to the Pleroma is not one of personal achievement but of alignment with the divine flow.

Experiencing Divine Union through Meditation is another practice that brings the Gnostic closer to the Pleroma. In this meditation, the seeker envisions the self dissolving into light, merging with the divine presence that fills all things. This meditation is not an escape from the world but an immersion in the essence of the Supreme God, a way of experiencing oneness beyond the boundaries of the physical form. Through this union, the Gnostic touches the Pleroma within, feeling the peace and completeness that come from reuniting with the divine. This experience serves as a foretaste of the ultimate return, a glimpse of the boundless love and unity that await.

The Gospel of Judas portrays Judas as one who sees beyond the physical, who is drawn toward a truth that others do not understand. His path reflects the Gnostic's own journey to the Pleroma, a journey that requires seeing beyond the ordinary and embracing a higher reality. In following this path, Judas shows a willingness to sacrifice conventional beliefs for a deeper, more profound truth, a reflection of the Gnostic's own commitment to the path of return.

Embodying the Qualities of the Pleroma is another essential practice. The Pleroma is characterized by unity, compassion, wisdom, and peace—all qualities that reflect the Supreme God. By cultivating these qualities within, the Gnostic prepares the soul for its return, creating an inner state that mirrors the harmony of the Pleroma. This embodiment is not a denial of human experience but a transformation, a way of allowing the divine light within to shine through every thought, word, and action. Through this practice, the Gnostic lives in a way that honors the divine, making each moment a reflection of the eternal fullness.

Letting Go of the Illusion of Separation is also fundamental to the return to the Pleroma. The Demiurge's world thrives on the illusion of separateness, creating divisions between self and other, human and divine. The Gnostic learns to see through this illusion, understanding that all beings are interconnected, part of the same divine essence. This recognition allows the soul to dissolve the barriers that prevent it from experiencing the oneness of the Pleroma. By letting go of separation, the Gnostic steps into a state of unity, a recognition that the Supreme God exists within and beyond, permeating all of existence.

Developing an Attitude of Inner Completeness supports the soul's journey to the Pleroma. In the material world, there is a constant striving for fulfillment, an endless pursuit of external validation. For the Gnostic, the understanding that true completeness lies within brings peace, freeing them from the cycle of desire and disappointment. By cultivating inner completeness, the seeker becomes content in their connection with the divine, recognizing that the soul's fulfillment is found in its relationship with the Supreme God, not in external achievements. This state of contentment mirrors the fullness of the Pleroma, preparing the soul for its ultimate return.

In the Gospel of Judas, the teachings that Jesus shares with Judas suggest a perspective that transcends the ordinary, inviting Judas to see beyond the illusions of the material. This invitation echoes the Gnostic's call to the Pleroma, a reminder that the journey of gnosis is a return to the divine essence that lies beyond physical form. Judas's willingness to explore this path, even when it leads to misunderstanding and sacrifice, reflects the commitment required to transcend the material and embrace the eternal.

Living as a Beacon of Divine Light becomes a way of embodying the Pleroma while still within the physical world. By allowing the light of the Supreme God to shine through, the Gnostic becomes a living expression of divine truth, a reminder to others of the unity and peace that lie beyond. This practice is a form of service, a way of bringing the presence of the Pleroma into the world and helping others remember their own divine origin. By living as a beacon of light, the Gnostic prepares themselves for the return, creating a bridge between the earthly and the eternal.

Accepting the Mystery of Divine Unity is also crucial in the return to the Pleroma. The Pleroma is beyond comprehension, a state of wholeness that defies the limitations of human understanding. For the Gnostic, embracing this mystery is an act of humility, a recognition that the divine is both infinitely near and infinitely beyond. This acceptance allows the soul to surrender to the unknown, to trust in the Supreme God without needing to define or control. By embracing mystery, the Gnostic opens to the fullness of the divine, allowing the Pleroma to be experienced rather than understood.

The return to the Pleroma, then, is the fulfillment of the Gnostic path, a journey that brings the soul from separation to unity, from illusion to truth. Through practices of divine surrender, meditation, embodiment, and acceptance of mystery, the Gnostic prepares for this ultimate reunion with the Supreme God. This return is not a loss of self but a realization of the soul's true essence, a state of being where individual identity dissolves into the oneness of the Pleroma.

The Gospel of Judas invites the Gnostic to follow this path, to see beyond appearances and to embrace the call of the divine within. Judas's journey, marked by courage and inner vision, serves as a reminder that the soul's true home lies beyond the physical, in the boundless light of the Pleroma. For the Gnostic, the return to the Pleroma is not an ending but a return to the beginning, a rediscovery of the soul's original unity with the Supreme God.

This is the promise of gnosis—a return to the Pleroma, a reunion with the infinite. Through this journey, the Gnostic transcends the limitations of the material, experiencing a peace that is eternal and a unity that is all-encompassing. This return to the Pleroma fulfills the soul's deepest longing, bringing it home to the divine fullness from which all things arise and to which all things ultimately return.

Chapter 42
Achieving Inner Peace

In the Gnostic journey, inner peace is not merely the absence of conflict; it is a profound state of harmony that emerges from aligning the soul with its divine origin. This peace is a sanctuary within, a place where the Gnostic can find refuge from the turmoil of the material world and the illusions of the Demiurge. Achieving inner peace means reaching a state where the soul rests in its true nature, untouched by the fluctuations of the physical, and firmly rooted in the knowledge of its connection with the Supreme God. For the Gnostic, this inner peace is a reflection of the Pleroma, a glimpse of the boundless serenity that awaits beyond the illusions of duality.

In the Gospel of Judas, Judas's journey reveals the path to this inner peace, a peace born not from outward acceptance or worldly success, but from a deep understanding of divine truth. Jesus's teachings encourage Judas to look within, to seek truth beyond conventional boundaries, and to trust in the reality of the divine. This guidance suggests that peace is not given by the world but discovered within, a product of the soul's alignment with its higher purpose and a commitment to live in harmony with the inner light of gnosis.

One foundational practice for achieving inner peace in Gnosticism is *Inner Stillness*, a state of calmness that transcends the movement of thoughts, emotions, and desires. The Gnostic learns to quiet the mind, to let go of inner chatter, and to rest in a space of pure awareness. Through this stillness, the Gnostic can perceive the divine presence within, a presence that is always serene and whole. Inner stillness becomes a doorway to the soul's true nature, a way of connecting with the peace that lies at the heart of existence, unaffected by the illusions of the material world.

Detachment from Egoic Desires is also essential to inner peace. The ego, driven by the Demiurge's influence, seeks power, recognition, and control, constantly creating inner conflict and restlessness. By practicing detachment, the Gnostic lets go of the ego's demands, learning to value inner truth over external validation. This detachment is a process of releasing the attachments that pull the soul outward, allowing it to settle into a state of inner contentment. Through detachment, the Gnostic finds a freedom that is not dependent on circumstances, a peace that comes from knowing the self beyond the ego's constructs.

Acceptance of the Present Moment is another powerful practice for achieving inner peace. The Gnostic learns to embrace each moment as it is, without resistance or judgment. This acceptance is not passive but a recognition of the divine unfolding within every experience, an understanding that each moment offers a lesson or insight that can guide the soul's journey. By accepting the present, the Gnostic aligns with the divine flow, releasing anxiety about the future or regret about the past. This acceptance creates a state of openness, a place of peace where the soul can rest in the knowledge that it is exactly where it needs to be.

In the Gospel of Judas, Jesus's encouragement to Judas to see beyond the material reflects this practice of acceptance. Judas is invited to embrace a higher understanding, to let go of earthly attachments and to seek the deeper truths of the divine. This call to acceptance is a reminder that true peace is found not in resisting or controlling life but in surrendering to the wisdom of the Supreme God within.

Gratitude for Divine Presence is also a source of inner peace. The Gnostic practices gratitude, not only for specific blessings but for the presence of the divine within all aspects of life. This gratitude is a way of recognizing the Supreme God's guidance, even in moments of challenge or sorrow. By focusing on gratitude, the Gnostic shifts their perspective from lack to abundance, seeing each experience as an expression of divine love. This gratitude opens the heart, creating a space where peace can flourish and where the soul feels supported by the infinite presence of the Pleroma.

The *Practice of Non-Judgment* is also crucial for inner peace. Judgment, whether of self or others, creates separation and inner conflict, reinforcing the illusions of the Demiurge's world. The Gnostic learns to observe without labeling, to accept without categorizing as good or bad. This non-judgment allows the soul to move through life with compassion and understanding, freeing it from the burden of comparison and expectation. Through non-judgment, the Gnostic experiences a peace that is rooted in unity, a state of acceptance that reflects the harmony of the Pleroma.

Trust in Divine Order is another essential aspect of inner peace. The Gnostic understands that there is a divine wisdom guiding all things, a higher order that is often beyond human understanding. By trusting in this divine order, the seeker releases the need to control or predict outcomes, finding peace in the awareness that the Supreme God's presence is always at work. This trust is a form of surrender, a willingness to flow with life rather than against it. Through this trust, the Gnostic experiences a peace that is grounded in faith, a calmness that arises from knowing that everything unfolds according to a greater plan.

In the Gospel of Judas, Judas's unique journey reflects this trust in divine order. Though his path is misunderstood by others, he is guided by a deeper knowledge that transcends ordinary perceptions. Judas's willingness to follow this path, despite its challenges, exemplifies the Gnostic's own journey of trust, a journey that leads to a peace that is not disturbed by external opinions or outcomes. For the Gnostic, this trust in divine order is a source of strength, a way of staying centered in the face of life's uncertainties.

Engaging in Heart-Centered Meditation is also a powerful practice for inner peace. In this meditation, the Gnostic focuses on the heart, imagining it as a sanctuary of light and calmness. By resting in this heart space, the seeker connects with the divine essence within, feeling the warmth and compassion that flow from the Supreme God. This meditation creates a state of inner refuge, a place where the soul can retreat from the chaos of the material world and reconnect with its true nature. Through heart-centered meditation, the Gnostic nurtures a peace that radiates from within, a peace that cannot be shaken by external events.

Living with Intentional Simplicity supports inner peace by reducing the distractions and complexities that clutter the mind and heart. The Gnostic chooses simplicity in thought, action, and surroundings, creating an environment that reflects the clarity and peace of the divine. This simplicity is not about renunciation but about focus, a commitment to keeping the soul's attention on what truly matters. By living with simplicity, the Gnostic finds a freedom that is unburdened by excess, a peace that comes from aligning life with the soul's highest values.

Service to Others from a Place of Inner Peace is another way of deepening this state. By extending compassion, understanding, and kindness to others, the Gnostic allows the peace within to flow outward, creating harmony in their surroundings. This service is not about obligation but about sharing the divine love that the soul experiences within. Through acts of service, the Gnostic discovers that peace grows when it is shared, that inner tranquility becomes more profound when it radiates outward as an expression of the divine.

For the Gnostic, achieving inner peace is not an end but a continual practice, a state of alignment that is maintained through conscious choices and inner awareness. Through practices of stillness, acceptance, gratitude, non-judgment, trust, and simplicity, the Gnostic cultivates a peace that transcends circumstances, a sanctuary that reflects the eternal fullness of the Pleroma. This peace is a reminder of the soul's true nature, a reflection of the harmony that exists in the Supreme God's presence.

The Gospel of Judas serves as a guide on this path, illustrating the importance of inner peace as a foundation for spiritual growth. Judas's journey shows that peace is found not in the external but in the inner alignment with divine truth, a truth that liberates the soul from fear and brings it into harmony with the eternal. For the Gnostic, this inner peace is a taste of the Pleroma, a state of being that connects them to the infinite, regardless of the challenges of the material world.

Achieving inner peace, then, is both a goal and a path, a way of living in alignment with the divine while still within the physical. Through this peace, the Gnostic prepares for the ultimate return to the Pleroma, creating a life that reflects the unity, love, and completeness of the Supreme God. This peace is a gift of gnosis—a reminder that, even amid the world's illusions, the soul can find its true home within, a sanctuary of light that transcends all separation and leads the way back to divine fullness.

Chapter 43
The Spiritual Ascension of Judas

The Gospel of Judas presents a narrative that reinterprets Judas not as a betrayer, but as a chosen disciple with a unique understanding of Jesus's teachings and a willingness to undertake a path of profound transformation. In Gnostic thought, Judas's journey is one of spiritual ascension, a movement from ignorance to gnosis, from separation to unity with the divine. This ascension does not refer to physical elevation but to an inner process of awakening, a realization of the divine essence within, and a return to the true knowledge of the Pleroma. Judas's role becomes symbolic of the Gnostic path itself—a difficult yet illuminating journey that leads the soul beyond the material illusions of the Demiurge and into a deeper understanding of the Supreme God.

Judas's ascension is marked by his willingness to question and to see beyond appearances, reflecting the Gnostic view that spiritual growth requires inner courage and a commitment to truth. While the other disciples misunderstand Jesus's teachings, Judas dares to seek answers directly, embodying the Gnostic ideal of an unquenchable thirst for divine wisdom. In the process, he steps outside conventional boundaries, challenging traditional beliefs and societal expectations. This journey of ascension transforms him, making him a bearer of secret knowledge, one who is willing to see the world not as it appears but as it truly is.

One essential aspect of Judas's spiritual ascension is his *Embrace of Divine Knowledge*. Rather than following doctrines or traditions, Judas seeks a direct experience of truth, a form of gnosis that transcends mere belief. In this pursuit, he comes to understand the nature of the Supreme God and the Demiurge, recognizing the illusions that bind humanity. This understanding is not an intellectual achievement but a profound shift in consciousness, a revelation that frees the soul from the constraints of the physical. Judas's embrace of divine knowledge symbolizes the first step in Gnostic ascension—a willingness to let go of surface truths and to seek wisdom that originates from within.

Acceptance of Sacrifice is another significant element in Judas's journey. The Gospel of Judas suggests that Judas's role, though difficult and misunderstood, is a path chosen with purpose and intention. This acceptance of sacrifice represents the Gnostic understanding that spiritual ascension often involves letting go of personal desires, attachments, and even identity. Judas's willingness to undertake this role reflects the Gnostic path of surrender, a readiness to release the self-centered aspects of the ego in service of a higher truth. Through this sacrifice, Judas transcends the ordinary concerns of the physical world, aligning himself with the divine purpose that leads to spiritual ascension.

Transcending Conventional Judgments is another essential practice in Judas's path. In traditional interpretations, Judas is judged and condemned for his actions; yet the Gnostic view invites a deeper understanding. Judas's journey illustrates the importance of moving beyond external judgments, recognizing that true transformation often requires breaking free from societal norms and accepting a path that may be misunderstood by others. This transcendence of judgment is a hallmark of Gnostic spirituality, where the soul seeks inner truth over outer validation. Judas's journey reminds the Gnostic that ascension requires the courage to follow one's own path, even when it defies common perceptions.

The *Rejection of the Material World* is also central to Judas's transformation. The Gospel of Judas implies that Judas understands the illusory nature of the physical world, recognizing it as the domain of the Demiurge. This awareness reflects the Gnostic teaching that the soul's true home lies beyond the material, in the boundless fullness of the Pleroma. By rejecting the physical in favor of the spiritual, Judas aligns himself with the eternal, a choice that prepares him for ascension. This rejection is not a denial of existence but a renunciation of attachment to the material, a willingness to focus solely on the pursuit of divine wisdom.

In the Gospel of Judas, Jesus reveals to Judas mysteries that are hidden from the other disciples, guiding him toward a deeper understanding of the divine. This relationship reflects the Gnostic path of *Direct Revelation*, where knowledge is gained through personal experience rather than through external teachings. Judas's journey illustrates that ascension requires a direct connection with the divine, an openness to receive insight from the inner source. This direct revelation becomes the foundation of Judas's transformation, providing him with the gnosis needed to transcend the limitations of the material world.

Embodying Divine Will is another practice central to Judas's spiritual ascension. In the Gospel of Judas, Judas's actions are portrayed as part of a divine plan, suggesting that his role, though challenging, aligns with a higher purpose. This alignment reflects the Gnostic understanding that true ascension involves surrendering one's own will to the divine will, trusting that the Supreme God's wisdom guides all things. Judas's willingness to act in alignment with this divine will, even when it leads to personal loss, exemplifies the Gnostic's commitment to truth over comfort, a dedication to the spiritual journey over personal gain.

Inner Illumination and Self-Realization mark the next phase of Judas's ascension. Through his unique understanding, Judas experiences a form of inner illumination, an awakening that reveals his true nature beyond the ego. This self-realization is the core of Gnostic ascension, where the soul comes to know itself as an expression of the divine. Judas's journey serves as a reminder that spiritual transformation requires not only understanding but inner realization, a direct encounter with the divine spark within. Through this realization, the soul transcends the boundaries of the self, experiencing a unity with the Supreme God that brings it closer to the Pleroma.

The *Reintegration with the Divine* is the final stage of Judas's spiritual journey, symbolizing the Gnostic goal of returning to the Pleroma. Judas's path leads him to a place of inner peace and unity, a state where he is no longer separate from the divine but fully immersed in it. This reintegration is the fulfillment of Gnostic ascension, a return to the original state of wholeness that lies beyond duality and illusion. Judas's reintegration reflects the Gnostic understanding that the journey to gnosis ultimately leads the soul back to its source, a place where all divisions dissolve and only the divine remains.

In the Gospel of Judas, Judas's journey stands as a testament to the Gnostic belief that spiritual ascension is not about worldly achievements but about inner transformation and divine union. His willingness to embrace difficult truths, to sacrifice personal desires, and to seek direct revelation exemplifies the qualities needed for true spiritual growth. For the Gnostic, Judas's path is a model of courage and dedication, a reminder that the journey to the Pleroma requires a deep commitment to inner truth and a readiness to transcend the limitations of the physical world.

The Power of Inner Faith is also essential to Judas's journey, as he trusts in the divine guidance he receives even when it defies conventional beliefs. This faith is not blind adherence but a deep inner knowing, a trust in the divine presence within that guides the soul to higher understanding. By cultivating inner faith, the Gnostic strengthens their connection to the Supreme God, finding peace and clarity in the midst of the world's illusions. Judas's journey shows that faith in the divine is a foundation for ascension, a source of strength that carries the soul through the challenges of the path.

Embracing Mystery and the Unknown is also part of Judas's spiritual ascension. The path to gnosis is not linear, and much of it lies beyond the grasp of rational understanding. Judas's willingness to follow Jesus into unknown realms reflects the Gnostic's readiness to embrace mystery, to surrender the need for certainty in favor of direct experience. This openness to mystery is essential for ascension, as it allows the soul to encounter the divine without imposing limitations or expectations. Through embracing the unknown, the Gnostic experiences the boundless nature of the Supreme God, a reality that is both infinite and intimate.

For the Gnostic, the spiritual ascension of Judas is both a personal and universal journey, a movement that mirrors the soul's own path toward the Pleroma. Through practices of divine knowledge, sacrifice, detachment, illumination, and reintegration, the Gnostic follows a path that transcends the physical and leads to ultimate unity with the divine. Judas's journey serves as a guide for those who seek true transformation, a reminder that the path to the Supreme God is one of courage, surrender, and profound inner awakening.

In the end, Judas's spiritual ascension is a story of liberation, a testament to the power of gnosis to free the soul from the illusions of the material world and to bring it into the light of divine truth. This journey to the Pleroma is the ultimate fulfillment of the Gnostic path, a return to the fullness of the Supreme God, where the soul finds its true home in the infinite and eternal. Through this journey, the Gnostic discovers that spiritual ascension is not a destination but a state of being, a place of unity and peace that exists beyond all separation, a realm where the soul and the divine are one.

Chapter 44
The Legacy of Gnosticism

The legacy of Gnosticism is one of profound insight, resilience, and an enduring pursuit of spiritual truth. Emerging alongside early Christianity, Gnosticism offered a mystical perspective on divinity, human purpose, and the nature of reality that challenged established norms. While largely suppressed by orthodox traditions, the core teachings of Gnosticism—self-knowledge, divine connection, and liberation from material illusions—have survived across centuries, inspiring seekers to look beyond the visible and find truth within. The Gnostic legacy is one of resilience, a hidden but powerful thread that has continued to influence spiritual thought, philosophy, art, and modern spirituality.

At the heart of Gnosticism's legacy is its emphasis on *Inner Knowledge, or Gnosis*, which calls each seeker to experience truth directly rather than accepting external dogma. This knowledge, described as a direct, intuitive understanding of the divine, transcends intellectual belief, encouraging the soul to seek wisdom that speaks to its deepest nature. Gnostic texts like the Gospel of Judas embody this emphasis on inner discovery, presenting teachings that invite the seeker to look within, to see beyond earthly appearances, and to seek a deeper reality. This focus on personal gnosis laid the groundwork for movements and teachings that would later prioritize individual spiritual experience, from mystical traditions to modern spirituality's emphasis on self-realization.

Another lasting element of the Gnostic legacy is its *Radical View of Divinity*, which distinguishes between the

Supreme God and the Demiurge, the flawed creator of the material world. This dualistic perspective offered an alternative to traditional monotheistic views, encouraging a vision of the divine as transcendent, unknowable, and beyond human limitations. The Demiurge, as the creator of the material realm, was seen as the source of limitation and suffering, while the Supreme God existed as pure goodness, unity, and light. This radical cosmology has influenced later philosophical and spiritual traditions, shaping ideas about the nature of good and evil, and inviting seekers to view material reality as an illusion to be transcended in favor of higher, spiritual truths.

Gnosticism's *Emphasis on Personal Freedom* has also left an enduring mark. In rejecting external authority and encouraging direct experience of the divine, Gnosticism empowered individuals to seek truth independently, outside the confines of formalized religion. This perspective resonates with contemporary values of spiritual autonomy, encouraging a path of self-discovery that prioritizes personal growth and inner knowing over external validation. For the Gnostic, freedom is found in the soul's liberation from ignorance and illusion, a journey that leads to authentic connection with the divine and an inner peace that transcends worldly pressures. This ethos of freedom has inspired spiritual movements that challenge authority, champion individuality, and advocate for direct experience over institutionalized belief.

The legacy of *Mysticism and Symbolism* in Gnosticism has also had a profound influence on art, literature, and philosophy. Gnostic texts are rich with symbolic language—archetypes, visions, and cosmic metaphors that communicate spiritual truths in ways that defy conventional expression. This symbolism invites interpretation, encouraging the seeker to look beyond the literal and to engage with deeper meanings. This approach has inspired artistic and literary movements, from the mystical poetry of the Middle Ages to the allegorical works of modern writers and filmmakers. The Gnostic use of symbols as windows into the divine has influenced how later generations understand and communicate spiritual insight, fostering a legacy that values depth, mystery, and the power of inner vision.

The *Concept of Salvation through Knowledge* is another central theme in the Gnostic legacy. Unlike orthodox traditions that emphasize salvation through faith or adherence to rules, Gnosticism teaches that liberation comes through direct knowledge of one's divine origin. This salvation is not about escaping punishment but about awakening to the truth of the soul's connection to the divine. The Gospel of Judas reflects this understanding, showing a path where Judas's unique insight and connection with Jesus reveal deeper spiritual realities. This concept of salvation as enlightenment has resonated across various mystical and philosophical traditions, from Sufism to Buddhism, and remains a core principle in modern approaches to spirituality that emphasize awakening and self-realization.

The Gnostic *Challenge to Established Authority* is another significant aspect of its legacy. By questioning established beliefs and the institutions that enforce them, Gnosticism fostered a spirit of inquiry that refused to accept surface explanations for reality. Gnostic texts often portray Jesus as a teacher who reveals hidden truths, challenging the conventional wisdom of the disciples and inviting them to look deeper. This challenge to authority has inspired countless seekers to question received wisdom, fostering a spirit of exploration that encourages the individual to seek truth beyond the confines of dogma. This perspective has influenced reformers, mystics, and independent thinkers throughout history who have sought to restore spirituality to an experiential and personal foundation.

Interfaith Influence also marks the Gnostic legacy. Gnostic themes resonate with aspects of other spiritual traditions, such as the Buddhist emphasis on liberation from suffering, the Hindu concept of maya (illusion), and the Sufi pursuit of divine union. This universality suggests that Gnosticism tapped into timeless truths that transcend religious boundaries. By encouraging a journey of inner awakening and divine connection, Gnosticism aligns with the core teachings of other mystic paths, fostering a legacy that connects it with spiritual seekers from a wide array of backgrounds. This interfaith resonance has contributed to the modern embrace of Gnostic ideas, as people increasingly seek wisdom that transcends sectarian divides and offers a more universal path to inner truth.

The legacy of *Inner Transformation* in Gnosticism speaks to a process of spiritual awakening that transforms the seeker's perception of themselves and the world. This transformation is not about adhering to external rules but about transcending the ego, releasing attachments, and realizing one's divine nature. Gnostic texts emphasize this inner work as essential for spiritual freedom, presenting a path where the seeker must confront their own limitations, purify their intentions, and cultivate a direct relationship with the Supreme God. This approach to transformation has influenced self-help, psychology, and modern spirituality, encouraging people to view spiritual growth as an inward journey that changes not only beliefs but the way one experiences reality.

In the Gospel of Judas, Judas's journey reflects the essence of this Gnostic transformation, as he is led to a unique understanding of Jesus's teachings that go beyond the material. His willingness to see beyond appearances and to embrace a higher truth, even at personal cost, embodies the Gnostic ideal of transformation through gnosis. For the modern seeker, Judas's journey becomes a symbol of the challenges and rewards of inner transformation, a reminder that true spiritual growth requires courage, commitment, and a willingness to transcend one's limited perceptions.

The *Resilience of Gnostic Teachings* is also part of its enduring legacy. Despite centuries of suppression and persecution, Gnostic texts and ideas have survived, resurfacing through rediscoveries and adaptations. The discovery of the Nag Hammadi texts in 1945 brought Gnostic writings to a global audience, allowing people to encounter these teachings directly and experience their insights for themselves. This resilience reflects the timeless nature of Gnostic wisdom, a testament to the enduring appeal of its message of liberation, self-discovery, and divine connection. In modern times, Gnosticism has experienced a resurgence, with many finding in its teachings a path that speaks to their own spiritual longing for authenticity, independence, and direct experience of the divine.

The legacy of Gnosticism is also evident in *Contemporary Spirituality's Emphasis on Personal Experience*. The Gnostic approach, which values personal experience over institutional authority, resonates with the modern movement toward self-directed spirituality. Today, many people seek spiritual paths that allow them to explore their own experiences, to find their own answers, and to connect with the divine in ways that feel authentic and personal. This approach echoes the Gnostic emphasis on inner guidance, creating a legacy that encourages spiritual autonomy and the courage to explore beyond established boundaries.

In essence, the legacy of Gnosticism is a call to inner freedom, self-knowledge, and direct communion with the divine. Through its teachings on divine knowledge, inner transformation, and liberation from the material, Gnosticism offers a path that resonates with the timeless yearning for truth and meaning. The Gospel of Judas serves as a reminder of this legacy, presenting a vision of spirituality that is deeply personal, transformative, and attuned to the hidden mysteries of existence. Judas's journey exemplifies the Gnostic ideal—a seeker's willingness to defy convention, to ask questions, and to follow the path of inner knowing, no matter where it leads.

The legacy of Gnosticism is a testament to the power of gnosis, a reminder that within each person lies a spark of the divine, a source of wisdom and light that waits to be rediscovered. Through its influence on art, philosophy, mysticism, and contemporary spirituality, Gnosticism continues to inspire those who seek truth beyond appearances, encouraging a life that is authentic, reflective, and attuned to the divine. This legacy invites each seeker to embark on their own journey, to trust in their own inner knowledge, and to find the Supreme God within, a presence that transcends all boundaries and that guides the soul back to the infinite light of the Pleroma.

Chapter 45
Daily Gnostic Practices

For the Gnostic, spiritual practice is not reserved for special occasions or formal rituals alone; rather, it becomes a way of life, a daily commitment to inner awakening, self-knowledge, and communion with the divine. These daily practices are subtle yet powerful tools that help the Gnostic maintain their connection to the divine essence, cultivate awareness, and strengthen the soul's resilience against the illusions of the material world. Through these practices, the Gnostic continually realigns with their true purpose, experiencing life as a journey toward the light of the Supreme God and the ultimate return to the Pleroma.

In the Gospel of Judas, Judas's path reflects a deep commitment to this kind of lived, inner practice. His journey is marked not by public displays or adherence to external rules but by a private, inward devotion to understanding the divine. This quiet, personal dedication exemplifies the essence of daily Gnostic practice—a continual turning inward to seek the wisdom and peace of the divine that lies beyond the material. For the modern Gnostic, daily practices serve as anchors, a means of grounding the soul in its true essence while navigating the complexities of life.

One foundational daily practice for the Gnostic is *Morning Centering*, a moment of grounding that sets the tone for the day. Upon waking, the Gnostic takes a few moments in stillness, breathing deeply and tuning into the presence of the divine within. This centering is not about achieving immediate results but about creating a space of inner calm and alignment. By beginning the day with this intentional pause, the Gnostic reminds themselves of their purpose, cultivating an awareness that carries throughout daily interactions and experiences. Morning centering becomes a quiet affirmation, a commitment to live in harmony with the divine presence within.

Inner Reflection through Journaling is also a valuable daily practice. The Gnostic may keep a journal where they record their thoughts, insights, and dreams, exploring the deeper meanings behind their experiences. This practice of journaling is not about recording events but about seeking hidden truths, understanding the ways in which daily life reflects inner states and spiritual lessons. Through journaling, the Gnostic builds a relationship with the soul, uncovering patterns, symbols, and intuitions that guide them on the path to gnosis. This written reflection becomes a mirror, revealing the progress of the soul's journey and helping the seeker remain true to their inner purpose.

Practicing Silence and Inner Listening throughout the day allows the Gnostic to cultivate a state of receptivity to the divine. Silence, for the Gnostic, is not simply the absence of noise but a sacred space where the soul can listen to the subtleties of inner guidance. By taking moments throughout the day to enter into silence, the Gnostic quiets the mind and opens to the presence of the Supreme God within. This practice of inner listening strengthens intuition, allowing the seeker to hear the quiet voice of the divine that often gets lost in the busyness of life. Silence becomes a source of wisdom, a space where the soul finds refuge and reconnects with the eternal.

In the Gospel of Judas, Judas's private conversations with Jesus suggest a similar practice of listening and receptivity, as he seeks answers that are not readily available to others. This inner openness, reflected in Judas's willingness to question, is a reminder to the Gnostic of the importance of silence and attentiveness on the path to gnosis. For the seeker, this practice of listening cultivates a deeper relationship with the divine, an ongoing conversation that unfolds in the heart.

Daily Acts of Compassion and Kindness also form a cornerstone of Gnostic practice. Gnosis teaches that all beings are connected within the divine fullness of the Pleroma, and by extending compassion, the Gnostic acknowledges this unity. Acts of kindness become more than simple gestures; they are expressions of the soul's alignment with divine love, a way of embodying the qualities of the Supreme God. Each act of compassion strengthens the Gnostic's awareness of the interconnectedness of all life, fostering a state of peace that transcends the illusion of separation. This practice transforms ordinary interactions into moments of divine communion, reflections of the love that flows from the Pleroma.

Mindful Breathing and Presence is another daily practice that keeps the Gnostic grounded in the present moment. By bringing awareness to the breath, the seeker reconnects with the body, the mind, and the divine spirit within. Mindful breathing is a simple but profound way of cultivating presence, a reminder that the divine is accessible at all times. Throughout the day, the Gnostic may return to their breath, using it as an anchor to release stress, refocus the mind, and bring a sense of calm to each moment. This practice deepens the connection to the present, allowing the seeker to experience each moment as sacred, a reflection of the eternal now that is the Pleroma.

Incorporating *Contemplation of Divine Symbols* into daily life is also a powerful Gnostic practice. The Gnostic may choose a symbol that resonates with their spiritual path—a symbol of light, the Pleroma, the divine spark, or a vision from Gnostic texts. By contemplating this symbol in quiet moments, the seeker strengthens their connection to the divine, allowing the symbol to become a portal to deeper understanding. This contemplation is not intellectual but experiential, a way of connecting with the truths that lie beyond words. Through these symbols, the Gnostic accesses the qualities of the divine, allowing them to permeate daily consciousness and deepen the soul's inner alignment.

Evening Reflection and Gratitude closes the Gnostic's day, offering a time for quiet review and appreciation. At the end of each day, the Gnostic takes time to reflect on experiences, lessons, and moments of insight. This reflection is a gentle examination, not focused on judgment but on understanding. By expressing gratitude for the guidance received, the challenges faced, and the peace experienced, the seeker cultivates an attitude of openness and humility. This evening practice of reflection reinforces the soul's connection to the divine, allowing the Gnostic to rest in a state of peace, ready to begin the journey anew each morning.

Living with Awareness of Divine Light in All Things is a daily practice that helps the Gnostic see beyond appearances. By consciously looking for the divine presence in people, nature, and everyday interactions, the Gnostic cultivates an awareness of the unity that underlies all existence. This practice transforms the ordinary into the sacred, allowing the seeker to view the world as a manifestation of the divine fullness. In each encounter, the Gnostic sees a reflection of the Pleroma, a reminder that the Supreme God is present in all things, guiding the soul toward higher understanding.

Offering Blessings is another way the Gnostic shares the peace and light they experience within. This practice involves silently offering blessings to people, situations, or even the self, sending love, compassion, and healing to all beings. By offering blessings, the Gnostic creates an energy of positivity and connection, a way of contributing to the collective journey toward enlightenment. This practice reflects the Gnostic understanding that all souls are connected within the Pleroma, and that by lifting others, one also lifts oneself. Blessings become a silent prayer, an extension of the divine spark within, a way of spreading the love of the Supreme God into the world.

In the Gospel of Judas, Judas's quiet, contemplative approach to understanding Jesus's teachings reflects this daily commitment to inner practice. His dedication to finding truth, even in the face of misunderstanding, exemplifies the Gnostic spirit of perseverance, of continually seeking the divine within and honoring the soul's path. For the modern Gnostic, these daily practices serve as touchstones, simple yet profound ways of maintaining the soul's focus on the divine amidst the distractions of life.

Ultimately, daily Gnostic practices are a way of embodying the teachings of Gnosticism, of making each moment an expression of divine awareness. Through acts of kindness, moments of silence, reflection, and mindful breathing, the Gnostic lives in alignment with the Supreme God, creating a life that is an ongoing journey toward inner peace, wisdom, and union with the Pleroma. These practices are not about perfection but about presence, a continual return to the soul's true nature and a deepening of the connection with the divine.

This approach to daily life becomes a living testament to the Gnostic path—a reminder that every moment holds the potential for awakening, every interaction a chance to reflect the divine. Through these simple yet transformative practices, the Gnostic finds a way to live fully, peacefully, and authentically, experiencing the joy of the journey and the quiet assurance of the soul's ultimate return to the light of the Pleroma. This daily devotion is the heartbeat of Gnostic spirituality, a path of inner transformation that leads the seeker closer to the boundless presence of the Supreme God.

In the journey of Gnosticism, the seeker has walked through teachings, revelations, symbols, and mysteries that offer a glimpse into the nature of existence and the soul's purpose. These teachings, as explored in the Gospel of Judas and broader Gnostic thought, invite each soul to awaken, to see beyond the illusions of the Demiurge's world, and to embrace the light and unity of the Supreme God. But as this journey reaches its culmination, the focus shifts from knowledge alone to *integration*, a state where gnosis is not only understood but embodied, not only sought but lived in every aspect of being.

The final integration is a process of making the divine real in daily life, a fusion of inner insight with outer action, allowing the soul's awareness of the Pleroma to transform each thought, word, and deed. For the Gnostic, this integration is the completion of the journey, the moment where the mysteries, revelations, and practices become a natural expression of the soul's true nature. It is here that the seeker truly begins to live as a being of light, experiencing the material world with compassion and wisdom, while anchored in the eternal fullness of the divine.

Living from a Place of Divine Awareness is central to this final integration. Gnosis is not an abstract concept but a living truth that permeates the soul's perception. The Gnostic seeks to cultivate a state of awareness that recognizes the divine presence in all things, even within the limitations of the material world. This awareness allows the Gnostic to move through life with a sense of peace and purpose, seeing beyond surface appearances to the divine reality that underlies all. This awareness is not separate from the world but transforms the Gnostic's relationship with it, allowing them to experience every moment as a part of the journey toward the Pleroma.

Maintaining Inner Balance in the Material Realm is another aspect of this integration. The Gnostic, having gained insight into the nature of the Demiurge's world, understands that material existence is transient and often illusory. Yet, instead of rejecting the world entirely, the Gnostic learns to engage with it without attachment, to navigate its challenges while remaining anchored in the eternal. This balance allows the seeker to live fully in the present, appreciating the beauty and complexity of life without becoming ensnared by it. In this way, the Gnostic remains free, experiencing life as a journey of growth and learning while holding fast to the truths of gnosis.

Embodying Compassion and Divine Love becomes a natural outcome of Gnostic integration. The Gnostic understands that all souls carry the divine spark, each one a part of the Supreme God's fullness. By extending compassion, patience, and kindness to others, the Gnostic reflects this unity, offering love that is not possessive but pure, a love that seeks to uplift and heal. This compassion is a reflection of the Pleroma, a way of living that brings the divine presence into every interaction. Through this embodiment of love, the Gnostic serves as a bridge between the material and spiritual realms, offering a glimpse of the divine fullness to those around them.

The practice of *Continual Self-Reflection and Refinement* supports this state of integration. For the Gnostic, the journey of self-knowledge is ongoing, a lifelong dedication to understanding and refining the soul. This reflection is not rooted in judgment but in curiosity, a willingness to see clearly and to grow. By remaining attentive to inner thoughts, motivations, and actions, the Gnostic ensures that their life remains aligned with the divine, that each choice reflects the soul's dedication to truth. This self-awareness strengthens the soul's resilience, allowing it to stay rooted in the Pleroma even amid the shifting tides of the material world.

Living with Gratitude for the Divine Journey is also a hallmark of Gnostic integration. The Gnostic acknowledges that each experience, challenge, and insight is a gift from the divine, an opportunity for growth and understanding. By cultivating gratitude, the Gnostic remains open to the flow of the divine, experiencing life with appreciation and humility. This gratitude transforms even the mundane into the sacred, allowing the seeker to see each moment as an expression of the Supreme God's presence. Through gratitude, the Gnostic maintains a joyful heart, an openness to the beauty of existence and the mystery of the divine.

In the Gospel of Judas, Judas's journey illustrates a profound transformation, a movement from questioning to understanding, from isolation to connection with the divine. His path embodies the essence of Gnostic integration, where the soul's search for truth leads to a state of unity with the divine. For the modern seeker, Judas's story serves as a reminder that the path of gnosis is not about escaping the world but about seeing it through the eyes of the divine, a perspective that brings peace, wisdom, and compassion into daily life.

Trusting the Divine Process and Embracing Mystery is another essential aspect of final integration. The Gnostic acknowledges that the Supreme God and the Pleroma are ultimately beyond human understanding, a reality that transcends the limitations of thought and language. By embracing mystery, the Gnostic lets go of the need for control or certainty, trusting in the wisdom of the divine. This trust allows the Gnostic to surrender to the flow of life, to experience peace even in uncertainty, and to open to the infinite possibilities of existence. In this surrender, the Gnostic finds freedom, an acceptance that brings them closer to the divine fullness.

Being a Vessel for Divine Knowledge is the final expression of Gnostic integration. Through their journey of self-knowledge, the Gnostic has come to understand that true wisdom is not possessed but shared, a gift that flows from the divine. By living as a vessel for this knowledge, the Gnostic offers insights, compassion, and understanding to others, serving as a light in the world. This sharing is not about teaching dogma but about embodying the qualities of the Supreme God—peace, love, and truth. In this way, the Gnostic becomes a guide for others, not through instruction but through example, living a life that reflects the divine fullness of the Pleroma.

In the end, the final integration is the fulfillment of the Gnostic path, the moment when inner transformation becomes outer expression. Through practices of divine awareness, compassion, self-reflection, gratitude, and trust, the Gnostic creates a life that is a living testament to the truth of gnosis. This integration brings the journey full circle, allowing the soul to experience the unity, peace, and love that are its true nature.

The Gospel of Judas offers a vision of this integration, presenting a story that invites each seeker to see beyond appearances and to trust in their own journey. Judas's transformation, his willingness to follow a path that defies conventional understanding, is a reminder that the Gnostic path requires courage, humility, and a dedication to truth. His story reflects the ultimate goal of Gnostic spirituality—not an escape from life but a transformation of it, a way of seeing that brings the divine into every moment.

As the Gnostic completes this journey, they come to understand that the Supreme God is not a distant being but a presence within, a source of wisdom, peace, and love that guides each step. The return to the Pleroma is not a physical departure but a realization, an awakening to the truth that the soul has always been part of the divine fullness. Through this final integration, the Gnostic experiences the ultimate liberation, a freedom that comes from living in harmony with the divine, from embodying the light of the Supreme God in every aspect of life.

This is the culmination of Gnostic practice—a life lived in unity with the Pleroma, a state of being that transcends duality and rests in the eternal. Through this integration, the Gnostic fulfills their purpose, creating a life that is a reflection of divine truth, a testament to the power of gnosis to transform and liberate. In this state, the soul finds peace beyond understanding, love beyond condition, and wisdom that flows from the source of all things.

The legacy of the Gospel of Judas and the teachings of Gnosticism invite each seeker to embark on this journey, to discover the divine within, and to live as a beacon of light in the world. Through final integration, the Gnostic experiences the ultimate return to the Pleroma, a state of divine fullness that completes the journey and brings the soul home to the infinite love and unity of the Supreme God.

Epilogue

As you close this book, a cycle completes, but the journey may just be beginning. Through each page, you ventured into the complex layers of a hidden truth, a wisdom that reveals itself not as an imposition but as a light illuminating the path to a deeper understanding of yourself and the universe around you. What was uncovered here does not end with the final words; it is a constant invitation to an awakening that goes beyond what the senses can perceive and the mind can conceive.

As you bid farewell to the words and teachings that Judas shares with you, understand that, more than a historical figure, he becomes a symbol for all who dare to walk the less-traveled path. His story, transcending the role of villain or hero, resonates as the journey of everyone seeking true knowledge, that which frees the soul from the prisons of ignorance and illusion. Judas is no longer just a name; he is an echo of the human soul's yearning for something beyond appearances, a call for all of us to see beyond the visible and to hear beyond the audible.

This work, in its essence, urges you not only to read but to feel, to experience a truth that unveils itself subtly and powerfully. At this point, you are invited to internalize the teachings of this book, to allow each lesson, each question, each vision of a "Hidden God" to become part of your very being. The path of self-knowledge and spiritual freedom is not merely a goal but a constant practice, a dedication to discovering that the divine is not distant but present in every breath, in every thought that dares to question established truths.

Now, as you leave Judas and the Hidden God behind, you may find, within your own life, the silent presence of this ineffable truth that permeates all things. May every act, every choice, become an expression of the awakening that has been planted within you through these pages. May judgment, illusion, and fear give way to compassion, understanding, and clarity.

What you have learned here is a starting point for a new way of seeing the world and yourself. May your journey continue, now transformed by the silent wisdom of this God beyond gods, a mystery that, though hidden, remains accessible to all who are willing to look within. The return to fullness, to the Pleroma, begins with each decision to see beyond the obvious and to live a life in harmony with inner truth.

And so, we bid farewell to Judas, not as traitor or hero, but as a messenger who reminded us of the power of questioning and seeking. And you, who walked alongside him in this reading, now carry the seed of this revelation. The invitation remains: proceed on your journey. This book ends, but the search for truth is eternal—a flame that never dies and will always guide you back to the mystery of existence.